"Maybe we just need to take a break for a while."

Rick continued pacing. "Why do you think we should do that?" His words tumbled out slowly, but the thoughts of losing Patty Jo raced through his mind. "Is it something I've done? Maybe something I've said? Or does this have to do with anything about me visiting your family?"

Patty Jo took a step backward. Rick was making her feel uncomfortable.

"Of course not, Rick," she said, turning all this over in her mind again. She didn't enjoy thinking on her feet as Rick did, but she usually got there. "It's just that I've got so much to do this semester that I don't know how I am going to fit everything in."

Rick's heart sank. He couldn't stand the thought of losing her.

"Tell me the truth," he said, grabbing her by the arm. "Does this really have anything to do with school, or is it just an excuse to get rid of me?" His hand tightened around her arm. He had a very strong grip.

Rick's behavior and voice were unfamiliar to Patty Jo. She had never seen him act like this or talk to anyone in this manner. In fact, she had never seen him lose his cool, nor had she ever seen him out of control. This was just not the Rick she knew.

Rick's voice got louder. His grip began to pinch into Patty Jo's arm.

"Tell me the truth," he insisted again. "If it is being with me that bothers you that much, then we can do something about that."

Also by Dale Hudson

All I Wanna Do Is Kill

Die, Grandpa, Die

Dance of Death

KISS AND KILL

DALE HUDSON

PINNACLE BOOKS
Kensington Publishing Corp.
http://www.kensingtonbooks.com

PINNACLE BOOKS are published by

Kensington Publishing Corp.
850 Third Avenue
New York, NY 10022

All Kensington Titles, Imprints, and Distributed Lines are available at special quantity discounts for bulk purchases for sales promotions, premiums, fund-raising, and educational or institutional use. Special book excerpts or customized printings can also be created to fit specific needs. For details, write or phone the office of the Kensington special sales manager: Kensington Publishing Corp., 850 Third Avenue, New York, NY 10022, attn: Special Sales Department, Phone: 1-800-221-2647.

Pinnacle and the P logo Reg. U.S. Pat. & TM Off.

ISBN-13: 978-0-7860-1862-8
ISBN-10: 0-7860-1862-3

First Printing: February 2008

10 9 8 7 6 5 4 3 2

Printed in the United States of America

For my mother,
Katherine Hudson,
who has given all her life
so her children and family
could have so much.

Acknowledgments

Much of what is in this book I give credit to my friend and researcher Jo Clayton. A lot of the records, interviews, and photos were the result of her efforts. Without her encouragement and advice, this book would have never existed.

I particularly want to thank Patty Jo Pulley's niece, Connie Winslow; Patty Jo's parents, Elva Mae and Albert Riddick; Patty Jo's sister, Rita Corprew; and other members of Patty Jo's family for their help, cooperation, and assistance.

Other people deserve special mention: District Attorney Joel Brewer, Officer Keith Isom, Joan Kirby, Joel Clayton, and the family of Trooper Joe Wright.

Thanks also goes to my Agent Peter Miller and the folks at Kensington Publishing Company; my banker Richard Causey; my attorney Ralph Stroman; and my accountant Morgan Lewis. In addition, I particularly want to thank my friends and colleagues at all the Southern Cross Community Service offices for their help, understanding, and patience.

And finally my gratitude and love to my wife, Deborah, and to my children DJ and Deegan for their support and encouragement. This book could not have been written without their sacrifice and cooperation.

Prologue

Rick Pulley was forty-seven years old. In all of his wildest dreams, he had never imagined himself sitting beside an attorney in a criminal court of law and waiting for a judge to set his secured bond. As he was being escorted into this North Carolina courtroom, Rick was experiencing an incredibly strange feeling. He kept his head up, even though strangers whispered, pointed, and stared at him. Once he sat down at the defense table and the hearing became official, all of this nightmare seemed even more bizarre.

Judge Narley Cashwell's deep and husky voice boomed throughout the courtroom. "Ladies and gentlemen, we're here for the purpose of a bond hearing and I'm going to recognize the district attorney for his arguments."

Rick sat silently beside his defense attorney, Theresa Pressley, and listened to the district attorney (DA) go on and on about how Pulley had murdered his own wife and how he presented a danger to society. As the room started spinning, Rick started thinking, *Why is he saying all of this stuff about me?*

Rick had been incarcerated since February 2003, two months after the skeletal remains of his wife were found under a bridge. Patty Jo Pulley had last been seen on

May 14, 1999, when she was reported missing from their Ringgold, Virginia, home. Her pickup truck was found a few days later, eleven miles from where her remains were stumbled upon by a state surveyor 3½ years later, in December 2002.

The more Rick listened to the DA, the angrier he got. He had been left with the impression that in the nearly four years since his wife, Patty Jo, had been reported missing from their Ringgold, Virginia, home, the police still hadn't solved their case. Rick had always been the primary suspect.

Yet, even now, Rick believed there were some logical explanations and solid testimony the police had never considered that would exonerate him and end his wretched nightmare.

So why are they still looking at me as the suspect? Rick wondered. *Why aren't they out pursuing other leads and arresting the real killer?* He viewed the whole process as incredibly unbelievable.

From the start, Rick claimed he had nothing to do with Patty Jo's disappearance. He told his lawyer the night his wife disappeared had been an absolutely bone-chilling and indescribable event—a turmoil beyond belief that he would never be able to fully describe.

At a preliminary hearing in October 2003, Rick's attorney filed a motion for a speedy trial. Like all defendants, Rick was presumed to be innocent and had a constitutional right for his case to be heard in a reasonable time period. Judge Cashwell scheduled Rick's trial to begin six months later, on April 29, 2004, and then proceeded to set his bail.

"Four hundred thousand dollars," Judge Cashwell announced. Fearing that Rick might flee to another country, he added, "The court is also requesting that the defendant surrender his passport and reside with his mother in Raleigh, North Carolina."

Once again, Rick was frustrated and felt abused by the

justice system. He had been in jail for almost eight months, how could he arrange to meet such a steep bail? It was a bitter pill for him to swallow.

Rick had been under more stress than ever before. Even Patty Jo's family, who were at first Rick's most impassioned defenders, had now turned bitterly against him. For the past week, just knowing he had to appear in court and face her family again for the bond hearing had been one continual dark night for him. The hearing itself, he had imagined, would be enough of a terrible ordeal, but having to be humiliated in front of people he had known and loved in his past was unbearable.

Because of all the stress, Rick had not been eating. He had not been sleeping. He was irritable. His only consolation was that in a few months all this mental turmoil he had endured—for what seemed like an eternity—would finally be over. He believed the trial would clear him of all injustice and prove to everyone that he had not murdered his wife.

There were some in the courtroom who believed Rick was innocent. Defense Attorney Pressley was one of those who stood behind Rick and supported him.

"There are a few cases where the defense attorney truly believes their client is innocent," Pressley told reporters after the bond hearing, "and this is one of them."

Pressley was disappointed that Rick hadn't gotten his day in court. She further told reporters that she would rather have gotten a trial than bond, that there was no justice without a trial. What Rick really needed to prove his innocence was a trial.

Whoever Rick Pulley was—victim or killer—there didn't seem to be a lot of middle ground in the courtroom that day. Rick had succeeded in putting a lot of time between himself and the events of May 14, 1999. Yet, now, across all that time and space, the past had reached out to claim him. From the life he had once lived as an evangelical minister and gospel musician, from what seemed like eons away, the voices were calling him back to give account of his past sins. Back to the coldest and darkest hours of his life, back to the terrifying night in which his wife had lived the final, terrible moments of her life, and back to the days when he had struggled just to keep his sanity.

But Rick Pulley had no choice. He was being carried back four years into his past, being transported back to a time that hung over him like a black cloud. It was as if the American justice system had pushed a button on a time machine and it had whisked him away to the weathered and tangled paths of his past, to whatever it could discover, and to wherever it might lead, and he was literally holding on for dear life.

Eugene Ricky Pulley was in for the battle of his life.

Chapter 1

VIRGINIA IS FOR LOVERS!

At least, that is what the popular bumper sticker said on a number of vehicles at the River of Life Church parking lot in Ringgold, Virginia, on May 15, 1999.

The "Virginia is for Lovers" had been part of a very successful long-term campaign for thirty years, and although the slogan had never been restricted to just romance, it was often perceived by many tourists as the very reason to visit Virginia. There were, however, dichotomies in the Ringgold church parking lot that Saturday morning, which projected a different image of love and romance in Virginia.

Thirty-seven-year-old Patty Jo Pulley had planned to run errands in Danville at about 6:00 P.M. on Friday, May 14, then later meet her husband Rick Pulley, the youth and music director of the River of Life Church, at the Dan River High School and watch a play. She was driving Rick's red 1991 Ford F-150 pickup truck. Rick said he had waited at the play for his wife, but she never showed.

Rick then returned home and waited on Patty Jo there. Gradually, when she failed to return home, he contacted friends and, ultimately, the police. The police called Patty

Jo's disappearance "suspicious," but all they knew, at that point in time, was that she was missing.

It was almost noon and the temperatures outside were heating up as the sun bore down on the Ringgold church parking lot. The people gathered in the parking lot—many of them teenagers—were huddled together in small groups, talking and praying. Others were pacing, drinking yet another cup of black coffee and staring out across the parking lot toward the parsonage, where Rick and Patty Jo lived. Rick was inside the house, distressed, and being consoled by his pastor and colleague, Randy Sudduth, and other church members. Sitting in the living room by the phone, they waited for a call—a reassuring word—anything that would ease the dread everyone felt.

Patty Jo—"PJ," to those who were close—led a busy life. In addition to assisting her husband with the music and youth activities at the church, she was always scheduling appointments and events for the church's ministries. She and Rick also traveled as a music ministry team, and she taught piano lessons and cleaned houses for extra income.

But Patty Jo was a graduate of Meredith College, an independent, private women's college in North Carolina. She had earned high marks in their rigorous curriculum and leadership development programs in music education. She was a very responsible and resourceful person. Organized, efficient, and dependable in the ten-plus years she and Rick had served at the Ringgold church, Patty Jo had earned a solid reputation as the "go-to" person if one wanted to get something done.

With a dull sense of acceptance, Rick and Patty Jo's friends realized there was the possibility that on the previous night she hadn't been in any of the places or with any of the people who made up her world, as they knew it.

"Maybe she drove to Danville last night and had car trouble," a short, moonfaced lady with long dark hair suggested.

A younger girl with red-rimmed eyes, who had some of the same features as the older woman, wiped away her tears with a tissue. "She could have gotten stranded on Route 58," she added. The girl, who looked to be about sixteen, said she had taken private piano lessons from Patty Jo, and didn't know what she was going to do if something had happened to her.

"I'm wondering if she just got sick and fell asleep in her truck," another girl, standing beside the younger girl, chipped in. "In my psychology class, I read something about a condition know as fugue, where someone suffers from amnesia and walks around for a week or more, not knowing who she is."

Every rational thought or possibility that could explain how Patty Jo was alive somewhere safe, and coming home soon, was mentioned among the people in the parking lot that day. Her friends could have never imagined her leaving without telling anyone where she was going, that she would have just left of her own volition and stayed away from the people who loved her. It just didn't make any sense.

But at this point, when time was so relentless and so unforgiving, the discussion of Patty Jo's disappearance turned from hopeful explanations to one with guarded explanations. As there is in almost every case when the truth is not known, with each passing moment the fear and apprehension grows more palpable, and then the unknown component in the puzzle surfaces. The explanation that no one in the parking lot wanted to face, that no one even wanted to consider, finally reared its ugly head. It was the same question they would later ask at another time and ponder again and again in private, even though they believed it to be outlandish and improbable. But, when people are desperate and looking for anything to dissipate their fears, every question has to be asked. Every possibility has to be considered. Every theory has to be challenged: "You don't think Rick had anything to do with all of this, do you?"

Finally the question had been asked, but then, as quick as it had been asked, it was answered. Granted, Patty Jo's disappearance was unusual and it didn't make any sense, but the last thing anyone wanted to think was that her husband had anything to do with it. The general consensus came back as "No way. Totally out of the question." Patty Jo and Rick had been happily married since 1982. And, since that time, they had worked together, had traveled together, and had performed Christian music, all without conflict, in hundreds of churches as far east as the Mississippi River. Patty Jo had always said she believed she and Rick had been brought together for a reason. She said they had a mission, that they both had the same purpose for existing, and that they both answered to a higher calling from God.

Patty Jo Pulley was not the type of person who would walk away from those commitments. Nor was she the type of person who would walk out on her husband, her family, and her church friends—the people she cared about the most.

There were those in the parking lot that day who admired and respected Patty Jo. They loved and appreciated her friendship. There were also those present who loved her husband and had an allegiance to him. With an optimistic sense of hope, the Pulleys' friends waited and prayed that at any moment they would receive word that Patty Jo was safe. Surely, she had to be alive and stranded somewhere on the road between Ringgold and Danville. That made all the sense in the world.

"I am positive Patty Jo would not leave on her own accord," a friend would say later that afternoon to the police. "She is not that type of person. If there is any way she can get in touch with her family and let them know where she is, then she will do it."

Chapter 2

The habit of thinking in terms of "right" and "wrong" often colors one's perspective of human behavior that is unfamiliar, strange, and different. One commonly characterizes behavior as "normal" or "abnormal," even though it has been proven that humans react to similar situations in as many different ways as there are people. The remarkable thing about human nature is how one often picks out innocent episodes in another's past and suddenly interprets them as revelations of how that person must have gotten off the beaten path, mentally and emotionally, and then gone awry.

Although Patty Jo's friends had nothing tangible to go on, there were still some missing pieces of the puzzle they had not grasped. In private, they questioned one another and questioned themselves about Rick and his relationship with Patty Jo. Even though they knew it was an intrusion into the Pulleys' personal lives, they still, however, felt the urgency to look at Rick for some clues as to where she might have gone. It didn't matter if she and Rick had argued, and maybe had a few skeletons in their closet—everyone had those—the only thing that mattered now was Patty Jo's whereabouts and that she be brought home safely.

Rick's parents' divorce in the 1950s was somewhat nontraditional. He remembered in those days, it was a man's world, where the husband was the breadwinner and the head of the family, and it was the husband who went out into the world and worked. The woman's role was a housewife—with basically all the responsibilities inside the home, including those of raising children. But the wife did not have her own money to spend and depended totally on the husband and his salary. At the time, it was rare for a husband and a wife to share roles.

Although it was unusually frowned upon in the 1950s, Rick's parents did divorce, and he and his mother, Shirley, moved to Raleigh, North Carolina, where they lived with his mother's sister and her husband. In 1956, Raleigh, the state's capital, had grown very little during the 1900s, and the only jobs available to women were either as a laborer on small farms or a blue-collar worker in light-manufacturing and food process plants. All the good office jobs for women, such as secretaries, receptionists, and support work, were already taken. But with the development of the Research Triangle Park in the early 1950s, along with the plans for the construction of a freeway, soon to be known as the beltline—which would encompass highways I-440, US-1, and US-64—as well as speculation of a new International Business Machine (IBM) Complex, typing pools in big offices—mainly women typing letters, correspondence, and official contracts—became a hot commodity.

Rick's mother was fortunate to find employment in a Raleigh insurance agency and was happy to know that her weekly take-home pay was more than enough to insure her and Rick a comfortable life. Just before Rick enrolled in elementary school, he and his mother moved in with his grandparents so she could be closer to work and so he would always have someone to look after him.

"As a child, I lived in a quiet middle-class neighborhood in Raleigh, attended Emma Conn Elementary School, and did all the normal things all the other children did in my neighborhood. I believed in Santa Claus, the Easter Bunny, and the tooth fairy. I played games, climbed trees, and grew up watching television shows like *Bonanza, Gunsmoke, Lassie,* and *The Andy Griffith Show.* All these shows had heroes and good guys, and they portrayed everyday, honest people who always said and did the right thing. Of course, all of us kids wanted to be the good guys in the white hats, who rode in on their horses, and saved the day with their six-shooters. We emulated people like Andy and Opie Taylor, who lived the good life and who always, somehow, managed to get themselves and their friends out of trouble. The funny thing about the fictional town of Mayberry, North Carolina, is that in all of the episodes that were televised, it never rained in Mayberry."

But Rick said that life was no different for him than any of the other children in the neighborhood.

"Because my grandparents were there to help out, my mother had more time to interact with me than before, and it was nice to talk, play games together, or sit around the dinner table after eating and just be together. Even though I didn't have the security of a two-parent family home, my mother and grandparents were always there for me."

Rick said that the two big morals his family always taught him were from the Golden Rule: "It was 'do unto others as you would have them do unto you,' and 'treat your neighbor as you would want to be treated yourself.'" It was also from his family that Rick learned authority was to be respected and appreciated, and this always included the police, his teachers, and any of his elders.

"Oddly enough, my grandfather worked as a prison guard at the Central Prison, and it was from him that I learned a lot about the law and how criminals were punished. In those days, there were a lot less laws and rules for both children and adults, but those laws were enforced by the society and the families.

"On the other hand, people helped one another and looked out for one another then. Families and neighbors cared for each other and treated kids as if they were their own. Children were encouraged to be active and join in organizations, like the Boy Scouts and the 4-H Club, so as to learn good citizenship.

"One of the big sayings in those days was 'Children are to be seen and not heard,' and, like everyone else I grew up with, I had rules, duties, chores, and homework. As a whole, I had a happy childhood and always enjoyed a loving family. And, in the process, I became a more responsible child and never caused my family any problems."

Chapter 3

The 1960s and 1970s was not only a very special time in history, but a significant time in Rick Pulley's life. During those years, many changes in American society were taking place. It was a time of rebellion, the Vietnam War, and countercultural behavior in which young people like Rick were questioning everything, including authority, corporations, the government, and other aspects of everyday life. Essentially, a revolution of the status quo, what was going on during the 60s and 70s was characterized more by the music than anything else.

During the mid-1960s, several bands from Great Britain were creating a buzz in the United States. The British Invasion, as the music industry termed it, featured most of the prominent bands that defined this movement, such as the Beatles, the Rolling Stones, the Who, and the Animals. These musicians, with their catchy tunes and boyish good looks, were trendsetters, and they had the young teens of the decade, literally, swooning in their presence.

Rick Pulley had watched these bands perform on television and had listened to their songs being played on the radios. Like all young teens growing up in the 1970s, he idolized these pop singers and imitated their hairstyles, dress, and language. After all, it was the beginning of an American cultural transition in style. Television programs, like *American Bandstand,* were being watched by 20 million people and setting the standard for all teens. The 1970s music was representative of a movement to express oneself, and Rick, like millions of other teens, was mesmerized by it.

Up until then, Rick's hairstyle and dress had been very conservative. His hair had been either buzzed short or combed to the side with a part. With hair oils, he had learned to style his hair so as to train it to stay in place. All that changed as Rick began to let his dark hair grow long and curly. His clothes were also changing. He began wearing loud colors and plaids, open-necked shirts, and loose longer jackets without a tie.

In junior high school, Rick had taken a few guitar lessons and did well for his age. He seemed to have a good ear for music and could easily pick out the different guitar chords and notes. He particularly enjoyed rock-and-roll music, which was characterized by the use of electric guitars, with a strong rhythm and an accent on the offbeat. Rick's heart and soul were captured by the music revolution of the 60s and 70s. The youth-oriented and harmonious voices from such performers as McCartney and Lennon enthralled him.

When Rick was in the ninth grade, he demonstrated a talent for music on the standardized achievement tests and was invited to play percussion in the school band. As he practiced on the different instruments and received instructions on how to keep a steady beat, he eventually gravitated toward the drums as his primary instrument. Rick practiced hard and relished the opportunities to play in the different bands at school. He was invited to play in some garage bands locally and developed quite a reputation as a budding musician. Soon his identity was being defined by his love for music and the talent he displayed. Rick saw himself as something of a band geek, but he loved every minute of it.

Rick was a likeable guy in high school and he was popular among his peers, but his classroom grades were nothing more than average. There was always the constant cry from Rick's teachers that he was an underachiever. If he would only put his mind to it, then he would have been a straight-A student.

The comments about Rick's lack of effort in his schoolwork appeared continually on his report cards. However, Rick was happy enough just to get by, and was satisfied with a few A's, a couple of B's, and a lot of C's. School was no big deal to him. He enjoyed his music and that was what was really important to him.

Rick's second love next to music was sports. Although he was never a gifted athlete or a sports star, he performed well enough to hold his own in intramural games. His peers soon recognized that regardless of what sport Rick played, he always gave it 100 percent, and they admired him for that.

Rick didn't date a lot of girls in high school, but he did have a couple of long-term romantic relationships. He was always shy and insecure about his looks. Tall and skinny, with long, curly black hair, he looked like a young Howard Stern. Nevertheless, he did muster enough courage to get dates and attend both his junior and senior proms. He survived both of those events, and despite his self-consciousness about his dancing, he went on to live a pretty normal teenage existence afterward.

In 1973, Rick started skipping school a great deal. At first, it was to play basketball and music, but, later on, he started cutting classes just because he could get away with it. Although he still maintained decent grades, and thought no harm had been committed, he was informed toward the end of the year by the school principal that he had missed too many school days and that he would not graduate with his class. While Rick was very disappointed, he used the setback to inspire himself and redouble his efforts when he returned.

The following year, Rick did very well, and he earned the respect he had lost from the adults and the teachers who had monitored his life. Afterward, he was proud of what he had done, feeling like the "comeback kid." This was a milestone in his maturation process and it provided him enough confidence so as to move on with his life and enroll in Louisburg Junior College.

Chapter 4

Located about thirty miles north of Raleigh, Louisburg Junior College is the oldest chartered two-year, church-related, coeducational college in the nation. Related by faith to the United Methodist Church, this college of less than five hundred students and twenty staff members is touted as the model church-related college for nurturing young men and women intellectually, socially, physically, and spiritually. Its main task is to provide a bridge for students to make a successful transition from high school to senior colleges and universities.

Rick Pulley had enrolled in the business curricula at Louisburg Junior College and was making admirable grades in his classes. He enjoyed his classes, sang in the glee club, and took piano lessons. Yet, it still wasn't enough to satisfy a growing passion he had acquired for music in high school. He greatly missed the opportunities he had to play in the bands and tried to fill the void by either playing golf or participating in pickup basketball games. Even though he had never played basketball in high school, he was serious enough about the game that he tried out for the college team as a walk-on. Although he only made it to the first cut, many of the players on the team said he was good enough to have been chosen for the team.

The only trouble Rick ever got into at Louisburg College was a bit out of the ordinary, but typical for Rick. If Rick had a flaw—a crack in his armor—then it was his momentary lapses in judgment. That was evident during his childhood and high-school years, and it reappeared his freshman year at Louisburg.

Rick had managed to secure an envied position as a reader for a visually impaired English teacher. In between classes, he would assist the teacher with his paperwork and preparation of class material and exams. Serving as the professor's eyes, he had proved himself both capable and trustworthy—that is, until he made a serious error in judgment.

Robert Brown (pseudonym), one of Rick's class mates at Louisburg, had previously shared with Rick how he was struggling in a certain English class. One afternoon, he and Rick were walking back from the gymnasium when he asked, "Is it possible you can help me out with this class?"

Rick grew silent. He acted surprised, then inquired, "Why are you asking me to help you?"

Robert looked at Rick like he was a head case. "Because I know you work for the teacher," he said as a matter of fact.

Rick's eyes moved reflexively away from Robert, giving himself more time to think. He cleared his throat, then offered him a couple of suggestions and a few study tips, hoping that would pacify him.

Robert's contorted face turned red. "Come on, Rick," he said weakly. "That's of no help to me. I'm going to be honest with you, I just can't get the hang of it." He talked a moment longer about the difficulty of the class exams, then admitted he was flunking the class. "Look, if I don't pass this class, then they're not going to let me graduate."

Rick listened to Robert and acted concerned, but didn't like what his class mate was asking him to do. "I'm sorry," he apologized, staring straight ahead and unsmiling, "but there's nothing more I can do to help you."

It was Robert's turn to grow silent. He stared at Rick for a few minutes; then with a pitiful persistence, he begged. "Please, Rick, I'm asking you as a friend to help me out this one time. Just this one final exam, and I will never ask you for anything again—"

Rick cut him off in midsentence and didn't appreciate being placed in such a predicament. "I'm sorry, there's nothing I can do to help you," he snapped back, in a voice so unbelievably cold he didn't even recognize it as his own.

Robert's face tensed suddenly. He shifted his body uneasily, brought his hands to his face, then nodded. "Okay, you win, Rick," he said, as if his next alternative was a bullet to the brain, then turned and walked inside the dorm.

Rick stood outside the dorm and thought about the matter a few minutes longer. He remembered what it was like when he had made the mistake of cutting classes his senior year, and how the principal had denied him the right to graduate with his class. The pain was still there. Rick softened. Suddenly feeling sorry for his classmate, he changed his mind and decided to help him.

Robert was inside his room, sitting on his bed, when Rick tapped lightly on his door. When he answered the door, he was relieved to see Rick, but even more so that Rick was holding the answers to the next English quiz.

"Here," Rick said hurriedly, and in a whisper, before relinquishing the answers. "Will this help you any?" He then admonished his friend to keep it a secret, adding, "Do you realize what the faculty will do to both of us if they ever found out this happened?"

Robert nodded his head. He was very grateful to Rick and vowed to keep the incident to himself.

Rick tried not to show his frustration. Instead, he drew in a quick breath, then said adamantly, "Just make sure you don't share those test answers with anyone, agreed?"

Robert smiled, nodding vigorously all the while.

Rick was sure the incident with Robert Brown would go unnoticed. After all, his class mate had sworn absolute silence. But several days later, after Rick had finished grading the English tests, he discovered, to his dismay, that over two-thirds of the class had missed the same group of multiple-choice questions.

At first, Rick could not imagine how that could have happened, and then it suddenly dawned upon him. He closed his eyes as a frightening thought suddenly crossed his mind. *Oh, my God, I hope Robert Brown didn't do what I am thinking he did.*

Rick feverishly went through the answer sheets a second time. He could hardly believe his eyes. Dropping his head into his hands and shaking it unbelievingly, he then took a deep, shaky breath. What he suspected was true. There could be no other explanation for what had happened.

With the English tests and answer sheets in hand, Rick left the office, walked to the dorm, and confronted Robert about their dilemma. The young man sheepishly admitted he had given the answers out to the majority of the students in the class, but never dreamed this would have happened. He couldn't explain it all to Rick, but said he must have copied some of the answers down incorrectly, and that was probably why half of the class missed the same multiple-choice questions.

Rick could feel the noose tightening around his neck. When he presented the graded test sheets from the quiz, the professor would know something fishy was going on, and it would all come back on Rick. The teacher would recognize that the answer key was seriously flawed and then Rick would have to admit he had indirectly shared the answer key with most of the class.

It was a bitter pill to swallow, but he knew what he had to do. He walked back to the professor's office and confessed what he had done. Rick set the test results on the professor's desk and stated, "There's something I have to tell you." Rick then leaned back in his chair, letting his eyes roll toward the ceiling, and owned up to his transgressions.

"But why did you do this?" the professor asked.

It was a question whose answer Rick would ponder for a long time. His lips now trembling, he said, "I don't know. I guess I felt sorry for the guy."

Rick was a broken man.

The professor sat silent for a few minutes until he figured out what to do. He told Rick he appreciated his honesty and suggested they both visit the disciplinary committee and plead his case. Although the professor didn't understand all the ramifications of the committee's action, he acted on Rick's behalf. He told the committee that up until now Rick had performed exemplarily and protested vehemently against any disciplinary action they considered levying against him. But the committee's response was clipped and quick. They didn't like the smell of things and didn't appreciate what Rick had done. This was not the kind of behavior they expected from their students and it would not be tolerated. Rick would not only be fired from his job, but he would be suspended for the last week of the semester and be given zeros for all of his final exams.

Rick felt a cold knot growing in his stomach. He sat quietly and listened as the men and women at the head of the room continued their judgment on him and doled out his punishment. He shifted uneasily in his seat, then turned toward his professor. Feeling both helpless and humiliated, he admitted he had royally screwed up this time. But there was nothing more he could say or do to change the situation. He would have to live with what he had done, then come back next year and prove he was worthy.

Rick escorted the professor out of the room. Rick told the educator not to worry, that everything would be okay. Rick Pulley would be back at school next year, and he would be stronger and better than ever.

Chapter 5

After Rick's unfortunate incident at Louisburg Junior College, he brushed himself off and started over again. Although he understood he was on treacherous ground with the disciplinary committee, and would be for some time, he did not allow that to deter him from continuing his education. After all, he was the "comeback kid." So even though Rick was put on probation at the college, he returned the following semester, kept his nose clean, and performed very well in his classes. Once again, he had proved to everyone he could do whatever was required of him.

Deciding it was time he put all he had learned about management to the test, Rick turned his energies toward a career. He had worked at the Big Star Foods grocery store throughout high school and during his two years of college, after classes, on weekends, and on holidays. It was during his sophomore year at Louisburg that the grocer store manager noticed his work and offered him a position in the Big Star's management-training program. Rick recognized this as a good opportunity, so he left college at the end of his second year with the assurance of not only a management job in the future with a good salary and good benefits, but a job with room for advancement.

In the 1970s, Big Star Foods, like other grocery store and food chains seeking to gain a foothold in the market, was aggressive and competitive. It was a big challenge to find the right person for the right job. Big Star was looking for young, trainable managers, with just the right sort of work ethics and business savvy that would give their companies a leg up on their competitors. With it becoming increasingly difficult for any business to hang on to their high-quality managers, they were recruiting young men and women from the nearby colleges and business schools.

As an incentive, Big Star offered Rick Pulley a generous entry-level package and promised ambitious plans if he would train for one of their future management slots. Rick had weighed all the negatives and added up all the positives before finally concluding there were great opportunities at Big Star for him. At Big Star, there was room for him to grow, to influence change, and to get creative in the workplace. He especially liked the descriptive phrases he had heard in the management-training program: "This is a team-oriented position where honesty, creativity and your input is encouraged."

Rick Pulley was everything that Big Star Foods was looking for, and thought they had found. Rick had a good personality, always had a smile, and had displayed good character. He was a career-oriented team player, and the recruiters at Big Star saw in him not only supervisory skills, but someone who could roll with the punches, either landed or pulled. He also seemed to possess a sense of compassion and humanity, the patience and the ability to train and counsel, and the flexibility to direct and be directed.

The philosophy of Big Star in the 1970s that guided their search to Rick Pulley, one of their ideal job candidates, made it known that management wasn't all about technical skills, but more about people—people who would fit into their culture and who would embrace their company's philosophy. In addition, it was people like Rick Pulley, whom they had found to possess not only good managerial skills, but who were trustworthy, ethical, and moral. People who would set good examples.

Rick had talked a good game during his Big Star interview and made a good impression on the committee. He was considered a good prospect and they enrolled him in the management program. But once he started working, the management discovered he lacked a certain amount of maturity and wondered if he had the necessary skills the company was looking for. Questions about his commitment and abilities soon rose to the surface. Was Rick really a team player? Could he acquire the skills needed to empower his employees and build a certain amount of loyalty from them? Would he be capable of creating growth opportunities and follow company policies as required of him?

In all fairness to Rick, at the same time he had started his management-training program, he had also begun to take inventory of his spiritual life and evaluate his religious beliefs. In the seventh grade, he had walked forward in a Baptist church and was baptized (immersed in water) upon his profession of faith. He had professed Christ as his Savior and confessed his sins. Throughout high school, he attended a small Methodist church with his girlfriend. He had maintained his faith and read his Bible nearly every day, but something was still lacking in his life.

During this perplexed period in his life, Rick had always seen himself as an ethical person. He had never smoked, drank alcohol, or used drugs. But he recognized the missing ingredient in his life was that he had never fully dedicated himself to God through Jesus Christ. With the help of a friend, he began more fervently seeking the words and wisdom of Jesus, and exercising the gifts of the Holy Spirit. It was as if God had literally opened the heavens and poured out His blessings on Rick. Before that moment, he had been blind and could not see, but now the scales that had covered his eyes had fallen away. He could see clearly now and could see that he was not only a new person in Christ, but that God had given him a new mission and a new goal in life.

Rick got more involved in the church and became a serious student of the Bible. He began playing music again and started listening to other Christian singers. In the 1970s, there was a new wave of music that was sweeping across America's churches. It was a kind of revolution against the older and traditional church hymns. In an odd sort of way, it was a form of music not unlike what Rick had known and played in the 1970s. This new sound of Christian popular music arose from nontraditional churches and incorporated a variety of musical styles, including rock music, contemporary country music, and age-old gospel. Similar to the 1970s music, this unusual blend was very popular among teens and was characterized by electronically amplified instrumentation, a heavily accented beat, and relatively simple phrase structure.

Rick found himself on old turf. This was his kind of music and once word got out about his musical talents, he began receiving opportunities to sing and play guitar in local churches. Gradually he began to envision himself employed as a full-time Christian speaker and entertainer.

With Rick's increasing love for Christ also came a laying aside of his earlier ambitions as a grocery store manager for Big Star. As his opportunities to play his music increased and his talent developed, his desire to work a "normal" job decreased. Gradually he lost all interest in the management program and his desire for any job that called for more than forty hours a week. Rick viewed any activity that interfered with his newfound faith and his music ministry as out of the will of God and a deterrence.

Though Rick continued to work for Big Star and make good money, he was still free to pursue his dreams and to play a greater role in his church. Soon he was taking on leadership roles and volunteering for teaching responsibilities at the Methodist church in Raleigh. It was during this time in his life that he met Patty Jo Riddick, and suddenly everything took on a new perspective.

Chapter 6

In the fall of 1980, eighteen-year-old Patty Jo Riddick and several of her classmates from Meredith College walked into the Sunday school class at the United Methodist church in Raleigh, where Rick Pulley and four other single guys sat in chairs and stared at them with open mouths. The room quickly exploded with a burst of electrifying joy that only long weariness followed by sudden triumph can inspire.

"I can't believe it," a blond-haired boy with an angelic face, sitting next to Rick, whispered. "God has finally answered our prayers."

Rick smiled, then glanced toward the girls as they took their seats. He quickly singled out, then focused on, the pretty one, with long, glossy brown hair and the good figure.

Rick's pastor stood at the lectern and called the class to order.

"Can I have your attention, gentlemen?" The young pastor's words hung in the air like new laundry. "I'd like to introduce you this morning to Patty Jo Riddick and several of her college friends she has brought with her."

The pastor stepped aside and waited as each of the girls stepped forward to the lectern. One by one, they stated their names and what course of study they were enrolled in at Meredith College.

"Now, all of you know that I spend a few weeks during the summers playing music at the Circus Tent in Kill Devil Hills," the pastor continued after the girls had introduced themselves. "Well, last summer while I was there, I met Patty Jo and was very impressed with her abilities as a musician. After I learned she was a music education major at Meredith and lived here in Raleigh, I didn't waste any time inviting her to become our choir director."

A resounding "yes" arose from the boys in the classroom, sounding as if it were all from one voice. The pastor smiled and folded his muscular arms across his chest. "I can see from your responses that none of you are opposed to this decision."

Everyone in the classroom laughed.

Rick let his eyes settle upon the pretty one again, the one his pastor had introduced as Patty Jo. It would be months before he would finally tell someone what he saw that day, but he said what appealed to him most was Patty Jo's soft and delicate features. Then he said he looked closer and found she had an innocent, sort of vulnerable look.

Earlier that year, Rick's high-school girlfriend had broken up with him. She did not fully understand his embrace of certain aspects of the Christian charismatic movement and told him that wasn't going to work in their relationship. There were certain beliefs typical of those held by Pentecostal Christians—specifically what are referred to as spiritual gifts—and that was fine for Rick, but not for her. Many of these gifts, especially speaking in tongues, prophesying, and supernatural healing, were profoundly opposed by those belonging to Protestant and Roman Catholic Churches. Rick's girlfriend happened to fall along those lines. Many of the charismatic Christians Rick knew, and was acquainted with, had experienced some of that opposition from family and friends. They had chosen to join separate churches and denominations, or either form their own. Their doctrines were influenced by the Wesleyan/Holiness tradition, which encouraged the practice and manifestations of the Holy Spirit as was seen in the first-century Christian Church. Rick believed he had a great deal in common with other Christians who had embraced the charismatic movement, and found their worship styles, preaching styles, and altar methods very satisfying.

Though Rick's girlfriend had broken his heart, he did not renounce his faith. He remained true to his charismatic beliefs and continued the same fervent passion for its doctrines. In time, he believed he would be delivered from his hurt and that would help him rise above it all. God would eventually send someone to him, who would embrace him and accept his unique style of faith.

After Sunday school was dismissed, Rick and his friends followed the girls from Meredith into the sanctuary for worship. Rick would scramble for a seat and purposely position himself directly behind Patty Jo. With his face nearly touching the back of her hair at times, he would sing out, loudly and boisterously, hoping she would hear his strong and clear baritone voice. Maybe then, he would later confide to his friends, Patty Jo would invite him to sing in the choir. Rick told his friends he was confident this technique would help get him a prominent seat in the choir loft.

Rick's attraction to Patty Jo was given a major boost when he found himself talking to her for the next couple of weeks in the Sunday school class. He had thought at first that she might be a bit aloof, given that she was a paid staff member, but she surprised him with her friendliness. He still wanted to be in the choir and had hoped she would have asked him by now, so he continued his impromptu auditions. Almost as if it was a routine, he would stand behind Patty Jo in the worship service, lean into her and sing. Of course, it was always loud enough for her to hear every single note.

Finally, after one of the services, Patty Jo turned around and took a closer look at Rick. He wasn't very tall, just about six feet, nor did he have a muscular physique, like her previous boyfriend back home. But he had warm green eyes and a luxurious head of black curls. At that moment, she said, he was about as attractive and handsome as anyone she had remembered seeing.

"Would you like to join our choir?" she finally asked him.

Rick nodded and could only squeeze out, "Okay, if you insist," but, inwardly, he marveled at her invitation. For the first few weeks, he was the first choir member to arrive at practice and the last one to leave. He found Patty Jo very easy to talk with, and appreciated the fact that she was such a very vibrant and positive person. Even though she said what was exactly on her mind, always stating her feelings and expressing her personal opinions, he still found her very refreshing. Gradually he and Patty Jo opened up to each other, and were talking as if they had known each other since kindergarten.

"No, I'm not dating anyone at the moment," Patty Jo had told Rick after choir practice one Wednesday night. "I did date a guy all the way through high school, but that relationship ended when I left for college. My studies at school and my job at this church are enough commitment for me, so I'm not really interested in another relationship right now."

Rick shared a few brief stories about his previous girlfriends and how the romance had gone out of those relationships way too soon. He laughed, then said that he wasn't looking to get into another relationship either, that he had been burned in the wars of love too many times. He also let Patty Jo know that all he ever had longed for was a woman who would truly love him for what he was and accept his charismatic faith.

Patty Jo said she admired him for not allowing anyone to change who he was and stand between him and his relationship with Christ.

Rick told Patty Jo that he had been receiving invitations from a number of churches and local youth groups for him to visit, play his guitar, and sing. He then played some of his music, telling her how the teens had been reacting to this particular brand of Christian music.

"You really ought to see how they respond," Rick said to her. "I can truly see God manifesting His Spirit and ministering to these kids through this music. For me, it's really been a life-changing experience."

Rick was careful. He knew he had a tendency to get so excited and caught up in his emotions that he often leapt without thinking. In the past, he had made a lot of his decisions based on emotions rather than common sense and that had gotten him in trouble. He didn't want to make a mistake like that again.

But all the stars seemed to be aligned that night. And it seemed so right and natural for him to ask, "Hey, Patty Jo, would you like to go and sing with me at a Fellowship of Christian Athletes' banquet?"

Patty Jo stared at Rick, wondering if he really meant what he said.

"You mean the two of us?" she sputtered. "Like, uh, me and you go out and perform as a group or something?"

Rick shook his head. He sat up in his chair, then drew closer to Patty Jo. He paused and watched her body language. He sat directly in front of her, their faces were nearly touching. "Sure, that's exactly what I mean." He smiled, trying to relax and sound confident. "You and me. We can both go out and play together."

Patty Jo eased back in her chair as if to draw a breath from the unencumbered air. It wasn't that she didn't want to join up with Rick—in fact, she thought it would be fun and exciting—but she wasn't so sure as to how this would affect her job as the church's choir director.

"I'm not sure that's a good idea, Rick," Patty Jo said reluctantly. "I don't know how the church would feel about that."

"Oh, come on," Rick prodded her. "What can anyone say about it? It's not like were going out on a date or anything. We're just singing and playing Christian music together."

Finally, after weighing all the issues and believing there was no real harm in it, Patty Jo agreed. "Okay, I'll do it," she declared. "But you know how much of a perfectionist I am. Just promise me we're going to practice our music and rehearse our songs. We've got to practice and practice again until we get every single note right."

"I promise," Rick agreed.

Patty Jo was truly a gifted musician. By the time she was a senior in high school, she had already taken piano lessons for ten years and dance for thirteen years. After graduating with honors from Gates County High School, she had applied at the prestigious Meredith College and was accepted. Because she loved music and people, and especially liked working with children, she chose music education as her major. Even though Meredith was considered one of the best values for quality education in the South, their tuition and room and board fees were very expensive. But the admissions and scholarship committees at Meredith were so impressed with Patty Jo's talents, and the fact that she had been an honor student every year in high school, that she was approved immediately for the college's financial aid program. She would prove to be a good investment.

The music education program Patty Jo was enrolled in at Meredith College was one of the best in the nation. She was learning basic performing skills in keyboard, voice, and approximately fifteen other musical instruments. She was also being equipped to teach on multiple grade levels and handle a variety of ensembles (choir, band, orchestra), as well as provide instrumental instruction to individual and small groups. Her course of study was not an easy one, though, as it required her to learn how to design music curricula, evaluate progress, and utilize recent technology, including computer-assisted instruction. In addition, she was also to learn how to inspire students and to communicate the values of the arts to the community.

As if that were not enough, Patty Jo's curricula included plenty of performances in solo and ensemble settings, and classes in how to master theoretical and historical studies, how to analyze music both visually and aurally, and how to compose pieces that illustrated a variety of styles and forms, as well as classes in how to acquire the skills to research and explain the historical and cultural setting of individual composers and specific musical works.

As Rick and Patty Jo practiced their music together, it was obvious he was clearly not in her league. Although gifted in his right, he didn't have the background or the training that she had acquired. But Rick never let that bother him. He recognized how talented and gifted a musician and songwriter she really was, and at the same time, he found himself being drawn to her for reasons other than music. She was attractive and smart. She was sensitive and caring. But, most of all, she had a deep and abiding allegiance to the Christian faith that matched Rick's.

By Rick's own admission, he was just a band geek. His experiences were limited to playing percussion for school bands and banging out beats and rhythms for garage rock bands. Although he had played the guitar and had sung solo in many small gigs, he still had his own style and way of doing things that was a bit amateurish. In his favor, he did have a natural love for music and enjoyed playing and singing. But, in no way, did he ever proclaim to be as accomplished and as professional a musician as Patty Jo. But as they practiced together, Rick noticed he and Patty Jo were developing their own unique style. It was as if the two were being transformed into one.

Patty Jo was a slender woman with soft brown hair and

come-hither hazel eyes—eyes that seemed to be looking into Rick's as often as they glanced at the music in their hands. Everything about her body language and the easy, casual conversation they struck up while they sat side by side in the church sanctuary seemed to indicate that she was as interested in Rick as he was in her. Even though Patty Jo's talent was significant, she never talked down to Rick or tried to intimidate him about his lack of formal training. She had a certain way of handling herself when she needed to admonish him that he appreciated. If she didn't like a particular harmony line or guitar riff that Rick played, she wouldn't hesitate to tell him so, but she did it with such a gentle spirit that she didn't make him feel less of a person afterward.

It was during their first performance when Patty Jo began to see another side of Rick. As she listened to him sing and play, she could hardly believe the full extent of his charisma. She had expected something entirely different out of this curiously shy and insecure man, who had sat behind her in church and entertained her with his impromptu rehearsals. But when he was onstage, he took on an entirely different persona. He had a kind of magnetism she couldn't describe. Not only did he look physically different onstage, but when he opened himself up to the Spirit, he took on a new confidence and countenance she had never seen before.

But what is it that is so different about him? Patty Jo marveled.

At the concert, Patty Jo sat at the piano and stared at Rick. As she listened and watched him entertain the crowd, she tried to figure out exactly what it was that was so intriguing about him. Finally she realized it was that smile of his. When he flashed it, his whole face lit up. Yes, she was beginning to see something more in Rick that she really liked, besides his watery blue eyes and his dark, curly hair. He had such an infectious stage personality that he made everyone feel alive and happy. Suddenly she could hear buzzing in her head, and it just wasn't the noise inside the building.

"You were awesome, Rick," Patty Jo exclaimed after the meeting was over. "You really know how to get a crowd going. God can really use a person like you to minister in song."

"Wow, coming from you that means a lot," Rick exclaimed. His voice began to take on a different ring. "But it's not me up there on the stage, it's the power of God working through me."

Patty Jo didn't know how to respond. All this charismatic stuff was new to her—this indwelling and empowerment of the Holy Spirit—but she got the connection.

Sweat was running down the side of Rick's face. His head was spinning like a roulette wheel, but he saw where the ball needed to drop. His voice was as excited as his face, but he hoped Patty Jo could see what he was trying to say with his eyes: in more ways than one, they could be a team.

At the same time, Patty Jo knew no one would understand this special revelation besides she and Rick. A small voice had spoken to her and it was in that small voice she recognized God had brought her and Rick together for a purpose. She had always trusted God and believed He had a reason for doing the things He did in her life. Now she could see that somehow He had a much bigger plan for both her and Rick's lives than they had ever imagined.

Chapter 7

Nineteen-year-old Patty Jo had set aside her concerns about how the people at the church would react to her and Rick's relationship. Their first date was at a ritzy steak house in Raleigh, where they both ordered prime rib. He made fun of her when she told the waiter she wanted her prime rib to be cooked well done, and then laughed out loud when she smothered it in ketchup. Only country girls ruined their meat with ketchup. But all jokes aside, he admired her independent spirit and her willingness to do and say what she wanted. Inherently, he envied that about her character, and hoped as they grew closer, that part of her would somehow rub off on him.

It just seemed like a natural progression for Rick and Patty Jo to continue dating. As they got to know each other better, they discussed what they were both looking for in a relationship. For him, maybe it was their strong spiritual attraction that he appreciated the most. For her, maybe it was the fact she enjoyed Rick's attention and that she didn't feel alone anymore. As the two talked and got to know each other better, they developed a mutual bond of respect and admiration.

Rick and Patty Jo continued performing together through the winter of 1980, playing at least one or two concerts each month, up to the time of her Christmas vacation. Rick was still working at Big Star and Patty Jo was still attending Meredith. On the last day of the college semester, they met at their favorite restaurant and celebrated Christmas. Patty Jo gave Rick a UNC sweatshirt, and he gave her a Christian tape, a book, and a bottle of ketchup.

After their dinner, Patty Jo pulled in closer to Rick and asked, "Will you come visit me over the holidays and meet my family?"

"Sure, you know I will." Rick smiled.

Patty Jo's college friends had warned her to be cautious, that maybe she and Rick were moving a little too fast, but she had shaken her head and laughed. The more time she spent with him, the more she liked him. He was the dearest, sweetest, most romantic man she'd ever known. All he seemed to care about was her happiness, and she'd never known anyone like that before. She told her friends she had never imagined herself falling in love so quickly, but she had.

"Would you mind checking the air in my tires before we leave?" Patty Jo asked. The next day she was driving home for the holidays and wanted to make sure she didn't have a flat along the way.

"Not a problem," Rick said to her, retrieving an air gauge from the inside pocket of his car. After he checked her tires, he handed her the gauge. "Why don't you put this in your car and use it as often as you like."

Patty Jo giggled like a little schoolgirl. "Does this mean we're engaged now?"

Rick was taken aback. At first, he went quiet, and then in a surprised voice, he asked, "What did you say?" But before she could reply, he reiterated, "Did I hear you say something about being engaged?"

"Yeah, you heard me right," Patty Jo said without faltering.

Rick's heart was thudding so hard, he thought he

could see the front of his shirt shaking. He wore a smile, wide and pleasing. He told Patty Jo it would be two weeks before he could take the trip to visit her, and those days would be long and painful ones for him. He also knew that he was in love with Patty Jo and that he wanted more than anything to make her his wife.

The long awaited period for Rick to visit Patty Jo finally ended. Rick picked up his check at Big Star, packed his things in his car, and then drove the four-hour trip from Raleigh to Gates County. He had missed being with Patty Jo and was eager to spend what little time he had left of the Christmas holidays with her.

The day Rick arrived in the rural county of Gates, North Carolina, he was shocked to see this area hadn't changed a lot since the two hundred years it had been formed. Gates County was located in the northeastern section of the state, and bordered the state of Virginia. It had been part of an area originally called "Albermarle," which was later split into three separate entities. In the earlier years, pioneers had tried to make a living off the land, which was riddled with snakey swamps and sandy soil, and it would not produce. The lack of fertile farmland made many of the settlers bypass Gates County to areas farther south, where the land was richer and had fewer wetlands. But those who stayed behind and worked the land became a strong and resourceful lot. Persevering and determined to make a living, despite the odds of a difficult life, the settlers discovered their resources in timber and pine tar.

In the last quarter of the nineteenth century, the railroad did open Gates County to new opportunities. Shipment by railcar was more efficient then and allowed the logging operations to move their timber cheaply to the pulpwood markets; the farmers to ship their produce and crops of peanuts, corn, soybeans, and cotton more readily; and the small shop owners to burgeon into prosperous communities. Up until 1979, Gates County remained pretty much the same until the railroads ceased running through the county, after highways and interstates made truck shipment cheaper than the rails.

Amazingly, Gates County had remained close to the same since the days of the early pioneers. Other than their obvious changes in technology, the county still relied on their timber industry and agriculture business more than any other commercial enterprise. Six of the nine largest manufacturers in Gates County were all related to, and were relying on, the timber business, while the remainder of the jobs were related to agriculture.

Gates County had not only remained the same since the late-eighteenth century, but its population hadn't doubled in the past two hundred years. In 1790, there were 5,372 people living in the county, and in 1980, there were less than 10,000 people.

As Rick drove through the countryside of Gates County, he got the feeling that Patty Jo lived not only in a small town, but a tight-knit community, where everybody knew everybody, and everybody knew everybody's business as well. She had talked about her hometown often, always joking that nothing big ever happened in Gates County since the railroad company had first laid its tracks in the 1870s. Rick wasn't sure if he could live in a place like this.

"Maybe one day we'll get a second stoplight," Patty Jo had told Rick. "I just hope it is one that works and actually changes colors."

Rick drove through Gates County, where he saw large farms crowded with combines and dotted with tractors and trailers. He circled a few blocks, then searched for a strip mall, thinking maybe there would be a Big Star grocery store nearby, but he didn't see one. What he did see and discover were parts of the everyday scenery: people sitting on their porches, drinking ice tea, or standing around in their yards talking, while young children cartwheeled and played jump rope.

Geez, things sure do move at a slower pace here, Rick thought.

It was a long four-hour trip. Rick was hungry, so he stopped and grabbed a bite to eat at one of the barbeque restaurants. While he was there, he talked with a few people and tried to get a feel for the local life. Gates County reminded him a lot of Mayberry, the fictional town in the popular television series *The Andy Griffith Show,* where one could find Andy, Barney, Floyd, and Goober hanging around the barbershop on any Saturday morning, just laughing and having a good time. Everything seemed to be in black and white.

In Gates County, families were close and they enjoyed being together. It didn't matter what the occasion was that brought them together, just so long as they were together.

When Rick arrived at the Riddicks' home, a large number of Patty Jo's family and friends had already gathered to greet and meet him. It looked as if the Riddicks were having a family reunion. He was not accustomed to the traditions of large families and close neighbors, and felt out of place. He was shocked to see his visit had turned into a family event.

"Wow, how many people did you say lived in Gates County?" Rick asked Patty Jo when she met him at his car. He surveyed the crowd, then added, "And how many of those are here today?"

"Why," Patty Jo asked, laughing out loud. "Do you think all of these people came here today just to meet you?"

Rick felt his stomach churning. He admitted this was a little more reception than he had expected.

Patty Jo escorted Rick from the yard and inside the house, where the crowd had gathered into the Riddicks' living room and kitchen area, where they were mingling. They were all waiting and eager to meet "that wonderful man from Raleigh" whom Patty Jo had been telling them about.

Once inside the house, Rick felt his face grow pale and his mouth turn awkward again. He felt weak at the knees.

"Hello, I'm Elva Mae Riddick." Patty Jo's mom was the

first to greet and hug Rick. Patty Jo's dad, Albert, followed with a hardy handshake, and a "Welcome to our home, son. Would you like something to eat or drink?"

Rick quickly deduced the Riddicks were simple people, and in the course of the day, he found them to be extremely sweet and frugal. In the hall, Patty Jo showed Rick a framed black-and-white photo of her parents, taken in front of a grocery store they had owned and operated in Gates County during the 1950s.

"When Mama wasn't working in the store with Daddy," Patty Jo explained, "she was at home doing her domestic chores and watching after my brother and sister." She pointed at two children in the picture, standing alongside her parents. "That's Billy, he was fourteen then. And that's Rita, she was eleven."

"So where were you when this picture was taken?" Rick asked sarcastically.

"Oh, give me a break," Patty Jo said, elbowing Rick in the side. "I wasn't even thought about for another ten years or so."

Patty Jo pointed to a photo of an infant with soft white skin, a thick head of black hair, and deep-set hazel eyes. "That's a picture of me a few weeks after I was born." Scribed at the bottom of the picture was *July 31, 1961; Chatham County Hospital; 5 pounds.*

Rick examined the photo closer. "I guess it didn't take long for you to become the center of attention," he quipped.

"Yep, not only was I the baby," Patty Jo remarked, "but my parents were in their thirties when they had me. I can assure you I got lots of love."

Rick had already gotten that impression from what Patty Jo had told him about her family dynamics. They were a close family and very protective of her. Maybe it was because she was the baby of the family, and that her brother and sister were much older than her and now had kids of their own, but, for whatever reason, Patty Jo was the most beloved of the Riddick children.

Rick learned a lot about Patty Jo that she hadn't told him. As a child, she was very outgoing and talkative, very friendly, and involved in whatever was going on around her. She had attended T. S. Cooper Elementary School in Gates County, not too far from Sandy Creek Baptist Church, where the Riddicks had been lifelong members. It was here, at both school and church, where Patty Jo got her first indoctrination of the Riddick way of life: always treat everyone fair; stick to what you say; and right is right, and wrong is wrong. There is no in between.

Patty Jo was very popular in school and church and well-liked by both her peers and her teachers. Her favorite subjects in school were creative writing and journalism, and she was named coeditor of her high-school newspaper. In addition to being an honor student, and serving as president of various clubs, while taking piano and dance lessons, she somehow found the extra time to participate and excel in athletics. Her senior year at Gates County High School, Patty Jo was cocaptain of the softball team and was named at the end of the season to the county's all-conference team.

Patty Jo had graduated from Gates County High School in 1979 with honors and had planned to attend East Carolina University, until she visited Meredith College's 225-acre campus and talked with the faculty about her love for music and their music education program. Patty Jo was the first in her family to attend college, and everyone was so proud of her. The Riddicks had high hopes for their daughter.

Patty Jo's maternal grandmother, Etta Britt, was living with Patty Jo's parents. Like most senior citizens, she had a wealth of experience to draw from and a keen eye for trouble. The only problem was that she compared every man she met to her late husband.

"So, young man, what are your plans for my grand-daughter?" Etta asked Rick candidly. She always spoke as if she had a license to say the first thing that popped into her mind.

Rick licked his lips and ran his tongue over his teeth. He wasn't sure what she meant. "I don't know, we've not talked a lot about it yet."

Etta looked at Rick with eyes perfectly clear. She wanted him to know that mentally she was still all there. "You can see that Patty Jo's got lots of friends here. Everyone loves her and she loves them. So I don't see no use in you taking her away from us."

Rick nodded his head slowly, as if to say: "Okay, I got it. I see what's going on here."

Patty Jo intervened. Raising a hand to assure Rick her grandmother didn't actually mean anything by that statement, she pleaded, "Grandma . . . please." She lowered her hand and dropped it around her grandmother's neck, then smiled and gave her a big hug. In a voice that conveyed all is forgiven, Patty Jo teased, "Don't be so mean, Grandma. He is scared of us enough already. Besides, he just got here."

Rick had a glum look on his face. His lips were pressed together so tightly that they almost disappeared. Awkwardly, with his backside jutting out behind him so there would be as little body contact as possible, he leaned forward and gave Etta a cautious arm-to-shoulder hug. It was as if he were giving a courtesy hug to a stranger in a reception line at a wedding.

Connie Corprew, Patty Jo's ten-year-old niece, sat on the couch next to her great-grandmother Etta and witnessed the entire incident. She had always looked up to Patty Jo as a big sister. When Patty Jo and her high-school boyfriend had gone to the movies, they always took Connie with them. Connie had attended all of Patty Jo's softball games, her dance recitals, and her piano concerts. She was there when Patty Jo first got her learner's permit and remembered how awful the ride home was due to Patty Jo's "lead" foot versus the dynamics of a sharp curve. Patty Jo had always been fun to be around, but Connie couldn't see what it was that attracted her to Rick. She thought he was a stick-in-the-mud.

"So how do you like him, Grandma?" Connie asked Etta when Rick and Patty Jo left the room.

Etta frowned. "Well, he's not a very friendly man. He's tall, a bit pale, and a mighty skinny man. Let's see, he's got a pointed nose and short, curly black hair. Do you think he is Italian?" She assured Connie she wasn't quite through with her final assessment of Rick yet, but she had just pointed out what she thought was the obvious.

"Italian?" Connie giggled. "I don't know, Grandma. What's him being Italian got to do with anything?"

"I don't know, he just looks Italian," Etta said.

"Well, if you ask me," Connie teased, "he reminds me of the Count on *Sesame Street*, only with curly hair."

Etta brought her hand down hard on her knee and doubled over in a belly laugh. "Yes, that bushy style of wiry hair just doesn't suit him somehow," she said, shaking her head. "To be sure, he's an odd-looking man."

"And when he looks at you with those bulging eyes, you can't help but wonder what he's thinking," Connie added. "Is he really that afraid of meeting with all of us? What does he think we're going to do to him?"

"I can't imagine," Etta said, shaking her head again. "Besides looking so odd, Rick seems so very soft and timid, not at all what I expected. The way Patty Jo talked about him, I thought he'd be more of a man, like Gary Cooper, Clark Gable, or—"

"Or great-granddaddy?" Connie chimed in. She'd heard that story a hundred times—probably a thousand times.

"Yes, like your great-granddaddy Britt and so many other men around here who happened to be strong from working on the farm or doing other outdoor jobs. I bet that Rick hasn't had a hard day's work in all of his life."

"How do you know?" Connie asked.

"I know because I felt his hands." Etta winked. "He's got soft, baby hands."

Though Rick offered to stay overnight in a motel, he was invited to spend the night in the Riddicks' home. His stay was brief—he said he had a lot of work to do back home in Raleigh—but he enjoyed the sense of the family.

After Rick left, Patty Jo could see her family was a little disappointed in him. Regardless of how hard they had tried to maintain normal facial expressions during that first meeting, she had detected some of their surprised reactions to him. She would later record in her diary: *I appreciate how warmly they welcomed him and tried to make him feel that he can be a part of our family. In time, they'll love him as much as I do.*

Chapter 8

It was during the winter months of 1980 to 1981 that Rick and Patty Jo's relationship blossomed, and they grew closer. After the Christmas holidays, Patty Jo returned to Meredith, where she and Rick continued their relationship and revived their music ministry. Although they had become a little more selective in the invitations they accepted, they still played two weekends out of each month.

Everything seemed to be working out well for Rick and Patty Jo. Rick had started envisioning a life with Patty Jo and believed their working together had been truly ordained by God. The thought of something happening to Patty Jo or the mention of their relationship ending terrified him. When Patty Jo once felt the pressure of school caving down on her, she called Rick and told him she needed to talk with him about their relationship.

"It's something important," Patty Jo said, with a certain hesitancy in her voice. "I feel God has laid on my heart, but I've been afraid to talk with you about it."

Rick sensed a breakup. He had been down this road before with his last girlfriend. This was the same song-and-dance routine she had used on him, so he knew what was coming next.

Rick's body was shaking when he arrived at Meredith College. Patty Jo had just finished registering for spring classes and was eating lunch in the cafeteria with her classmates when Rick burst through the doors and sat down beside her. Clearly out of breath, he asked in a panic, "What is it? What is it about our relationship that we need to talk about?"

Patty Jo stopped eating her food. She excused herself, got up from the table, and walked over to the salad bar, motioning Rick to follow behind her.

By then, Rick had turned mute and two shades of red, but followed a couple of steps behind her, as if he were a puppy trailing its mother.

"Keep your voice down, Rick," Patty Jo said. Both her hands in front of her, with her palms turned downward. "We just need to talk about a few things."

Rick was pacing back and forth in front of the salad bar. He was very angry. He didn't like being led on and then dropped.

"It's nothing like that," Patty Jo assured him. "I'm just having a hard time concentrating on school right now. And we've been moving so fast in our relationship that I think we're rushing things. Maybe we just need to take a break for a while."

Rick continued pacing. "Why do you think we should do that?" His words tumbled out slowly, but the thought of losing Patty Jo raced through his mind. "Is it something I've done? Maybe something I've said? Or does this have to do with anything about me visiting your family?"

Patty Jo took a step backward. Rick was making her feel uncomfortable.

"Of course not, Rick," she said, turning all of this over in her mind again. She didn't enjoy thinking on her feet, like Rick, but she usually got there. "It's just that I've got so much to do this semester that I don't know how I am going to fit everything in."

Rick's heart sank. "Tell me the truth," he said, grabbing her by the arm. "Does this really have anything to do with school, or is it just an excuse to get rid of me?" His hand tightened around her arm. He had a very strong grip.

Rick's behavior and voice were unfamiliar to Patty Jo. She had never seen him act like this or talk to anyone in this manner. In fact, she had never seen him lose his cool, nor had she ever seen him out of control. This was just not the Rick she knew.

Rick's voice got louder. His grip began to pinch into Patty Jo's arm.

"Tell me the truth," he insisted again. "If it is being with me that bothers you that much, then we can do something about that."

Patty Jo assured Rick her greatest concern was for her schoolwork. And, in no uncertain terms, she told him she didn't appreciate being talked to in this manner. "You're hurting my arm," she said, pulling away from him.

Rick's teeth were clenched. "Just tell me the truth," he insisted.

"Well, my grades have not suffered yet, if that is what you are asking. But a music education major is a challenging and time-consuming program. I'm not sure you understand all that is required of me. I think we just need some downtime."

Rick's face turned the color of a plum. "Patty Jo, if you leave me," he said in a low voice. "I swear I will kill you."

Patty Jo's eyes widened. "What did you say?"

Rick had been looking down at the ground, and when he looked up at her, his gaze was uncomfortably penetrating.

One of Patty Jo's classmates, Cassandra Martin (pseudonym), was standing nearby and overheard Rick threaten to kill Patty Jo. Not knowing what was happening or who this guy was, she ran over to the salad bar, grabbed Patty Jo by the arm, and pulled her away from Rick.

"Look, I don't know who this guy is," Cassandra said, thumbing back to Rick. "But you need to get away from him."

Rick looked embarrassed, much like a little boy when he gets caught stealing from his mama's pocketbook. "I'm sorry, I didn't mean anything by it," he apologized.

Cassandra had attacked him so quickly and so unexpectedly she thought it must have vaporized whatever anger he had. He dropped his head immediately and turned to face Patty Jo, who had remained strangely quiet throughout the whole ordeal.

"Can we take this outside?" Rick asked. He grabbed her by the arm, only this time there was no force, and pulled her toward him.

Cassandra took several steps toward Rick, but Patty Jo waved her off.

"It's okay, Cassandra," Patty Jo assured her. "He's my boyfriend. We're going steady and just happened to be having an argument. I know he didn't mean what he said. He's just mad at me."

"But he shouldn't threaten you like that," Cassandra said, backing away from her. "He's got some serious problems, if he talks to you like that."

Rick kept his head down the whole time, never looking up to make eye contact with Patty Jo's friend.

When Patty Jo had convinced Cassandra all the wind had been knocked out of Rick's sails, and he was really as meek as a lamb, she then turned and joined her classmates.

Patty Jo was already embarrassed to the nines, and didn't want to cause another scene. She grabbed Rick by the hand, then led him away from the salad bar and out the door.

Cassandra Martin felt as if she had put herself right smack-dab in the middle of a lover's spat. She watched as Rick and Patty Jo left the building, hearing Rick say he was sorry for losing his temper. Cassandra felt bad about witnessing the incident, but wasn't sorry for what she had said to Rick. She did exactly what any other person in the same position would have done. When she finished her dinner, she and several friends walked past Rick and Patty Jo. He was crying, apologizing, and saying he was just so afraid of losing her.

Chapter 9

In late February 1981, Patty Jo stepped outside the rehearsal building at Meredith College and found the wind had picked up. The temperature in Raleigh had been dropping slowly all day. It had started raining after lunch, so gradually the rain had turned cold, showing signs of freezing.

As Patty Jo raced through a collection of faceless gray buildings, headed north and west across the campus, then wound her way up a hill toward her dorm in the cold, she thought about how awkward and incomplete she felt, having not seen Rick.

"Rick, I can't stand being away from you," she would confess to him later that night on the phone. "I just need to be with you."

After Patty Jo had admitted she could not bear being away from Rick, their agreement not to see each other during the week was made null and void. On occasions, Rick would drop Patty Jo off at her dorm at around 11:00 P.M., only to find his phone ringing when he entered his apartment. She would call him on the phone many nights and say to him that she was doing her homework in the bathroom, then keep him on the phone until two or three in the morning. It was obvious, they had become more attached to each other than ever before.

Now that Rick and Patty Jo were back on the right track, he started making plans for his and Patty Jo's summer music tour. He thought it was a good idea for him to start reserving some concert dates; then they could start traveling as soon as school was out. It was Patty Jo's sophomore year at Meredith College, and he knew there was plenty of time and opportunities for them to develop their talents, and he believed they should forge ahead. The summer's steady course of work would definitely put them further along in their plans for becoming full-time Christian contemporary singers.

But Rick's plans for a summer tour were brought to an abrupt halt when Patty Jo revealed she had received a letter from the Outer Banks. For several years, she had been invited to audition at the Circus Tent. Each year she had auditioned, she had been chosen to perform Christian music with other groups of musicians who entertained visiting tourists, along the sandy 130-mile sweep of barrier islands on the Atlantic Coast. The majority of the islands were part of the Cape Hatteras National Seashore vacation lands, and Christian entertainers, like Patty Jo, would perform at a gathering place, the Circus Tent, to help make the summer a memorable event.

This particular year, Patty Jo had been given a special opportunity. The sponsors of the Circus Tent ministry had invited her to direct a group she had sung with the previous summers. She was also given the opportunity to be a part of the selection committee for performing musicians and to lead the group for the entire summer.

Patty Jo had loved her first experiences with the Circus Tent, and she knew the final decision was going to be a tough one. At first, she felt as if she was faced with almost the same choice as before, when she had to decide between Rick and school. Only now, she was being forced to choose between Rick and the Circus Tent. She did not want to make that choice again.

After Patty Jo explained her predicament to Rick, he agreed that the job offer was an important aspect of her college experience. He admitted he didn't like the part of the decision that put her in Kill Devil Hills (an area near the Outer Banks), and the part that left him in Raleigh. Rick admitted he didn't like being separated from Patty Jo, but conceded when she convinced him it was God's way of testing their love for one another.

The summer of 1981 was especially hard for Rick. He had grown to depend on Patty Jo for his strength and leaned heavily on her for stability. With her working in the Outer Banks, Rick felt helpless and hopeless. Nevertheless, he did survive those three long months, with the help of phone calls, letters, and occasional visitations.

One particular Sunday morning, Rick was feeling bluer than blue, only to walk out to his car and discover that two of his new tires had been stolen off his car.

Why would someone steal my tires when they knew perfectly well I was inside church and worshipping God?

Standing there, angry and perplexed, not knowing what to do or whom to call, Rick heard a familiar squeak in the distance. He turned around and saw Patty Jo's white Ford Pinto coming up the road toward him. Rick shook his head, then leaned against his car and watched as her vehicle eased over the speed bumps, looking like a rescue ship riding an ocean of waves to come and save him.

Rick laughed. "Well, aren't you a sight for sore eyes," he said, greeting Patty Jo as her vehicle pulled up beside him.

Patty Jo noticed Rick's wide smile and the surprise registered on his face.

"I thought you'd be glad to see me," she said slyly, "but I didn't know how much, until now." She looked down at Rick's car and pointed at his bare axles.

Rick reached through the open window and kissed

Patty Jo on the lips. "I just wish you knew how truly glad I am to see you."

"Well, I should hope so," Patty quipped, hugging him around the neck. "I got up at three o'clock this morning, just to make certain I caught you before church was over. So I'm glad you appreciate that."

"Trust me, Patty Jo. I appreciate you and miss you more than you'll ever know."

Rick and Patty Jo had an amazing day together. At the end of the day, they took a solemn vow: they would never stop loving each other. The next weekend, Rick drove down to North Carolina's coast and watched Patty Jo and her group perform at the Circus Tent. After the concert, they drove over to Gates County and spent the night with the Riddicks.

By now, Patty Jo's family had learned to overlook Rick's insecurities and ignore his odd behavior. "Oh, that's just Rick being Rick," they would say. "But if Patty Jo loves him, then we're gonna love him too." The Riddicks knew, in time, that Rick would fit in someday. Then he'd learn to love them too. "Just give it time, and pretty soon he'll be like family," Elva Mae Riddick would say.

Albert and Elva Mae Riddick had talked about Rick and why he was so insecure. They were aware that he was an only child from a broken home. Unlike Patty Jo, Rick had not grown up in a two-parent home, with two siblings, and lots of nieces and nephews around. Most of his life, he had lived in an apartment in Raleigh with his mother and his grandparents. He did not have the privilege of knowing his biological father. And after his grandfather died prematurely, it had been just him and his mother.

All the Riddicks knew of Rick's family and about his childhood was what Patty Jo had told him. She said that Rick's mother had been very fond of the bottle and that was why his father had abandoned them. According to Patty Jo, Rick's mother had been married several times, and each time he had tried to get along with his stepfathers, but it always ended in an argument. She didn't have proof that Rick had been abused by his stepfathers, but she suspected it.

On more than one occasion in church, Rick had related a horrible childhood story that involved one of his stepfathers. His eyes would mist over and his voice would start to break as he related his story: "My stepfather was so filled with the Devil that he killed my pet rabbit and served it to me for dinner. He then sat there all the time, laughing and forcing me to eat it."

When the Riddicks asked if Rick's rabbit story was true, she responded, "Of course, it's true. If it wasn't true, then why would Rick lie about it in church?"

According to Patty Jo, Rick felt insecure at her family gatherings. "It just makes me feel so overwhelmed," he had told Patty Jo after his first meeting with the Riddicks. Of course, Rick wanted to be a part of their family, more than anything, but he said he just didn't know how to give or accept affection from anyone, other than Patty Jo.

"I guess that's why hugging Rick was like hugging a tree," Connie Corprew, Patty Jo's niece, pointed out.

In due time, however, Rick loosened up. During his summer visits with Patty Jo, Rick put his best foot forward and did his level best to warm up to her family. It wasn't long before he had won them over, feeling comfortable enough to be the playful and loving person Patty Jo knew him to be. The attention he was receiving in return seemed to spur him on. It seemed to mean so much to him that he affectionately began referring to the Riddicks as "Mom" and "Dad." He even started calling Patty Jo's great-grandmother "Grandma," and her siblings, Billy and Rita, *his* brother and *his* sister.

When Rick wanted, he could be a real entertainer. As he became more relaxed around the Riddicks, he turned into quite a showman, always making jokes and playing around with the younger kids, acting like a kid himself. He had such a unique way of generating a variety of animal sounds, disguising his voice, and making weird and funny faces that he kept the children entertained for hours.

After one particularly long weekend with the Riddicks, Rick put his arms around Patty Jo's parents and cried. "I've never felt so loved before. Your family is the only real family I've ever had that has made me feel like this."

Elva Mae said she felt so sorry for Rick that she started calling him son. "Go tell your daddy, I said for him to let you drive his new car," she remembered saying. Rick would smile and take off running after Albert.

Connie Corprew was young when Rick and Patty Jo began dating. Like all young girls, she had her moments of rebellion and definitive periods when she struggled to find herself. There were times when she and her brother, Alan, rejected the love of their own mother and father and turned to Rick and Patty Jo for advice.

"The good thing about it was whatever we were going through, Rick and Patty Jo always seemed to understand," Connie remembered. "It was probably because they themselves were still young and they understood what it was like to have problems. But, for whatever reason, my brother and I would always listen to them. It didn't matter how big our problems seemed to us, Patty Jo would always seem to have a solution. She'd say, 'Don't worry. Everything is going to be okay,' and usually it would be."

The soft-spoken, awkward and shy Rick Pulley, whom everyone but Patty Jo had written off at Christmas the year before, was officially becoming part of her family. While Patty Jo continued her work at the Outer Banks, Rick would stay in Gates County with the Riddicks. They knew he and Patty Jo had been discussing marriage and were talking about the possibilities of having a future life together. They had been dating a little less than a year and a half, so the Riddicks were not surprised when Rick asked them for their daughter's hand in marriage.

At that time, there was no way of knowing what Rick and Patty Jo's lives together would be like, or if they would even have a life together. All the Riddicks really knew was what they saw at home, and what they saw was that Rick treated Patty Jo like a princess and he worshipped the ground she walked on. They told Rick they were happy to welcome him into their family and so pleased that a man like him—who had turned his life over to God and was so in tune to Him—was going to marry their daughter.

Chapter 10

In November 1982, a month or so before Rick and Patty Jo were to be married, they decided to make their first joint purchase. Early one Saturday morning, they drove to a piano and organ distributor, located between Raleigh and Durham, and inquired about buying a piano. Patty Jo was still enrolled at the college as an education music major with a piano focus, and even though she was considering switching to a voice major after she was married, she still would need a piano in their home. Otherwise, she would have to drive back and forth to the college and practice on one of their pianos. They had talked a lot about buying a piano and keeping it in their home after they were married.

"Good morning." A short, balding, pudgy man greeted Rick and Patty Jo as they entered the store. Pianos and organs were backed up against each other in the showroom, surrounded by walls of other musical instruments. It was the typical music store. The man introduced himself, then asked, "Can I help you with anything?"

"Yes, sir," Rick said, extending his hand. "We're looking for a nice practice piano for our home." He pointed toward Patty Jo, who was meandering among the other pianos, especially admiring a black baby grand on the far side of the showroom. "My fiancée is a music major at Meredith College, and she and I are going to be married next month."

"Well, congratulations," the store manager offered politely.

"Thank you," Rick acknowledged, then returned to the business at hand. "Well, she is going to need a nice piano so she can practice at our home."

"Oh, I'm sure we can find something to suit her," the man assured Rick. "Is this something you will be paying cash for, or are you going to want to purchase it in monthly installments?"

"Monthly installments," Rick told him.

The salesman escorted Rick past a number of pianos and directed him toward an upright studio piano with a high-gloss black finish. "Well, this is the model we sell the most of to our music majors. I know it is similar to the pianos in the practice rooms at Meredith College, because we've sold a number of these same models to them."

"This is a nice piano," Rick said, running his fingers down the keyboards.

"Oh, yes, it is a very high-quality piano," the man assured him. "You won't find another like it anywhere in this area, at this price."

Rick sat down at the piano and played a few chords. By now, Patty Jo was on the other side of the room, sitting down at the baby grand, tickling the ivories. There was a huge difference in the tone of the two pianos. There was also a huge difference in the price of the two pianos.

"Patty Jo," Rick called, waving to her. "Come over here and see what you think about this one."

Patty Jo jumped up from the piano bench, strolled over, and stood beside Rick. Recognizing the piano as similar to the ones at the college, she said, "Yeah, that's nice."

"Well, what do you think of it?" Rick asked.

"What do you mean, what do I think of it?" Patty Jo mocked playfully. "It's a piano. I'm in love with any piano." She sat down and started playing a Christian hymn. Heads in the store quickly turned in her direction.

"Oh, my," the man gasped, "you play very well."

Patty Jo thanked the man, then asked Rick if he liked this piano.

"Well, like the man said, it is a quality piano. I know you'd probably like to have that baby grand, but I think that is out of our price range. This would probably fit our budget—then we could trade up at a later date, if we wanted to."

Patty Jo nodded.

Rick sensed her disappointment, but knew the right decision for them was to settle with a piano they could afford.

"Now, what if we decide one day that we want a different piano?" Rick posed the question. "What if we wanted to trade up, say to that baby grand piano or something a little more expensive. How would that work?"

"That wouldn't be a problem for us," the salesman assured Rick. "I can guarantee you the piano you are buying now is a very fine instrument, and its value is not going to go down over the years, but it is going up. We would consider a trade-in."

"So what you're saying is if we sold it a few years later, then it would be worth more than we paid for it? That maybe we could use it as a down payment and trade it for a more expensive model?"

"More than likely." The salesman nodded. "We can work with you as long as the piano isn't scratched or damaged in any way."

Rick was sold. The piano was affordable, they could pay for it on time, and it would save Patty Jo a lot of extra time and money. This meant she could practice in their home and not have to worry about going to the labs at school. It would also be a nice lifetime investment for them.

After conferring with Patty Jo, Rick agreed to sign a contract. The salesman agreed to have the piano delivered to their home whenever Rick was ready for it.

The black studio piano would become one of Patty Jo's most prized possessions. It was something both she and Rick valued and wanted to take care of. It symbolized their financial commitment as husband and wife, and it represented their love and trust in each other. After all, why would someone purchase a piano and agree to pay for it over a long period of time, if they didn't intend to be together forever?

"That's my engagement ring you're looking at," Patty Jo would say proudly.

Of course, no one but the two of them knew that Rick didn't have enough money to put a down payment on the piano, so they decided to use the money he had been saving for her engagement ring.

But what did it matter? After all, Rick did buy the piano for Patty Jo.

Chapter 11

Eugene Ricky Pulley and Patty Jo Riddick were married on January 2, 1982. The formal candlelight and double-ring ceremony took place in the small Methodist church in Raleigh, where Rick and Patty Jo had first met. Patty Jo was twenty-one and in her junior year at Meredith, while Rick was twenty-six and worked as a grocery store manager.

During the ceremony, Patty Jo, in her long and beautiful white wedding gown and train, and Rick, in his formal gray tuxedo, starched white shirt, and bow tie, held hands and kissed. They acted like the perfect couple. Before the wedding, they had purchased two wide gold wedding bands. Inside the gold rings, they had their wedding date, *1-2-82*, engraved.

In front of all their friends and family, Rick and Patty Jo exchanged their vows: "For better, for worse. For richer, for poorer. . . . Until death we do part." Theirs was a commitment they honored and planned to keep throughout all eternity. They vowed before God, their family, and a church filled with witnesses that they would love, honor, cherish, and obey "until death do us part." A solemn oath was taken between Rick and Patty Jo that their lives and their marriage would honor God, that they would never allow anyone or anything to come between them, and they would love each other no matter what.

After a brief reception at the church, the newly married couple drove to the Outer Banks of North Carolina for their brief honeymoon. As almost a sign of the troubles to come for the couple, Patty Jo lost her expensive college class ring somewhere on the beach at Nags Head. She was never that careless and would never have misplaced something that meant so much to her. *How could I be that thoughtless?* she wondered.

After their honeymoon, the Pulleys returned to a normal routine in Raleigh. Rick went back to work at Big Star, and Patty Jo picked up where she had left off in her studies. In his job at the grocery store, Rick was making over $20,000 per year, enough for them to live comfortably. He had insurance, good benefits, and an incentive package. But material things were never important to Rick. He and Patty Jo still had their sights on a full-time music career, and spent every free moment they had playing or practicing their music.

"This is all we plan to do after Patty Jo graduates," Rick would announce at the end of all their musical performances. "So we covet your prayers for the future and we ask for your continual support."

While performing at the Outer Banks during the summer of 1981, Patty Jo had met Clay Davis, a pastor of a nondenominational church, and his wife. After they were married she introduced the Davises to Rick, and the two couples quickly found out they had a lot in common.

"You are so wonderfully talented," the Davises would say to Patty Jo. "And you have such a lovely voice that I know God is going to bless you both."

Rick praised his wife and told the Davises how much she had helped him. "She's taught me a great deal. I can remember when we first met, I couldn't even maintain a pitch. We had to work on that until our voices blended."

Rick then shared with the pastor and his wife how he

and Patty Jo had first met. It was God's plan that they become partners in a music ministry.

"I guess we just seemed to be right for each other from the very beginning," Rick said. "We've had this vision of singing together and we've never lost sight of it. We really feel this is what God wants us to do."

"So what is stopping you from doing this?" Pastor Davis challenged. "If God has called you to do this, then there is no way you can fail."

"We feel the very same way," Rick said enthusiastically.

"Say, maybe we can work something out." Davis looked at his wife as if suddenly a light had been turned on over his head. "We're moving to Winston-Salem, and we're starting a new church called Proclaim Christian Center. A big part of our ministry is going to be a home for unwed mothers."

The pastor leaned forward in his chair and smiled. He had a proposition for the Pulleys.

"Maybe you and Patty Jo can become a part of that ministry and fulfill your dream at the same time."

Rick was suddenly very curious. He had been praying for the right opportunity and maybe this was it. "How so?" he asked, not wanting to appear overly eager. "Can you tell us how all that would work?"

Davis spelled out a workable plan. "Well, first you would have to move to Winston-Salem and be a part of the church and all. Then we could get you signed up as house parents in the home—the one we're opening for pregnant teenagers. In exchange, the church will give you room and board, and all the freedom you need to advance your music ministry."

Rick and Patty Jo got very excited. Of course, that meant they would have to move and Rick would have to quit his job. And once he resigned from Big Star, there would be no turning back. From that day forward, they would be totally dependent on their music ministry and the church for support. It was a huge risk, but there were so many possibilities for them.

"So let me get this straight," Rick clarified. "Who would serve as directors at the home? You know, like who would ultimately be responsible for the girls, doing the paperwork and collecting all the money?"

"Oh, my wife and I will fill that role," Davis clarified. "You and Patty Jo wouldn't have to worry about anything but staying there with the girls and watching after them."

That was good, Rick said. He had never been very good at managing money.

"Well, don't worry about the money, God will provide," Davis said optimistically. "My wife and I will work out all those details and give you sort of an arrangement as to where you are free to travel a couple of trips every month. In exchange for your services, we'll give you free housing, food, and everything else that goes along with being house parents. But the most important thing is that you will also have the freedom to be able to travel and pursue your music ministry."

Rick smiled. A handshake—a gentleman's agreement—was all it had taken to seal the deal. "Oh, that sounds fantastic." He reached over and hugged Patty Jo. Finally, their dream was being realized.

After Patty Jo graduated in July 1983 with her B.S. in music education, Rick quit his job at Big Star, they packed up their things, and moved to Winston-Salem. The newly organized church was also sponsoring a coffeehouse, and the Pulleys had performed there on several occasions. They were very impressed with what they had experienced and trusted this was the right move for them.

For a year and a half, the Pulleys lived at the Haven Home for Girls, with five unwed mothers at a time (eighteen total girls), and cared for them before and after their babies were born. For at least a week each month, they traveled and performed throughout the southeastern United States, sharing their faith in music

and song. The only musical equipment they had at the
time was a very small sound system Rick had purchased
before they were married, an acoustic guitar, and the
piano they had bought on credit shortly before they
were married.

While Patty Jo was working on her music education
major, she had brought home all kinds of instruments, including a trombone, an accordion, and various stringed
instruments that she had to become familiar with, but she
didn't play any of those well. Her forte was the piano and
keyboard, even though she knew how to play the guitar,
and learned how to play the flute. Nevertheless, she and
Rick made the best of what they had and performed their
music with great fervor and excitement.

The greatest challenge the Pulleys' music ministry
faced during this time was financial. While working in
Raleigh, Rick had made middle-class wages and they had
lived comfortably. At the Haven Home, they were provided with food and housing, but they were not paid a
salary. The agreement was that the Pulleys were to be totally self-sufficient and that their music ministry would
support them. The plan, as agreed upon by Rick and
Patty Jo, was that any money and gifts collected, less their
travel and hotel expenses, were theirs to keep as salary.

The first year the Pulleys were self-employed, beginning
in July 1983, the total amount they collected from their
music ministry was less than $4,000. After all was said and
done, after all the hard work they had put in, and after all
the hours upon hours of practice they had invested, they
had gotten paid less than minimum wage. The Pulleys
were heartbroken to know that was all they had made.
And what was even worse, most of what they had made,
they used that to purchase additional equipment.

With Rick's salary and benefits irrevocably gone, he
and Patty Jo found it difficult to make a living. Had they
not had their housing and food supplies paid by the

girls' home, they would have been virtually penniless. It was, to say the least, a reality check.

After Rick and Patty Jo examined their situation, they accepted the fact that they had not planned on making such low wages. They wanted to believe Christian people would have been a little more generous. Yet, they were willing to trust God and accept whatever lot He had cast for them. They considered it a joy to live a sacrificially simple lifestyle for the sake of the Gospel. They had not gone into this venture to get rich, but to serve God. And their greatest joy was not seeing how much money they could make, but seeing people's lives changed as a result of their preaching, teaching, and music. Despite some initial discouragement, the Pulleys decided to set their compasses on the straight and narrow and continue pursuing their dreams.

Finally, in a few months, the Pulleys' situation did improve. Suddenly their ministry began receiving a lot of calls and they were getting special invitations to perform as far away as Louisiana and Mississippi. Even more opportunities would come their way, they assured themselves, if they only had the faith and if they only trusted in God.

"I'm afraid our budget is a little more lean than we expected," Rick told Pastor Davis when asked how things had been going. "But things are starting to pick up, so we are trusting this is what God still wants us to do."

The opportunities to minister did prove more fruitful for the Pulleys in 1984. As their music ministry grew, they were able to move from the Haven Home for Girls and lease a small house in an older neighborhood where several other families from the church lived. Fortunately, they were now traveling and performing at least three weeks out of every month—they were thriving spiritually and emotionally. Even though their finances were still low, they believed they were living a blessed life.

We are fulfilling our dreams and we are together all of the time, Patty Jo wrote in her diary. *I am continuing to pray for blessings, but God has already blessed us enough that I can't thank him enough for what he has done.*

Frequently the Pulleys' travels would take them near Patty Jo's parents in northeastern North Carolina. It was during these periods that they stayed with the Riddicks and used their home as a base of operations, which both lowered their expenses and gave them quality time with her family.

"Patty Jo's parents knew that I rescheduled our tours and seemed to appreciate the times I arranged our extended visits with them," Rick recalled. "My relationship with them was much closer and deeper than was most relationships between a husband and his in-laws."

If Patty Jo was aware that she and Rick were having a tough go of it, she never cried to her parents about it. Maybe in her striving to please God, to feel like she always had to accept whatever was His will and try to choose the right alternatives, the bitter irony of her thoughts did not surface. Even though she and Rick were living well below the poverty line, she never once complained or appeared to be bitter. Knowing Patty Jo had a degree in music education, one would have thought the logical remedy would be for her to get a job teaching and earn a respectable paycheck. But for reasons Patty Jo understood well, that was never an option.

As Rick and Patty Jo traveled all over the southeast, and as far as east of the Mississippi River, their only means of support was through love offerings. By no means were they getting wealthy, but they were finally making enough to pay their expenses, and then some. Still, by the time they added it all up, it wasn't what they had expected.

"There may be a lot of love in some of those churches you visit," a friend of Rick's once told him, "but there's not a great deal of offerings."

Rick's friend's commentary on the Pulleys' situation was very typical of what they had experienced in their travels. On some occasions, they would travel a long distance, play and entertain, and leave without hardly any money at all. That was not true in every case, though. Some places did give a lot and this helped to even out the contributions.

In late 1985, the Pulleys were in debt and were forced to confront their financial crisis. It was then that they realized and understood the importance of having a local church supporting them and their music ministry. After a series of events in their Winston-Salem church, when key members left the church and others moved away, the Pulleys decided to look elsewhere for a church home. They did not believe they were being led in the same direction as before, so they resigned from the group home. They began praying in earnest for another church to call home and to rely upon as their "ministerial covering."

As always, God began opening the doors.

In the course of the Pulleys' travels, they had performed in a lot of outdoor settings, in churches, and open storefronts. In the 1980s, their most enjoyable venues were the coffeehouses. They had heard about a certain coffeehouse that was located in Danville, Virginia, called the Gathering Place. Gene Smith had been leading that ministry and had invited the Pulleys to perform on a couple of occasions. After a few performances at the coffeehouse, Smith invited the Pulleys to Ringgold Christian Fellowship (RCF), where they played a couple of special songs or more on a Sunday morning. The next month, the Pulleys were asked to perform an entire weekend of music. It seemed as if the Ringgold church couldn't get enough of the Pulleys.

Chapter 12

The RCF church was perched on one of the many rolling hills in the small incorporated town of Ringgold. Located at the Virginia–North Carolina line in Pittsylvania County, just fifty miles east of the beautiful Blue Ridge Mountains in south-central Virginia, the church's piedmont location had always been blessed with a mild winter climate and moderate summer temperatures and humidity.

Named after Major Samuel Ringgold, a hero of the Battle of Palo Alto in the Mexican War, this unincorporated community is situated in the south-central Piedmont plateau region known as Pittsylvania County. The land in Ringgold and other surrounding areas in the county is rolling to hilly, with elevations averaging from four hundred to eight hundred feet above sea level.

Ringgold is in Pittsylvania County, and consisting of approximately 962 miles, it is the largest county in Virginia. The county surrounds the city of Danville and borders the counties of Halifax, Henry, Bedford, and Campbell in Virginia, and then nestles up to the counties of Caswell and Rockingham in North Carolina.

Today, Ringgold's population of less than four thousand is conveniently located in the south-central area of Virginia, about the same distance between Danville, Virginia, and Milton, North Carolina. Most of what goes on in Ringgold is printed in the *Danville Register & Bee,* and for the national news, sports, and weather, there are twenty-one newspapers and twenty-five licensed television stations within a hundred miles to choose from. Three-fourths of Ringgold's population is white, married, and has a high-school education. They live in homes appraised at somewhere close to $120,000, and work in jobs related to construction, transportation, or excavation businesses.

Nearly everyone who lives in Ringgold attended school together at Kentuck Elementary School or Dan River Middle School, then graduated from Dan River High School. They are a friendly and hospitable bunch, always eager to help anyone in need, but there is never any news posted in town about upcoming community events or festivals. It's rather entertainmentless. In fact, if one is looking for something to do, then the best bet is to stay on Highway 58, which runs east to west through Ringgold and into Danville, or turn on Highway 29, which runs south into Milton.

One of the most outstanding features nearby Ringgold is the Dan River. Flowing from its headwaters in the Blue Ridge Mountains of Virginia, the waters of the Dan River slow and widen not far from Ringgold in Rockingham County. The river then reenters Virginia and snakes back into North Carolina for a short distance in Caswell County before eventually joining the Roanoke River in Virginia. As with any river, the outstanding beauty and undisturbed wilderness is a natural tourist attraction for hikers, fishermen, and paddlers.

The Bible Belt also runs hard through Ringgold. Religion plays a huge part in the lives of its citizens. It's a town where belonging to a church and living by its principles is expected. Even a person's social status and worth in Ringgold is often determined by his/her standing in the church.

Ringgold Christian Fellowship began in the 1980s with a handful of Pentecostal Christians who lived in Danville. The Reverend Peter Newell (pseudonym) was hired as their first pastor. Originally, the congregation started as a small group of worshippers, but over time, the crowds grew so large for their meeting place that they began to look for a building site. Referencing the biblical passage, "A city on a hill can not hide its light," the church elders located an old farmhouse on a large tract of land in Ringgold. Thinking this would be the perfect spot for a church and a Christian community, the band of Christian brothers signed the necessary papers and had the deeds transferred over to the church.

After the land was purchased, a building was constructed that served as both the sanctuary for worship and an auditorium for a Bible school. The old farmhouse was repaired and remodeled to serve as the men's dorm, while an old chicken coop was expanded and converted into the girls' dorm. The rest of the land was subdivided into saleable lots and offered to church members for home sites.

Not long after the church purchased the first tract of land, they bought another farm. This large tract of land was also subdivided and sold to church members, who were, by now, multiplying rapidly. The first community was developed in Ringgold and was renamed Sonshine North, while the second one was developed in Milton and was renamed Sonshine South.

The Ringgold church prospered and continued to grow, adding to their numbers each year, until a scandal broke out in the community. There were problems with Pastor Newell and accusations were made against him. The information was made public, an argument ensued, and Newell was asked to resign from his position.

The church scandal left a lot of disgruntled church

members, many of whom withdrew their membership and put their homes up for sale. A determined remnant agreed to stay and try to rebuild what they had lost. Robbie Lear, the church's associate pastor, agreed to step in and take over this group of wounded souls. Lear united the remnant and promised to move them beyond this indiscretion.

When Rick and Patty Jo Pulley first arrived at RCF in 1984, they were there as members only. The Pulleys enjoyed just sitting in the congregation, listening to the teaching and preaching, and participating in church worship. They provided special music on a few Sundays, and it wasn't long after they arrived that Lear had gotten them involved. They were naturals for the worship team, and were the right candidates to help with the worship services.

Ringgold's services were a lot different than the mainstream denominational churches, in that there was not a choir or a choir director to lead the services. The worship leader was an individual appointed who selected songs and worship, and the activities he/she chose actually became the focus of the services. It was a very demonstrative time in the worship, as their definition of worship was more than just preaching. In a real sense, the activity director led the people in worship. Rick and Patty Jo would become part of that worship team.

In February 1984, the Pulleys made a critical decision in their career and moved to the Ringgold area to be a part of RCF. Initially, they lived in the same development outside of Milton where church members David and Jo Wilson and other church families lived. Soon after arriving to be a part of the church, the Pulleys volunteered to lead an intensive Christian-training program for teenagers called Teens in Training (TNT). This ministry got a number of other church members involved and they helped with housing and program needs. Two of their largest supporters were the associate pastor, Randy Sudduth, and his wife, Judy.

The church members recognized the contributions Rick and Patty Jo had made with their teen program, and Rick was hired on as a part-time youth director. Whenever the Pulleys were not traveling, Rick would schedule youth meetings at the church and was paid $60 per week as salary. Rick also volunteered to lead the worship ministry as well, even though he received no extra pay for that responsibility.

The Pulleys had traveled a lot in 1983 and 1984, but curtailed their performances in the fall of 1984 after Rick was asked to join the RCF staff full-time. Gradually the Pulleys slowed in their music ministry, but increased their work in the church, as if there had been a shift in focus from what they had initially believed God had been calling them to do and be. A year later, the Pulleys were invited by Pastor Lear to move into the large farmhouse beside the church. This was a tangible way the church wanted the Pulleys to know they supported them and their ministry.

The move into the farmhouse provided the Pulleys a place to live, and like their first agreement with the church in Winston-Salem, they once again survived. Rick was the only one getting a salary, which had been increased to $13,000 per year. The church had also agreed to pay a portion of their utilities, and even though they didn't make a lot of money, they felt comfortable with the arrangement. At least they had their basic needs taken care of and were able to make it on what the church paid them. The Pulleys' finances were tight, but the situation never became a sore spot between them and the church. Again, all that mattered was Rick and Patty Jo loved each other and were together.

"Our marriage is real," Rick would say to anyone who asked. "I would describe it as wonderful, amazing, and intensely happy. Don't get me wrong, I'm not saying our marriage is perfect—it's not, in a myriad of ways. We've had arguments and we've had our share of disagreements, but the things we argue about most are the insignificant things.

"Like, we'll argue about who is going to sing a part in a song that she wrote. I will say, 'I like that song,' and she will say, 'Well, I want to sing this part,' and I'll say, 'No, I want to sing that part,' and we'll fuss over who sang what in the song. We will argue about that occasionally—the songs we are going to sing. But our arguments are always pretty insignificant, and I call them arguments because we just both spoke our minds to each other."

When asked if Rick had ever gotten physical with Patty Jo, he responded, "No, never. Not even the first time." The reference to "the first time" suggested that, not only was Rick aware that his confrontation with Patty Jo in the cafeteria was violent, but that there might have been at least one more subsequent violent confrontation.

Rick said what was unique about his and Patty Jo's relationship was that they both were free to speak their minds. They were free to say whatever they needed to say to one another without fear of rejection or reprisal. "We'll say what we're going to say and then it's over and done with. The matter is gone and forgotten.

"Of all those that I've known in Patty Jo's family," Rick explained, "two of the people that she took after, more than anyone else, were her grandmothers. She had a unique combination of both of their personalities. Her [paternal] grandmother was as sweet and loving as a servant, and I never saw her angry at all. Her [maternal] grandmother was kind, but very outspoken. She always spoke her mind, and that was exactly the kind of person Patty Jo was. She was a combination of those attributes. She could be sweet as sugar, but if she had an opinion, she was never afraid to state that opinion.

"I am saying that Patty Jo did speak her mind, and by the virtue of her ability or her propensity to speak whatever was on her mind, or if she didn't like something, she said it. It didn't matter really who it was. You always knew where you stood with her. I always knew where I stood with her. I liked her candidness, and I believed her strength would one day help me to become more vocal, a much stronger person than I was. I wouldn't say that either of us were dominant, but I would say that Patty Jo did have a stronger personality in some respects than I did."

When Rick was asked why he and Patty Jo did not have any children, he said that had been Patty Jo's decision from the very beginning.

"Before we were married, Patty Jo made it very clear to me that she did not want to have children. She stated, when she was growing up, there was a big difference in age between her and her sister, Rita, and her brother, Billy. Patty Jo was born when her parents were older, and though I don't know the whole story—I think Rita and her husband divorced or something like that—but there came an occasion where Rita's children came to live with her and her parents. It was no reflection upon them at all, but I remember Patty Jo stating frequently that she just didn't want to have children for that reason.

"But then, as we sort of settled into what was going on in our lives, we realized on our own that it was better that we did not have children. We were always away from home and on the road. From the beginning of our marriage, we were traveling all the time and performing music. It just wasn't a situation that was conducive to raising a family.

"When Patty Jo was asked how many children she had, she would respond, 'I have eighteen children and eighteen grandchildren,' the same number of children and their babies at the girls' home. She always said she had enough children to look after, between the girls' home and the youth at the church, that she didn't have time for her own."

Perhaps another reason the Pulleys didn't have children was finances. Throughout their entire marriage, especially after Rick quit his job at Big Star in July 1983, they had struggled financially. To offset expenses, Patty Jo taught piano lessons and private voice lessons in their home. There was barely enough money to feed themselves, much less a child.

"When we were on the road, we could change the schedule if we got an opportunity to do some traveling. She could also call her students and say, 'I'm canceling next week's lesson,' and they would always understand that. She taught piano lessons, and even at some point, she started cleaning houses.

"People didn't understand why, with a music degree, Patty Jo would clean houses, but it was because she didn't want to tie herself down to a job that would not allow a flexible schedule. She found cleaning houses was a way not only to make relatively decent money, but it also gave her a flexible schedule. As a bonus, the people that she cleaned house for would work with her very easily, and if we had the opportunity to travel, she was able to cancel on short notice.

"Patty Jo's income total was about four or five hundred a month. And the way we split up the bills varied over a period of time. Our normal procedure was to sit down at the beginning of each month with our bills and discuss how much we owed and to whom. Rarely, at the end of tallying those bills, did we ever have enough money to actually pay all our bills at any given time. It was frequent that we were late paying bills. But we would look at the bills we had, and we hoped and prayed the money would come in that particular month to pay those bills. Later on, as things developed, and as our situation changed and more money came in, we would still do the same. We would again sit down with our bills, review all the bills, then decide what we could pay and what we couldn't pay at the time."

Patty Jo's family cautioned her that if Rick didn't assume his role as the husband and leader of their family, then they were headed for financial difficulties. At times,

Albert and Elva Mae stepped in and helped pay some bills that were outstanding. It was a sticky situation, and the Riddicks didn't want to discourage Rick and Patty Jo, but if they couldn't make a living in their music ministry, then they should have gone out and gotten real jobs.

"Patty Jo was raised much stricter and more structured than Rick," Patty Jo's niece, Connie, remarked. "Rules were important to our family, and were not to be broken. We believed in what was right and what was not. It was either black or white—there were no shades of gray.

"In our family, reputation was everything. People paid their bills, and they paid them on time. There was always an emphasis on each individual's consequences. Husband and wives were held accountable for their actions. Men were to be the breadwinners, the ones who worked hard to see to it the family's needs were provided.

"Men had careers, and they made enough money to support their families. Women were mostly expected to stay home, support their husbands, and be in charge of the home and taking care of the family. It wasn't that we were opposed to their music ministry—we admired them for that—but we didn't believe it made enough money to support them.

"We did know that Rick did not have the advantage of growing up with a strong male role model." Rick's grandfather had died when he was still young. "We assumed he never clearly understood that men had pretty much clear-cut goals and responsibilities, and that included their responsibility for income. We assumed he had never seen that, that the husband was to do whatever it took to make sure there was always enough money for all the necessities.

"But there are some men who grow up with strong women, who have seen the women accept total responsibility for everything, including the finances. The way Rick depended on Patty Jo, we thought he was one of those. We knew men who worked second and third jobs, just to make ends meet, but Rick was never one of those.

"Rick was also a little strange when it came to women. When we visited them after they were married, he would always choose to be around the ladies, regardless of what they were doing. He never engaged in activities with the men, but chose to do whatever Patty Jo was doing. When they came home to visit, it was always the same scenario—the men outside or in the den, while the women and Rick were in the kitchen."

One Sunday afternoon at a cousin's birthday party, Connie noticed her great-grandmother Etta Britt kept staring at Rick from across the room.

"Grandma, if you keep staring at him," she whispered, "you're going to spill your coffee on your skirt."

Etta composed herself, then said something Connie would never forget. "It's just that I've never seen a man behave like Rick does—always wanting to be around women. You know, that's not normal. It's not like any of the men in my day. . . ."

Connie put her hands to her face, acting as if this were her first time hearing her grandmother's roll call of all the great men in her life. "You mean, like granddaddy, Clark Cable, and Gary Cooper," she teased.

But the truth was obvious. Etta saw it, Connie saw it, and others saw it. Rick did like spending time with the ladies.

Etta frowned. "Well, I don't know why Patty Jo doesn't say something about it, but if it is okay with her, then it'll just have to be fine with me too."

"I guess Rick's need to draw comfort from women probably stems from his having been raised by women," Connie offered in his defense.

"Yes, I guess you're right," Etta agreed as she looked up at Connie. But, still, there was something that troubled her. "I do hope for Patty Jo's sake that is the only reason he acts that way."

The expression on Connie's face changed. The way her

grandmother talked about Rick's problem made her feel as if she knew more about Rick than she had revealed.

Unbeknownst to anyone at the time but Patty Jo, Rick had begun to dabble in 976 telephone sex sites a few years after they were married in 1982. Even though he did this secretly, and in the privacy of his own home, he knew this was not appropriate Christian behavior. It was not the sort of thing a minister and a leader in the church—particularly a youth minister—should participate in. Yet, Rick had developed a pang of desire for phone sex, something he couldn't seem to shake.

Rick did eventually own up to his sexual problems.

"It was basically a phone-sex-type thing," he admitted years later. "It was the first time that I had ever done anything like that in my life. At periods of time, that would continue to be a problem for me, and over the years, it would raise its ugly head up again. Yes, it was definitely something that I struggled with."

Chapter 13

As the Pulleys' church work evolved at RCF, doors again opened, and they began to see a lot of needs in the community that could be met. The church agreed to start an outreach program, and in 1985, Rick and Patty Jo started on-campus ministries at both Averett College (later renamed Averett University) and Danville Community College in Danville.

All the while they had been living in Ringgold, the Pulleys had been renting a small home at Sonshine South. In November 1986, RCF's pastor had offered them the use of the big farmhouse. Even though the church still used a lot of the spacious old house for Sunday school and other functions, there were a few rooms downstairs that were completed—mainly two bedrooms and a bath—that could be utilized.

The old farmhouse at RCF had at one time been used as a Christian school. When the Pulleys first moved in, there were still bulletin boards and chalkboards on the walls in all the rooms. Rick and Patty Jo took all those down and installed chair railing. Even though they were on a very limited, almost nonexistent, budget, they found a creative way to remodel. A lot of their labor for repairing and painting was donated by friends and church members. The Pulleys used the bulletin boards to make chair rails, and they repaired and refinished, plastered and painted, and refurbished all the rooms until the old house was completely renovated.

The Pulleys enjoyed living in their new home. It provided not only a stable base for their music opportunities, but it gave them a sense of belonging.

However, the house was not enough to make Patty Jo happy. Rick had not realized how unhappy Patty Jo would be when they stopped traveling full-time in the music ministry. It wasn't that she didn't enjoy working in the church with him, but church was his thing, and she just didn't find the fulfillment as when they had performed their music on the road. Rick thought about all the work and responsibility of being on the road versus the little income they had made. But, perhaps, a few additions to their group would enhance their programs and make things easier for the both of them.

In 1990, Jerry and Angel Cox (pseudonyms) joined the Pulleys' group, the Covenant Ministry, and began traveling with them on a regular basis. The Coxes were issued a small check from Rick after each trip so they could pay their expenses on the road. When they were not on the road, Jerry labored as a construction worker and used his income to help offset the difference between what Rick paid them and what he needed to pay his family's bills. Jerry was a huge help to Rick with the physical challenges of loading and unloading their equipment, as well as the setup and operation of the sound equipment and instruments.

Rick had learned a few things about marketing and sales while he was a manager at Big Star, and as a means of extra income for the group, he had started a merchandising table. He and Patty Jo had invested some of their money into studio time and had recorded several Christian tapes. These tapes, along with T-shirts, key chains, pictures, and other promotional materials, were being sold after the concert. Part of Jerry's job was to stock the merchandise table and collect the money when the items were sold.

It appeared as if the partnership of the two couples was working out. While Patty Jo and Rick continued performing as before, Angel was added as a keyboardist and background singer. If only Rick would have learned the value of the old saying "If you want to find out another woman's faults, then sing her praises to your wife."

And what started out as a good idea quickly turned sour.

"Rick, I am very angry with you right now," Patty Jo informed him one night after a concert.

"Why?" Rick asked, surprised. "What did I do?"

"You are ignoring what I say to Angel," Patty Jo explained in detail. "And you're taking her side."

In the past two years, Patty Jo had accepted Angel as part of the group, but she believed Angel was not as committed to the group as she was. Patty Jo was an accomplished musician with a trained voice. She was a perfectionist and would spend countless hours rehearsing and learning her music. The last thing she needed was someone in their group, singing and performing, who didn't feel as if she needed to practice. Patty Jo made that clear to Angel and told her she wasn't very pleased with her progress as a musician.

Rick didn't view Patty Jo's comments as cruel, and explained to Angel that this was just a part of her being direct. It was an open and honest assessment of Angel's progress—something that he and Patty Jo had done with one another from their first day of practice. He assured her it would help her improve as a musician, as it had him, but Angel didn't buy into that. That might have been okay for Rick and Patty Jo, as they were husband and wife, but she didn't appreciate Patty Jo's criticism and constant scrutiny.

"I don't know how much more of this I can take," Angel told Rick.

Rick took a deep breath, then let it out just as quickly. He was always a lot less direct with Angel than Patty Jo was. "Just don't worry about it. She didn't mean anything by it."

While Rick struggled to keep everyone in the group happy, and keep them focused on their goals, he found it difficult to buffer Patty Jo's feelings. Because he was trying to please both women, it wasn't too long before he found himself caught in the middle of their problems. It was an awkward situation for everyone involved.

Even bigger problems arose when Rick started giving Angel advice concerning her relational problems with Patty Jo. As far as he was concerned, the issues between Angel and Patty Jo were insignificant and petty. But to the two of them, he knew, they were very significant.

As Rick attempted to defend his wife, and maintain his friendship with Angel, he gradually got sucked in. Crossing over into the gray area that pastors and counselors consider the forbidden zone, Rick found himself getting attached to Angel. Knowing full well where this might lead, Rick plunged ahead in a feeble attempt to soothe Angel's feelings.

"I believe I was flattered by the pursuit of a pretty woman ten years younger than me" is how Rick described his motive for getting involved with Angel. "I had always been insecure about my looks, and that was why I stayed in the relationship until it became inappropriate. However, I believe Angel was motivated by a deep anger and bitterness toward Patty Jo. In her mind, I think, Angel believed Patty Jo was jealous of her. And that was why she thought Patty Jo was keeping her gifts and talents from developing and growing.

"When Angel first joined the group, she sought Patty Jo's approval. She wanted to do everything she could to satisfy her, but all of that changed radically after the first few concerts."

It was then that Rick stepped in and attempted to play peacemaker between the two women. For the benefit of the group, he wanted to see their relationship restored and healed. He felt Angel's feelings had been bolstered somewhat by him coming to her defense, but he learned later that Patty Jo had felt betrayed by her husband. She let Rick know immediately that her needs were more important than Angel's, and if he was going to take Angel's side every time they had an argument, then they should go back to when it was just the two of them.

"I wanted to see Patty Jo and Angel get along," Rick admitted. "I wanted them to work out their differences. I thought we had something good going with the group, and I wanted to keep us together more than anything else.

"It was in the summer of 1994, when the problems between Patty Jo and Angel really escalated. I started talking to Angel regularly, discussing the problems the two of them were having, and we started discussing other problems she was having that was specific to her life. During this time, she also started talking with me about her and her husband, and I guess I took on a role sort of as a counselor at that time."

Angel Cox was a very attractive, curvaceous girl, with long, dark hair. She had a very pleasing personality and made it clear to Rick she would do whatever she needed to do for the good of the group. That was too much of a temptation for Rick to overcome, and he took her at her word.

"Angel and I continued talking about our lives, even though I knew we were becoming attracted to one another. I started telling her how overwhelmed I felt with all my church work and my work with the music ministry. Out of her concern for me, she volunteered to help with my workload."

Rick told Angel she could help prepare and mail the promotional and publicity packets for the music ministry, as well as the discipleship packets to new believers. So they could be alone, he scheduled her to come by his house and work at his home office. Friday was normally a good day, as activities at the church slowed and Patty Jo cleaned homes until late in the evening.

As expected, one thing led to another between Rick and Angel, and they began engaging in inappropriate affection and inappropriate touching. According to Rick, that was as far as their relationship progressed. He did admit that they met over a half-dozen times in motel rooms, where they both got naked and masturbated each other, but stated they never engaged in sexual intercourse.

After three or four months of secretly meeting with Angel at motels and parks, Rick said, he woke up and saw the dangers of being involved in an adulterous relationship and what it would cost him.

What would happen if Patty Jo or the church ever found out? This is my marriage and my career that are on the line. The thought turned over in Rick's mind quite a few times. *This type of thing happened before with the church's first pastor and had caused the church to split.* He didn't want that.

"On numerous occasions, Patty Jo warned me that would happen. She said that a friendship could become too close, that this attraction could develop, and then problems would ensue between us. And, as if to add insult to injury, when we were off the road, I would ask Patty Jo to call and check on Angel because I believed she was fragile and depressed. A number of times, Patty Jo warned me about Angel and said that she was manipulating me to take her side.

"Angel and I never had sexual intercourse, but the inappropriate touching lasted three or four months. It ended after both [of us] mutually believed it should end, and I really don't remember who said it should end first, but I remember voicing the need to end the relationship, considering how it had progressed."

By Rick's own admission, his sexual problems had surfaced long before his relationship with Angel. As indicated by the phone sex incidents shortly after they were married, there was some form of sexual gratification that Rick was seeking. Additional intimacy issues developed over time and these began to affect his relationship with Patty Jo.

"In the early 1990s, actually," Rick remembered, "I began having a problem on occasions. It wasn't every time Patty Jo and I were together physically or sexually, but I began having a problem where it was just difficult to maintain an erection. Actually, it intensified after Patty Jo stopped taking the birth control pills in 1992 or 1993.

"I can't think of any great stressors that caused me to suffer from penile erectile dysfunction, but I do know it happened. This problem affected our intimacy and sex life in the obvious ways, but we maintained as best we could. We were able to have a very active sex life—I mean, we loved one another. We were passionate about one another, and we expressed that love to one another. It was a serious matter, but not in the sense of performance, not in the sense where that was an issue for either of us.

"As far as Patty Jo was concerned, it was more of an issue of whether or not I had a health problem. She thought maybe that was why I could not maintain an erection. She wanted me to see a doctor, that maybe it was my body's way of telling me there was something going on.

"But Patty Jo and I did not love each other any less because of my inability to maintain an erection. No, never. We continued to express our love and maintained a satisfactory sex life. Throughout this whole ordeal, we were still very much in love."

Chapter 14

After Rick's affair with Angel in 1994, Rick told Patty Jo they should disband the music ministry. Rick then informed her he was taking on the role as the church's associate pastor and planned on working full-time. The church would give him an extra $1,000 per year, as his duties also included the planning and promoting of worship, youth and college activities, and an array of other activities at the church. Sensing the need to stay close to Patty Jo, so as to stay out of trouble, Rick asked her to assist him with his work.

As Rick thought about it, he guessed Patty Jo could have been content with working at the church. She loved ministry of all kinds. She loved helping people. She loved caring for people, and whatever ministry they were involved in, she always found fulfillment.

Yet, deep down inside, he knew Patty Jo's greatest fulfillment was still music. She loved to minister in song. She wrote songs. She composed songs. She rearranged songs. That was something she enjoyed greatly and never seemed to tire of.

Rick, however, was moving in a new direction. Although he still loved performing, he had grown weary of their music ministry and was being driven by another passion. Pastor Lear had a great passion for foreign missions and he had instilled that same urgency and need for overseas work in Rick.

In 1987, Lear encouraged the Pulleys to travel internationally and get involved in missions. The Pulleys took their first mission trip that year to Haiti and the Dominican Republic, where they worked with the evangelistic teams in these Third World countries. Rick supervised crews of American volunteers and together they constructed churches and schools.

Rick was hooked on missionary work, believing he could make a difference in such impoverished areas. After his trip to the mission fields, he organized a mission program for teens, hoping they would gain a greater understanding for the Third World experience. Once Rick got involved in the regular outreach missions programs, he threw himself into it day and night. He started contacting and calling people, organizing and planning the trips, targeting different groups and churches for outreach.

In the late 1990s, Rick envisioned a change in his ministry. God was now directing him to minister to a group of nations, which included Romania. He announced to the church there would be an increased amount of his and Patty Jo's time that was going to be devoted to international ministries. Even though they loved traveling in the United States with their music, he had seen God calling them more and more into a ministry that would ultimately take them to all nations.

As always, the only obstacle to Rick fulfilling his dreams was finances.

In the late 1980s and early 1990s, the Pulleys' finances had never been stable. Sometimes they were up, and sometimes they were down—but mostly down.

In 1994, they had procured a credit card, and because they had such bad credit, it carried a high interest rate. It was very little credit, and a whole lot of interest.

"I think the bill limit wasn't much more than three

hundred dollars," Rick remembered. "But we still had a difficult time paying them. I was a horrible money manager and my problems at that particular time in our marriage was in justifying our expenses, as we were either moving into a house or trying to make one more attractive. We were doing different things to the houses, like buying furniture, and it was just a real struggle.

"Never having enough money to pay our bills was an obvious strain on our marriage. I guess Patty Jo struggled with that more than I did. We had always said, though, 'Where God guides, God provides,' but it was always difficult for us to make a decent living. Whenever we got to a place where we realized we didn't have enough money to pay our bills, we didn't question God. We questioned ourselves.

"The pattern I learned in the beginning of our marriage was that we would set aside all our bills and we would add up the money to determine if we had enough to pay our bills. I'd set aside a certain bill if we couldn't pay it, and for the moment, it would be out of sight and out of mind. That would become an awful habit for me to break."

Rick had a terrible habit of hiding his and Patty Jo's bills. She would frequently find a bill or get a call from a bill collector about a past-due item. Most of the time, he had simply tossed it in the trash or stuck it in a drawer somewhere. She would find the bills, take them to Rick, and shout, "Why hasn't this been paid? What are we going to do?" Rick and Patty Jo would then have to determine how they would come up with the money to pay the bill.

Patty Jo was a very proud person. She told Rick she hadn't gone to school, studied hard to get an education, and worked all these years to live a pauper's life. She reminded him of all the overdue bills they had had in the past, and how they had struggled just to make their piano payments. Their credit was so bad that they had to borrow money from her parents to buy their Dodge van, and even then they were late on half of those payments.

"Why can't we make enough money to pay our bills?"

Patty Jo wanted to know. "We don't pay any rent. We don't pay any utilities. We just have to pay for our general expense and our car payment, yet we can't seem to make ends meet."

Patty Jo was disappointed and angry. This was not how she had envisioned her life. The husband was supposed to work and make certain his family had enough money to take care of their needs. She had always supported Rick in everything he had wanted to do. Was it too much for her to ask him to be responsible enough to pay their bills? She didn't think so. In fact, she thought it was his duty as both a husband and a Christian to keep their financial matters straight.

Rick admitted he was a failure in this area. He vowed to change his ways and promised to set them on a road to financial recovery.

"I knew Patty Jo was frustrated with me, but she forgave me and we moved on. We valued our commitment to each other. She valued our relationship, she valued our marriage, and our happiness was never based on how much money we had. Our happiness was never based on my performance as a man, my failures or my struggles, or anything like that. But our marriage was based upon a commitment that we shared and that we believed in, and that we both valued."

The Pulleys' marriage was tested further in February 1995 when they attended a marriage conference at a Fort Caswell, North Carolina, Baptist retreat center. The topic of the seminar had been "oneness," where the leader stressed the importance of the husband and wives being one, the importance of their open communication, and the importance of couples sharing their struggles and failures. The focus was that the problems and arguments couples encountered within a marriage would not interfere with that oneness, with that experience, and that this type of oneness and sameness would strengthen a marriage. At the end of the seminar, the speaker then encouraged each couple to meet, inventory their marriage, and discuss any problems that might be affecting their relationship.

Rick was very encouraged. After lunch, he and Patty Jo talked about their marriage and their relationship; then he confessed to her about his affair with Angel Cox.

"I'm sorry I waited so long," Rick apologized. "I was just so ashamed, so embarrassed to tell you. I knew that it would hurt you when I told you."

Patty Jo was devastated. "Then why tell me at all, Rick?"

"Because after today I realized it was the Christian thing to do." Rick was being honest. "Husbands and wives shouldn't keep secrets from each other."

Patty Jo couldn't shake her anger. "But why now, Rick, of all days? Why on Valentine's Day?"

Rick didn't know how to answer that question, but provided a feeble attempt. "Uh, I knew at the time there were a couple of holidays coming up, like Thanksgiving and Christmas, and I didn't want to ruin them for you. I knew it would, uh, just totally ruin those holidays for you."

Patty Jo rolled her eyes. She didn't care about what he *thought*. That was more of Rick's excuse than a reason.

Rick told Patty Jo he knew this wasn't a justifiable reason, that he should have told her about the affair, but in his mind-set it was the only reason he had.

Patty Jo said she was hurt more than anything else. "After all we have been through together, how could you do something like this?" Then she felt betrayed and angry. "Didn't I tell you something would happen between you and Angel if you didn't leave her alone?"

Rick apologized. He didn't know what he was thinking. He should have walked away. "Flee from temptation, that's what the Bible says."

"Honestly, Rick, I've suspected it for a long time," Patty Jo said after she had gotten over the tears. Even though Rick claimed responsibility for the adulterous relationship, Patty Jo blamed Angel for what had happened. "She's got that sweet outward demeanor, but that is just a façade—just an act. I always believed she was vindictive and manipulative."

Patty Jo never felt the same about Rick after he confessed he had had an affair with Angel Cox. In the months and years that followed his 1995 Valentine's Day confession, her anger grew and became more intense. She reminded Rick about the previous incident where Pastor Newell's scandal had nearly annihilated the church. "Is that what you want for our church, Rick? Is that what you want for us?"

"No, no, no . . . ," Rick cried. "I'd kill myself first."

Out of grave concern for Rick and their church, Patty Jo refrained from any confrontation with Angel. She also had a fear that Angel's father, who Rick believed was a dangerous man, would retaliate if she caused any trouble for Angel and her husband.

Finally Patty Jo spoke with another minister's wife while at the couples' retreat and asked her for guidance. She was offered counsel and prayer, which helped her a great deal. She later apologized to Rick for the way she had acted and admitted her mistake was refusing to care for Angel.

"I neglected Angel and deferred that responsibility to you, even though I felt she was drawing you into something unhealthy," she said. "I want you to forgive me. And I pray that our marriage will be strengthened and our love deepened by this experience."

After Rick confessed his affair to Patty Jo, their marriage changed drastically. There were always the basic issues they had to deal with, but more important was the fact that they were paid workers in the church and still attended the same church as Jerry and Angel Cox. If word leaked out about Rick and Angel's affair, the church would not only suffer, but so would everyone else involved. Rick and Patty Jo would be asked to resign their positions, and their reputations as Christian ministers would be destroyed forever. There were plenty of people, for whatever reason, who would love to see both the church and Rick destroyed.

It seemed as if a pattern was developing in Rick's life. Every time God opened a door, Rick would do something to close it. He was constantly given an opportunity, yet he always seemed to paint himself in a corner. It was as if he, out of his own actions, deliberately drove himself into the ground so he could rise again. And, somehow, like the mythical phoenix, he always rose again. He always managed to talk himself out of a jam or find a window to crawl out of.

According to Rick, Patty Jo never considered leaving him.

"There was always a trust issue, which was natural for her to trust me, for her to question my trustworthiness, but divorce or separation was never discussed. I will say she was deeply hurt and deeply angry, but she made the choice to give me her love, to give me trust, and to give me her forgiveness. I promised her I would never stray again, and I didn't."

One never knows when love begins and how it is going to end, but there seems to always be something that comes along to fill in the gaps in between. The week Rick and Patty Jo arrived home from the February marriage retreat, their next-door neighbor Judy Sudduth brought over a three-month-old puppy. Rick had had several dogs in his adult life and absolutely fell in love with the puppy.

"What's her name?" Rick asked Judy. "She sure is a beautiful dog."

Judy handed Rick the puppy. "We call her 'Flowers,' but I'm not sure what her real name is."

As Rick continued petting the puppy, he remembered how easily he got attached to animals. He had owned several dogs in his youth, and found them to be very loving and loyal. Perhaps this was just the diversion they needed to help them get through their marital difficulties.

Rick turned toward Patty Jo and whimpered in a little boy's voice, "Can we keep her, please?"

Patty Jo shook her head. "No. With all we've got going on in our lives right now, we just don't have the time."

"Please, Patty Jo," Rick begged. "I don't see anything wrong with having a dog. I think it would be good for the both of us."

"Okay, Rick, tell me then who is going to clean up after her, feed her, give her water . . . all the things that a dog needs. Caring for a dog is a big responsibility, and I've got more than I can handle right now in my life."

Rick pleaded again. "Look, if you'll agree for us to keep the dog, then I promise to vacuum after her. I promise to feed her. I promise to brush her. And I promise to train her."

"I don't know, Rick."

"Please let's keep her," Rick continued, until Patty Jo finally relented.

"Okay, okay . . . we can keep her," Patty Jo said, finally giving in. "You can have the dog, but as long as we change her name. The thought of calling a dog 'Flowers' doesn't sit too well for me."

Rick and Patty Jo made a list of names and narrowed their choices down to two: One was "Grace" and the other was "Mercy."

"Because we valued our marriage at that particular time in our lives," Rick recalled, "those were the two names we came up with. We thought they not only depicted our situation, but they demonstrated the value of God's grace and the value of God's mercy that Patty Jo had showed me at that time. We finally decided on the name, 'Grace.'

"No one knew the significance of that name; only me and Patty Jo. When someone asked why we had chosen the name 'Grace,' we told them we had named her that because it was by the grace of God that Patty Jo had let me keep her."

Chapter 15

In the summer of 1995, Mary Sue Fields had completed her studies at the University of Virginia and was looking forward to spending a missionary trip with Rick and Patty Jo in the Dominican Republic.

Mary Sue had first met Rick and Patty Jo Pulley at a Christian conference in July 1982. She was twelve years old then, and she and her mother would drive from Lebanon, Virginia, and attend this particular conference every summer. She met the Pulleys, who had just gotten married earlier that year and they were serving as youth directors of the church. She remembered Patty Jo had turned twenty, and she thought Rick was about six years older than her.

Mary Sue was smitten with the Pulleys, and, in Christian terminology, they had witnessed to her. As a result of sharing their faith, she, too, became a Christian. Over the next couple of summers, Mary Sue and the Pulleys continued their friendship. She went back to the same conference each July, where the Pulleys served as the youth conference leaders. She quickly became very attached to them.

By her own confession, Mary Sue was probably one of the most zealous teenagers at the conference. She totally fell in love and admired the Pulleys. They were her biblical "ram in the bushes," the persons who taught her that Christ was God's ultimate sacrifice for humanity's sin.

"It would not have been an exaggeration to state that aside from my parents," Mary Sue recalled, "they were probably the two people on earth that I loved the most."

As Mary Sue grew older and attended high school, the Pulleys were still the youth leaders at that conference. When she first met them, they were living in Winston-Salem at a girls' group home. She had never visited them there, but she did correspond with them through letters and phone calls throughout the year. Later, when the Pulleys moved to Ringgold, Virginia, and when Mary Sue was a junior in high school, she was invited to visit them in Ringgold.

After Mary Sue's junior year in high school, the Pulleys were very settled in the Ringgold church, and invited her to TNT, which stood for "teens in training." TNT was to be a program led jointly by the Pulleys and Associate Pastor Randy Sudduth and his wife. The teenagers would learn how to work with the children and how to share the Bible. They would work with children in the morning classes with the Sudduths and go through discipleship training with the Pulleys in the afternoon.

"The Pulleys planned on teaching us the Bible," Mary Sue said, "and they were going to share their vision from the mission fields with us. In Christian language, they planned on sharing their hearts with us and discipling us, and I was very enthusiastic to that invitation."

In 1986, the first summer Mary Sue visited Ringgold, she lived with Randy and Judy Sudduth, and the Sudduths' boys lived with the Pulleys. The next summer, she returned to the program for a time and lived with the Pulleys.

"I had the opportunity to travel on the road with them when they went on music tours on the weekend," Mary Sue remembered. "I just spent a lot of time in prayer and counseling with them, and, quite frankly, I was just completely sold on them, their mission, and their vision. I thought there were no other persons in the world I wanted to be with at the time than Rick and Patty Jo."

After Mary Sue graduated from high school, she attended Carson-Newman College in Jefferson City, Tennessee, but she kept in contact with the Pulleys by phone. On one occasion, they visited Mary Sue at her hometown church in Lebanon. She was proud to introduce the Pulleys not only to her friends and family, but to her pastor, Jeff Williams, and his wife, Peggy.

When Mary Sue graduated from college and entered a graduate studies program at the University of Virginia in 1993 through 1995, she was much closer to the Pulleys, as Charlottesville was only about 2½ hours from Ringgold. On holidays and on long weekends, she would drive down and visit the Pulleys.

In the summer of 1995, before leaving for France to complete a summer internship teaching at the University of Nice, Mary Sue decided to accompany the Pulleys on a mission trip to the Dominican Republic. Although she had visited them many times in the course of her life, and considered them to be dedicated Christians, she started noticing a change that summer in Rick. There was a change in his behavior. He was not the same Rick she had known and loved most of her life. He was behaving like the Reverend Jim Jones, or some of the other cult leaders she had read about.

Since Mary Sue was not connected to the church, a lot of her visits often turned into a gripe session for Rick. He unloaded a lot of information on her about people in the church, whom he believed were persecuting him and trying to destroy him.

"There was always somebody in the church that was having problems with Rick," Mary Sue revealed about her and Rick's conversations. "Of course, he was always in the right and the other person was always in the wrong. At that stage of my life, I would have followed Rick and Patty Jo to the ends of the earth. I trusted them, and I believed their perspective on what was happening at the church, but as time went on, I began to question if all that was true.

"I felt controlled and misled. I realized the views that I had formed of the people in the church were based on Rick Pulley's views, not on mine, and that my career decision was somewhat controlled by Rick's ideas and plans for me. Patty Jo and I were close, and I even noticed that she started stepping in between me and Rick, asking him not to put so much pressure on me to make certain career decisions and other decisions for my future.

"I understand that Rick has on many, many occasions thought he was hearing from God," Patty Jo said to Mary Sue before they left on the trip to the Dominican Republic. "I do know he has a strong personal desire for you to move to Ringgold."

Mary Sue was floored. Why would Rick want her to move to Ringgold? There was nothing for her there.

"He wants you to move here and join him in missions work," Patty Jo told her. "He said God revealed that to him."

Suddenly it all came together for Mary Sue. "Oh, yes, he has been telling me that God has spoken to him and that God told him He wanted me in missions work."

Patty Jo shook her head, then bit down on her bottom lip. "Sweetheart, I want you to listen to me," she advised. "Do not let Rick control you and your life. Sometimes he wants what he wants, and his own will gets in the way. That is why it is so important that you listen for yourself and decide what God wants for you, and not what Rick has said. You need to hear the will of God and decide what you want for your own career."

That summer, Mary Sue and the Pulleys traveled to the Dominican Republic, taking a group of teenagers from their churches and other churches with them. Because

Mary Sue spoke some Spanish, she was listed officially as one of the chaperones. One evening, on a field trip, she got to experience a different Rick Pulley than she had ever seen before.

"Everybody was kind of milling around and getting ready to go to their cabin for bedtime," Mary Sue stated. "Rick pulled me aside and asked to speak to me. I had to kind of put it in perspective that all of our teenage years we were taught—a lot of it by the Pulleys—that young women and pastors didn't talk together, unless there was another person with them. So I was a little bit uncomfortable, apart from the group like we were, but at least we were in a public place.

"We were standing near our living quarters when Rick suddenly began to sob. He was crying and told me that he was struggling to define what our friendship was—what our relationship was going to be in the future. Well, I was just a child when Rick and I first met, and that is the same way I felt about him now. I wanted him to remember that I was *still* one of his youths in his youth ministry. Rick then told me how much he and Patty Jo loved me and cared about me, but he said he didn't know how to define our relationship."

What Rick Pulley said to Mary Sue struck her square in the face. She knew what he was driving at and she knew better than to fall for such foolishness from a guy her own age, but she didn't expect this from Rick, her pastor.

"All the time, he kept crying and weeping, then saying that he knew I was the youth and he was the pastor. It didn't take me too long to know that was just a setup for what *he thought* was going to happen."

At first, Mary Sue sensed maybe Rick had become jealous of her father again. On another occasion, he had said he had put himself into her father's position and often thought of her as a daughter. He had expressed great remorse that he had never fathered any children, pointing out to Mary Sue that Patty Jo had never wanted children, and now that he was at a certain age, he wondered what it would have been like to be a father. Maybe this was his motive for such strange behavior.

Mary Sue could have understood that, given Rick's age and his responsibility at the church, because at some point, he probably had thought of and treated her like his daughter. If that was the case, then Rick would have been angry with her father. He had said to her several times that he didn't think her father was as responsive to her as a father should be.

"No, this is not a father/daughter relationship," Rick clarified as Mary Sue struggled to figure out if their relationship was related to friendship at all. "And if it is a friendship, is it more a girlfriend/boyfriend relationship? We're not lovers, but it's much stronger than that."

Rick continued weeping as he stuttered and stammered, trying to define the concepts of his and Mary Sue's relationship.

Mary Sue was speechless. It wasn't the kind of conversation she was normally accustomed to having with Christian pastors. Rick had never behaved that way before. Suddenly a door opened from behind her, and Patty Jo stepped outside. Mary Sue then saw that she and Rick had been talking outside his and Patty Jo's bedroom. In all likelihood, Patty Jo had heard every word of their conversation.

Patty Jo came outside with a look on her face that Mary Sue had never seen before. She didn't speak or talk with either one of them. Mary Sue had never had any relationship problems with Patty Jo, and she wanted to tell her then why she was there with Rick, and what *he* had said to her.

"Ricky, I think it's time for you to come to bed," Patty Jo said very authoritatively. She gave Rick a dirty look, and he turned around and walked inside their quarters.

Patty Jo didn't say anything to Mary Sue, not even a "good night," and that struck her as very strange. She walked away from that experience very concerned Patty Jo believed she and Rick were romantically involved. There was nothing in Mary Sue's frame of reference that could have made her believe that Patty Jo would be suspicious or concerned, but the authoritative voice and that look on her face made Mary Sue very concerned about their friendship.

Before Mary Sue flew home from the Dominican Republic, she talked to a friend in Lebanon about the situation. "Gee, I hope Patty Jo didn't think that I was trying to seduce her husband, or that there was something inappropriate between us."

Mary Sue had driven to the Pulleys' home in her father's 1988 Ford Escort. After returning home from the missionary trip, she was scheduled to board the plan and fly to France. Mary Sue had agreed to leave her dad's car with them until she returned to the United States the following year. The Pulleys owned just the one car, a van, and the idea was that Rick could drive her dad's car until she returned from France. Mary Sue had also volunteered to leave the Pulleys her desk computer so they could use that as well.

"I promise you we'll take good care of both your car and your computer," Rick assured Mary Sue. "They will be a big help to our ministry here in Ringgold. And we'll deliver them to your father before you arrive on Christmas vacation."

Mary Sue flew back from France at Christmastime, 1995, for her two-week vacation. She landed in Washington, DC, where her mother picked her up at the airport and drove her home to Lebanon. When Mary Sue and her mother arrived, the Escort was not at her house.

Mary Sue and her mother drove to Ringgold and visited the Pulleys. She was worried that something had happened between them that she wasn't aware of. Fortunately, she arrived to find out that things appeared to be okay between the Pulleys, and before she left, Patty Jo and Rick pulled her aside and offered her a very special gift: an Irish ring with two hands and a jade stone in the middle and a heart with a crown over the top.

"Oh, my God, it's beautiful," Mary Sue exclaimed as she pulled out the ring from the brightly wrapped box.

Patty Jo smiled. She glanced first at Rick, then back at Mary Sue. "I don't know what you call this," she said. "I think it might be an Irish engagement ring."

The Pulleys talked about the symbolism of the ring, how they viewed the two hands as themselves with Mary Sue's heart in the middle, and the crown as being the Lord reigning over the top. Afterward, Mary Sue got the sense that their friendship was okay, that maybe she had overreacted to that incident in the Dominican Republic. She had wanted to talk with Patty Jo alone, but she didn't get the opportunity. They were too busy talking about all of her travels to France and other parts of Europe.

"Do you remember when we had our youth meetings when you were a teen?" Patty Jo asked out of the blue. She then reminded Mary Sue of the importance of purity and not having sex before marriage. There were dangers of premarital sex, and she knew this because she was pure when she married Rick. But for Rick, it was different. He had had other girlfriends and he had struggled with those relationships, even now that they were married.

"For the sake of your future husband, Mary Sue, I want to remind you how difficult it is for a couple when one of the spouses has had former partners. They'll always have struggles with intimacy because of flashbacks to old girlfriends and such. It's hard not to get jealous when that happens."

Mary Sue never expected such candor from Patty Jo.

"You're still single, Mary Sue. You can travel, do all you want to do, enjoy yourself and your life."

During Mary Sue's 1995 to 1996 school year in France, she received several phone calls from Rick. In the past, it had always been the three of them: Mary Sue, Rick, and Patty Jo. Now Rick seemed be narrowing it down to just the two of them.

"Can I talk to Patty Jo before we hang up?"

"Uh, she's not here," Rick would say. "She's at the house and I'm here at the church, calling you from my office."

Something in the Pulleys' relationship had gone very wrong. Priorities had shifted, and Rick and Patty Jo seemed to be distancing themselves from each other.

The Christmas plan for the following year, 1996, was for Mary Sue to fly into Washington, DC, then rent a car and drive to Charlottesville to spend the first night with a friend of hers. Rick and Patty Jo would drive up with her father's Escort and leave it there for her to collect in Charlottesville. Mary Sue had called ahead and confirmed if the Pulleys were still coming. It wasn't clear who was going to come, but Mary Sue was told *someone* would pick her up at her friend's house. But Mary Sue never expected Rick to pick her up that Friday. It just wasn't a normal thing that should have been happening between them.

"Where's Patty Jo?" Mary Sue immediately asked, when Rick pulled in the driveway.

"Oh, she had something else to do."

Mary Sue still felt uncomfortable and told Rick that.

"Yeah, one of the elders told me that it wasn't wise to drive up here and pick up a young lady alone," Rick joked. "But I don't care. Don't worry about it, it's fine."

Mary Sue had no choice. Rick was her pastor. Besides, she had no other way to get home. She and Rick had always had a pastor/friend relationship, but as they were driving home, they crossed cars with someone on a two-lane road, when Rick laughed and joked, "Oh, I know that guy from my community. He's going to comment and make gossip that I'm having an affair with a beautiful young woman."

But it wasn't a joke to Mary Sue. Maybe with someone else, maybe in another setting, but it was an abrupt change in what she had been taught over the years. Now that she was an adult, the only role for a pastor was to be a friend with a pastoral relationship. There was something out of the ordinary that struck her about Rick, that made her feel terribly uncomfortable. Probably if she had heard this from any other man in the world and not someone who was her pastor, it wouldn't have upset her as much.

After Rick and Mary Sue returned to Ringgold, they spent the evening with Patty Jo, and everything was fine again. Mary Sue had expected to spend a large period of the holidays with the Pulleys at that time, but the next morning after she woke up, took her shower, and was upstairs getting ready, she heard Rick downstairs calling her, saying, "Please come downstairs. I have something urgent to talk to you about."

Drawing from all those years she had spent in Bible study with the Pulleys, her first question was "Where's Patty Jo?"

"Don't worry, it's fine," Rick shouted back. "She's at aerobics. She'll be back a little bit later."

"Okay," Mary Sue said, trying to avoid Rick's request. "I'll come down when Patty Jo is back."

Rick was very insistent. He kept saying over and over how desperately they needed to talk, that there were things on his mind that he needed to say to her. "We just need to talk."

Mary Sue shrugged. "Okay," she said, trying to avoid the situation. "I'll dry my hair and I'll come down, and then we'll talk."

But Mary Sue didn't do that. Instead, she packed her suitcases that morning and she waited upstairs until Patty Jo came home that afternoon. Mary Sue got her suitcases and walked downstairs.

"I have changed my mind about attending that family event this evening," Mary Sue said, making a feeble excuse for not staying the night. "But I think I am going to attend the annual Christmas dinner tomorrow, so I best be heading out before I get snowed in."

Rick and Patty Jo stood in the hallway. Patty Jo didn't protest, but Rick was very insistent that she not leave and go home.

"You can't see it?" Rick started in again on Mary Sue. "Your family isn't really a family, or, at least, they don't treat you like a family. You're committed to staying with us now. You shouldn't go home. That's not the best thing for you or for us."

Rick was addressing Mary Sue in the same controlling, manipulative voice that she had heard gradually increasing over the years. Mary Sue had always been loyal to the Pulleys and very compliant. As long as she had known them, she had wanted nothing more than to please them.

"I had always listened to Rick's voice and did what he wanted without question," Mary Sue admitted. "But on that morning, I just felt a different sense in that I was going to make a decision, and that my leaving them would probably cause a breakup in our relationship and with the people in the church. I knew I wouldn't be able to explain to them why I had run away, but I was going to leave."

Patty Jo stood up and jumped in the middle between Mary Sue and Rick. She spread her arms, then looked at Mary Sue with such sadness that it nearly crushed Mary Sue, as if to say, "You're doing the right thing, sweetheart. Go now, while you are still strong and young."

Rick was crying and shaking, mouthing the words, "Don't go, Mary Sue. Please don't go."

"Let her go, Rick," Patty Jo shouted in tears. "She has to decide what she wants to do with her life, and not you."

Mary Sue hugged and kissed both Rick and Patty Jo good-bye, picked up her luggage, and ran to her car. She cranked up the engine and was about to pull away when Rick came bolting out the front door, running toward her car, in tears again. Just as he had spoken to her the night on the porch in the Dominican Republic, he spoke to her in the same manner.

"Please don't leave me," he said, almost as if he were begging. "You cannot go. Please, you're hurting me."

It wasn't an issue that Mary Sue needed to discuss with the Pulleys any longer, but the delusion that Rick had—that God had shown him that "there were somehow things in my past, some deep dark hidden sins that I hadn't shared with him"—was a little too much.

"What was even worse," Mary Sue would reflect years later, "was that Rick believed, not that I needed to share them for me, but that I needed to share them for his sake. That it would hurt him if I didn't open up, and God had told him that."

"I didn't share these things with you about my past," Mary Sue finally told him, "because you had put me on a pedestal and I felt that I had to be perfect for you."

"Oh, God, I'm sorry if that was the case," Rick apologized, his face wet with tears. "But you have to do it now, Mary Sue. You have got to open up."

Rick reminded Mary Sue about the sermons he used to preach during Christian Youth Fellowship and teach at TNT. One of the sermon topics was about wearing masks, and the Greek word *"porneia,"* which indicated infidelity and fornication.

Over the past fifteen years, there had been a lot of sermons Rick had preached to Mary Sue, to young people in church and at their concerts, about how the modern Christian Church had so many problems because the Christian people wore masks. This was one of Rick's favorite sermons.

"We hide behind masks," Rick would always say. "And we are not honest with other people. We don't share what really is happening in our lives, and there are too many secrets. There are too many feelings that aren't shared, and that is why I am giving you this as a mandate—that you teenagers be open with pastors like me."

For the first time, Mary Sue believed she clearly saw what was going on behind closed doors in Rick Pulley's life. She sat in her car, looking at Rick, and thought, *Maybe I'm finally catching some glimpses of what it means for someone to hide behind a mask and pretend to be something else. And it is because of Rick's hypocrisy that I am going to flee from a relationship that was the most important to me in my lifetime.*

"Sorry, Rick," Mary Sue said, rolling up her window. "I have to go."

The expression on Rick's face changed, and suddenly turned cold and hard. "God told me that you're not telling me everything."

Mary Sue was hurt. She had counseled with her pastor at the Lebanon Community Fellowship Church, Jeff Williams, and she knew Rick knew him well.

"Is this something God has revealed to you, or did Jeff Williams tell you this?" she demanded to know.

"It was God that told me this," Rick declared boldly.

Mary Sue shifted her car in drive and pulled away from Rick. She didn't even turn to look at him in the driveway, but kept on driving until she finally reached Lebanon, five hours later.

"More than half of that drive, I spent in tears," Mary Sue recalled, "realizing later that I had just left the most important relationship of my life. And, what was worst, I would not be able to explain to anyone why I had done that. I could never conceive of myself explaining to Patty Jo exactly why I wasn't going back.

"I was almost twenty-six years old at the time of the incident and an educated graduate student, yet I wrote in my journal after that evening, 'How am I going to tell Patty Jo? What am I going to say to her?' And I finally did write something—maybe not the most appropriate language— but I did write about how I would tell a woman how I think her husband has become creepy. That I didn't run away because of her, but I ran away because of him.

"I knew I couldn't speak to Randy or Judy Sudduth

about Rick. Even though Randy was now the senior minister, I still had no inkling of an idea that anybody in that church would understand the shift that I had witnessed in Rick Pulley. It was a gradual shift, but something, nonetheless, that was so real and so dramatic that I was willing to walk away from the relationship forever."

When Mary Sue left the Pulleys' home in 1996, she carried everything with her that was hers. The only thing she did not carry was her computer. After she completed her teaching in France, and returned back to the States in the fall of 1997, she left messages at the Pulleys' home, telling them she would like to have her computer back for her studies and, ultimately, give it to her father.

Mary Sue had heard a rumor that the Pulleys were coming to her parents' church in Lebanon. The scuttlebutt was they were talking to the pastor, Jeff Williams, about them being hired for a position at Lebanon Community Fellowship. Mary Sue contacted the Pulleys again and asked that they bring the computer with them when they came.

When the Pulleys arrived in Lebanon, they didn't have Mary Sue's computer with them. Rick, however, had sent her a messages that it was very important for their ministry, and that maybe she wasn't hearing from God, that she needed to leave the computer right where it was.

Eventually the Pulleys packed it up in a box and mailed it to Mary Sue. At that point, however, Mary Sue didn't care. Although terribly heartbroken, she had finally ended her relationship with Rick and Patty Jo Pulley.

Chapter 16

In the 1990s, life was not faring well for the Pulleys. Their music ministry had ended, they were having relational problems, and the River of Life Church (as the church was now being called) was growing skeptical of Rick. They were questioning his spiritual commitment.

Even though Rick and Patty Jo were both working at the church, they still struggled financially and had numerous delinquent bills arriving at their home. They would take turns trying to manage their finances, and most of the time, it was a losing cause. The tab for their Romania trip was eventually paid for by the church, with the understanding that a portion of Rick's salary would be withdrawn for a month until that amount was settled. Because the money for the trip was being deducted from Rick's salary, they didn't have enough money to pay their April bills.

"The bills started adding up," Rick recalled. "I tried to pay them, but we didn't have any money. The payment that we were most concerned with was the van payment. We were two months behind on it, and I began to receive calls about our past-due amount.

"Patty Jo and I even discussed selling her piano. We thought the value had increased by now, but we later found out it hadn't. We had moved at least ten times since we had been married, and that piano was so hard to move because it didn't have wheels on it. We wanted to trade it in for a baby grand piano, but couldn't afford it."

Both the pastor and the elders had talked to Rick about the pressures that were piling on him. They advised him he was taking on too much, that he should concentrate on just a few areas of ministry, and not attempt to save the entire world. Rick should focus more on getting his life and priorities in order.

As a result of that conversation, Rick and Patty Jo began to feel as if the church was sending them a message, and felt as if their contributions to the church ministry were being minimized.

In 1997, the Pulleys were also told that the pastor and the elders had met and that Rick and Patty Jo would have to move from the big farmhouse they had been living in for the past ten years. Pastor Randy Sudduth had sold his house a couple of years earlier to escape some debt, and he and his family had since moved into a small home that the church owned. The church now wanted Rick and Patty Jo to switch homes with the Sudduths.

"We offered to switch houses when Randy first moved in the small house," Rick said in his defense, "but the elders assured that wasn't necessary. We were told the larger farmhouse was our home and switching was out of the question. At that time, we had sold our older furniture and were buying newer furniture as we redid the farmhouse. We did this in order to create additional space and provide a greater capacity so we could extend hospitality to our guests."

Almost every weekend in the 1990s, the Pulleys had had overnight guests. The dining room in the farmhouse could seat as many as thirty-five to forty people, and Patty Jo enjoyed entertaining such large numbers. People they had met on the road would come and spend their entire vacation with the Pulleys. In addition, they housed all of the guest ministers and visiting missionaries, as well as their families and guests. Patty Jo considered this a calling upon her life and valued the opportunities to serve. When they were informed they had to switch homes with the Sudduths, they both took it personally. Patty Jo was hurt more than Rick. She felt as if they had been evicted.

"Patty Jo and I were hit very hard by the request to switch houses," Rick explained as his reason for the bitterness toward the church. "We understood the practicality of it—the pastor and his wife had several children, and we had none. Yet, we still felt underappreciated and even betrayed. It was at that time that we began praying about leaving the church.

"At the same time, our hearts were growing stronger in a desire for a ministry to the nations. We had spent significant time in Haiti, the Dominican Republic, and Romania and had seriously considered a move to either of the three to work with our own contacts there. We also wanted to continue our goal of exposing young people to the mission field on a short-term basis."

Rick made a few calls to several people and tested the waters about a move and change in a ministry position elsewhere. The most promising and appealing of these places was with Jeff Williams at the Lebanon Community Fellowship Church.

"We spoke seriously with the pastor of the church there and he received positive responses from his leaders and even began raising the money for a pastoral position," Rick said. "We did not speak to anyone at Ringgold about a possible move, but we did speak to others in the ministry for advice and counsel."

But there were other problems the church and Rick were experiencing. One in particular was Rick's proposed March 1998 trip to Romania. Two years prior, he and Patty Jo had taken their first trip to Romania. While they were there, they had visited a group of missionaries and were excited to hear that one of the single missionaries was actually considering marrying a Romanian woman.

That same year, the missionaries that the church were supporting in Romania flew home for furlough during the holidays, and the Pulleys learned those missionaries had indeed gotten married. They had gotten everyone in the church excited about the ripe mission fields in Romania and had talked to the Pulleys about going back with them in March. The idea was for Rick and Patty Jo to accompany the missionaries back to Romania for the purpose of doing an outreach with the college students that would be returning at that time.

Apparently, with all the leadership changes that had taken place in the church, there was some misunderstanding as to who was in charge. In the past, when Robbie Lear was pastor, the Pulleys had basically just gone in their own directions. After stating what they felt like they should do and what they felt God was leading them to do, they'd plan these events, and do them, and then discuss them later. If there were any funds needed for the events that were to be allocated from the budget, and if there was budget money available from the church, then they would budget that money.

"After talking with the couple from Romania," Rick recalled, "we began to discuss pretty quickly our plans and what we wanted to do and how much air fare we were going to pay. We had found a good rate, a good air fare rate, that would fly us to Romania, so we purchased the tickets in January.

"I went to Richard Gardner, who was serving as the church administrator, and told him about our trip. He knew about our plans of going to Romania with the missionaries, and had helped us do an outreach. He then agreed to reimburse us the costs for the plane tickets, keeping in mind that we were going to be raising some money, maybe through fund-raisers or through offerings in the church, to help offset the cost of the expenses of the trip."

In December 1998, the Pulleys discussed their Romania

trip with Pastor Randy Sudduth. They asked him if they could do a fund-raiser to help pay for their tickets.

"I knew there was no money in the church budget," Rick explained. "There had been a drop in the offerings and the church was struggling with its own financial obligations. So I asked if we could take up special offerings for us and for the trip specifically, and he waited, until the last Sunday before we left for Romania, to come and talk with us."

"Rick, I'm afraid the elders did not believe this trip should be a church-sponsored trip." Randy tried to break the news gently. "But the church is not going to help you."

Rick was red in the face. He was losing his temper.

"Why didn't you come to us sooner, Randy, and let us know that then? We've already committed to the trip and it's too late to get our money back or start a fund-raising project."

"How did you pay for the tickets?" Randy asked.

"We put them on our credit card."

"Then just call your credit card and cancel the purchase," Randy suggested.

"It's not that easy. We've already committed to go and they are counting on us in Romania."

Randy took a deep breath. Rick always seemed to get himself into jams, but Randy didn't think the church should bail him out this time.

"Rick, this is what we've been trying to tell you all along. The church doesn't have the money to do all the things you are requesting. This trip to Romania is another example of why we believe you should back off from additional responsibilities, and concentrate on the work here in Ringgold. The elders and I both have talked to you on several occasions about you doing too much and our concerns that you were burning out."

Rick was offended. He and Patty Jo had already stopped leading the two college campus ministries they had started a few years back. What else did they want him to do? Stop serving God altogether?

"I think you're blowing this all out of proportion here." Randy downplayed it. "Maybe you are suffering from ministerial burnout and just need a break. You just need to relax and take it easy for a while."

Rick had heard about these ministerial sabbaticals. He'd heard of ministers who had agreed to a leave of absence, only to come home one night with a note on their door: *We no longer need your services. Please vacate the parsonage.*

"No, that's not happening," Rick said. "I refuse to go on any kind of leave. There's nothing wrong with me."

Patty Jo tried to calm Rick. She didn't see it as a bad thing, but maybe as an opportunity for them to travel some. Maybe they could visit her folks, or ride down and visit the folks at the Circus Tent at the Outer Banks. It would be nice to have a period of time where she and Rick could worry about their needs and no one else's for a while. After all, he would get paid for the entire year. Maybe he could get a job, like the manager of a grocery store. They could make some money, pay off some bills, and put something back for the future. It sounded like a good plan to her.

Rick explained further that he wasn't really opposing a sabbatical, but he was resisting because there was so much work to do. It would be almost impossible to get everything done before he could set up a sabbatical.

"We actually had discussed a yearly sabbatical every so often for all the people that were in the staff, including Randy," Rick explained. "I wasn't resistant to that type of sabbatical. It was just the timing of it. I was in a place where my leadership style was changing. I was developing or attempting to develop leadership within the groups that I was working with. I was working in the youth ministry. I was bringing more individuals on to help with the youth— more adults or young college students primarily—and had been giving more and more responsibility over to them.

I was attempting to take on more of just an advisory or oversight role of that ministry, but it would still need me to be there."

Rick admitted he didn't handle it well.

"Yes, I was angry at Randy, but the way I saw it, it was just a manifestation of my outspokenness at the time. I don't remember being angry about the request for me to take a sabbatical. I do remember being upset over the notification that the church was not going to be helping with the trip to Romania that we were taking just two weeks later."

Rick had never told Randy about his sexual conduct. Even after he was nominated and ordained an elder, he still never confessed to Randy anything about his relationship with Angel. It was something that he didn't think needed to be reconciled. He and Patty Jo had talked about it and worked things out. That was enough for him.

Chapter 17

Cassandra Martin could hardly believe Rick and Patty Jo Pulley were living in Ringgold and were employed at the River of Life Church. Martin had known the Pulleys when she, too, was a student at Meredith College. She had unfortunately witnessed an argument between them and heard Rick threaten to kill Patty Jo.

Cassandra lived in Semora, North Carolina, not in Ringgold, but her children had attended some of the activities at the church with their friends. After hearing Rick was associate pastor at the church and leading a lot of the activities, she was mortified. She was afraid of him and could not imagine him being there, especially working with her children.

"I hear the church has been having some problems with Rick Pulley," she cautiously mentioned this to her friend. She wanted her friend, who was a member at the church, to know that if the truth were to be told, Rick had not been up to speed for a long time.

"I'll never forget how he threatened Patty Jo," she told her friend. "It is always something that I've kept in the back of my mind, and every time I see the Pulleys, I can't help but think about that."

Over time, Cassandra bumped into Rick at the youth activities. One night, when she stepped inside the church to watch a play rehearsal, he asked one of the other adults to tell her he wanted to see and talk with her in private.

From across the aisle, Cassandra studied Rick's face as he stared at her with a slanted little smile. His face was much fuller than she had remembered, making his eyes look narrow. All she could see were two thin slits of blue.

"You tell him I am not interested in meeting with him," Cassandra said politely. She watched Rick's face change after the adult delivered her message. He sat down near the piano and started rubbing his face and head with the tips of his fingers. It was clearly the gesture of a perplexed man.

Later, whenever Cassandra saw Patty Jo at the church and started talking with her, Rick would suddenly appear from nowhere and their conversation would abruptly end. She vividly remembered times when Rick had been working with the children at the church, how he would have temper tantrums. In front of everyone, she saw him throw things and yell at Patty Jo.

Rick and Patty Jo had also performed at another local church that Cassandra had attended. During the on-stage activities, Rick would even have temper tantrums. She had witnessed that and it scared her to death.

"Patty Jo never came right out and said Rick had been abusing her," Cassandra Martin would say later, "but she would drop hints that she had a great fear of Rick. After all I witnessed, I can see why. The man was dangerous."

Cassandra took her children to the church during the summer of 1998. The church had constructed a pool adjacent to the old farmhouse and she would take her children there to meet their friends and swim. One day, she saw Patty Jo at the pool. She approached her slowly, then stood and looked at her body closely. Patty Jo had bruises on both her arms and her legs, as well as her face.

"Can I sit here beside you?" Cassandra asked, not knowing if Patty Jo would want her to be there or not.

Patty Jo's eyes moved reflexively toward a two-way radio resting beside her chair, and she quickly moved it behind her before she sat up and started chatting.

Cassandra found it odd that the entire time Patty Jo was talking, she appeared to be nervous and was looking around, as if she thought someone—maybe Rick—was going to catch her talking with Cassandra and scold her for that. Maybe that was why the radio was there, Cassandra suspected, for Rick to keep tabs on his wife.

Martin had also noticed bruises on Patty Jo before and had asked her friend if she knew how that had happened. Her friend had ignored the question and never did give her an answer. Martin made a mental note to ask Patty Jo about her bruises the next time she saw her.

"Oh, my goodness, Patty Jo," Cassandra said to her a few days later at the pool. "What happened to you that caused all those bruises?"

Patty Jo looked embarrassed. Her voice was oddly tight, almost strangled.

"I fell down some steps," she said weakly.

Even though Cassandra had no reason to be upset, she was barely holding back her tears. Finally she said to Patty Jo, "Are you okay? Is there anything I can do to help you?"

Almost as if Patty Jo believed what she was saying might get back to Rick, she told Cassandra, "I'm not going to live very long. So if anything happens to me, make sure they look at Rick."

Martin listened carefully—first once, then again a second time, as Patty Jo repeated her statement. Cassandra never could understand why any woman would let anyone treat her like that. She would have eventually figured out for herself what Rick was doing to Patty Jo, but she was just too stunned to believe he had hurt the person he supposedly loved.

The thought of Patty Jo dying at the hands of her husband was something Cassandra Martin didn't really want to consider. The image of Patty Jo's small body being beaten was a particularly disturbing one, and once that thought came into Cassandra's mind, it was very difficult to get it out.

Chapter 18

The Pulleys had made a vow to stay together and they had worked hard to put their lives back in order. They had dissolved their music ministry, and that had left Patty Jo free to help Rick with his church work. Their general consensus was that perhaps one of the reasons why Rick was having all these sexual problems, and had strayed from the home fires, was due to his workload and the amount of stress he was subjected to as a result.

On May 2, 1999, Patty Jo traveled with church members Walter and Nancy Jackson to Maggie Valley, North Carolina. Rick said he didn't travel with them because he had lots of responsibilities with the church and several meetings to prepare for. And that he was also developing some material and preparing for another summer mission trip to the Dominican Republic. "But had I known Walter was going, then I would have gone," Rick later said.

While Patty Jo was out of town, Rick decided to take a day off for some personal time. He thought it would be nice to surprise his mom in Raleigh. As he was driving toward Milton, he passed by Hyco Lake, and said he suddenly felt the desire to pray.

"About ten miles from our house, I pulled over on the

side of the road, over to the Hyco Lake area. There was a small campground down by the lake, and this is where I stopped, on the road adjacent to the water, and I just began to pray. And it wasn't something that was unusual, but it was something that was out of the ordinary."

Rick would agree his sudden urge to stop and pray was odd, but he said that it wasn't unusual for him to have some sort of a sense in his heart that somebody needed prayer, somebody needed a phone call, or some sort of special care. And it wasn't odd at this particular part of the day when God revealed that the persons needing prayer were him and Patty Jo.

"There wasn't anything specific," Rick stated, "like I heard God saying something. But it was just a sense in my heart that there was a spiritual attack that was coming upon our marriage and falling on Patty Jo. As a result of that feeling, I prayed, and then I just went home.

"Later on, in the evening, I was watching television, and I received a phone call and I answered the phone. When I answered the phone, there was a voice that was disguised. It sounded like a male's voice, using a falsetto-type sound, and the voice said, 'Your wife is having an affair.'"

Rick called the person a liar, and said he began to pray. He hung up the phone, but didn't don't know if the person hung up or if he hung up first. He looked at his caller ID band, but there was no number on the caller ID.

After Patty Jo returned home the following day, Rick said, he told her about the mysterious caller. He said she asked him what was said, and that he related the information about her having an affair.

"It was never a thing where she was defensive at all," Rick related. "I wasn't challenging her or accusing her. I was just relating something that I thought was a spiritual experience, where I felt like God was warning me that the attack that I assumed that time was coming."

Rick said that Patty Jo wondered who it was that had called. Rick said they had received some strange phone calls in the past and so they wondered who it was that had called this time. Rick related other strange calls from the past.

"We had, through the course of our ministry, received some phone calls from 'who knows.' This was before the days of caller IDs so we never really knew who they were from. We had received phone calls from people that would sometimes leave a message on our answering machine. Sometimes they would say something directly to one of us.

"There were some threatening phone calls from time to time. I remember one in particular, there was a threat to kill our dog. There was also another that threatened to rape Patty Jo.

"But I never called the police as a result of those. We had some suspicion as to where those phone calls might be coming from. There were some young people in our neighborhood who were on the fringe, so to speak, with the church. They weren't really members of the church, some of them had been members in the past, but these weren't members in good standing by any means. Occasionally they would come to a youth meeting and they would be disruptive.

"There was even an occasion where we'd have to ask some of these people to leave and there were also issues where these people were getting involved in some mischief. At first, they were riding lawn mowers through our yard. Then they all got motorcycles and they'd ride through our yard and through the church property. They would ride skateboards on the church property, and they would do tricks and try to damage things. There were a couple of times when I had to ask them not to do that—nicely, but firmly. I mean, sometimes they would challenge me and I'd have to say, 'I'm sorry. This is the way it has to be. You can't do this on church property.' So it might have been some of these people. We didn't know for sure."

Rick and Patty Jo clearly needed some downtime together. The following weekend of Mother's Day, they visited his mother on Saturday and took her on a picnic. The next day, after church services in Ringgold, they put Grace in the car and drove to Gates County. The Riddicks had always gathered together at their farm on Mother's Day and celebrated with their traditional first barbeque of the season. After enjoying a day with Patty Jo's family, the Pulleys spent the week with her parents.

"Patty Jo, you've lost a lot of weight," Elva Mae Riddick pointed out to her child. "Your cheekbones are showing. You don't look healthy."

In 1994, after Patty Jo and Rick disbanded their group and stopped traveling, she started working out, doing aerobics, and dieting. She also stopped taking her birth control pills, believing the pills had been contributing to her weight gain.

"Yes, Mama, I have lost a lot of weight," Patty Jo said, smiling. "But it's not because I'm sick, it's because I'm too fat."

Rick had been trying to diet as well, but got caught on an upward spiral of weight gain. As much as Patty Jo tried to get him to exercise and diet, he still seemed to be gaining weight and getting heavier all the while. Occasionally he would lose a few pounds, then gain it back just as quick.

Patty Jo kept encouraging Rick to lose weight. For health reasons, she wanted him to be thinner. She even suspected his weight gain might be contributing to his erectile dysfunction.

Patty Jo knelt beside her mother, grabbed her by the hands, and looked at her lovingly. "It's going to be okay, Mom. I'm down to a size eight in my clothing, and that's not too small for me. You're just used to seeing me overweight."

Elva Mae smiled. She just wanted to make certain her daughter was okay.

"Yes, I feel fine, Mama. I'm enjoying my new size. As a matter of fact, when I get home, I am going to ask Rick for some money so I can go shopping. I was thinking of getting a new pair of jeans and a new shirt."

After breakfast the next morning, Patty Jo gave Rick her list of visits. She wanted to visit her brother, Billy, at work, then stop by the high school and visit with the principal and a few of her old teachers. Her class was preparing for a reunion and she had a lot of ideas she believed would help make the event memorable. Patty Jo also wanted to visit her grandmother Etta Britt, who was now living in a nursing home, and her aunt Charlotte, who was suffering from cancer. Later that evening, they returned to the Riddicks' house and cooked dinner for the family. During the meal, Rick and Patty Jo shared all the wonderful opportunities God had given them. They talked about the all-nations ministry and their ministry at their Ringgold church.

"We're hosting conferences at the mission center for several groups next weekend," Patty Jo exclaimed. She rattled off an endless list of chores and errands, but her eyes were bright with enthusiasm. "With all that music and celebration, it is going to be so exciting."

Patty Jo also stated that one of her chores next week was to drive to the Norfolk International Airport, where she would meet and then transport a Haitian pastor and his wife back to Ringgold. She was ecstatic about the opportunity and was thrilled to hear about all the missionary work being done in Haiti.

On Tuesday morning, May 11, 1999, Connie Winslow (PJ's niece who, by now, had married and had children of her own) took her sons to school and drove over to her grandparents' house to say good-bye to Patty Jo. She was a criminal justice major at Elizabeth City State University and her first class did not begin until noon. When she arrived, her grandmother Elva Mae and Patty Jo were walking, while Rick finished packing. Suddenly Grace jumped out of the van and dashed into the road.

"Oh, my God!" Patty Jo screamed to Rick. "Grace is

out in the road." She continued calling frantically, until Rick caught up with the dog and called her back to the van. Patty Jo leaned against the van and breathed slowly. Her face said it all. She didn't want to go back to Ringgold just yet; she wanted to stay a few more days in Gates County with her family.

Rick grabbed their last bag and loaded it into their minivan, then started the ritual rounds of hugging and kissing everyone good-bye. Because the mornings were still cool, Patty Jo was wearing the same lightweight pink sweater she had worn at Christmas. When Connie embraced Patty Jo, she felt the softness of her sweater and smelled her homemade cream perfume. Patty Jo called the fragrance, "Lilac Lovely."

Elva Mae was the last to hug Patty Jo. "I don't know when I will get to see you again," she said, holding on as tight as she could. She kissed her daughter's right cheek and asked if Patty Jo would call her when she got home. "I just want to make sure you make it home okay."

"I will, Mama," Patty Jo promised, pressing her smiling face against the window as she waved good-bye.

Elva Mae, Connie, and the rest of the Riddick family stood in the yard and waved good-bye until the minivan finally disappeared. They had no way of knowing it would be the last time they would see Patty Jo alive.

Chapter 19

The following week of May 14, the River of Life Church staff were busy making necessary phone calls, shuffling through paperwork, and completing last-minute deadlines in preparation for their conferences. Campus Harvest, a Christian ministerial team of college students from Durham, had previously organized and booked a weeklong event at the church. Their regional district was sponsoring conferences throughout the eastern United States, and this particular conference at Ringgold had been reserved for approximately fifty people. Many of the attendees were scheduled to arrive on Sunday morning, May 16, where they would be housed at the church's mission center and remain throughout the week, until the following Saturday.

Because of the number of people involved in the training conference—a number that exceeded the usual number of the River of Life Church's capacity—a great deal of work and preparation were required of the church's staff. Extra beds and mattresses would have to be moved into the mission center to accommodate all the guests. Patty Jo was serving as the church's hostess for all guests and coordinating all special events related to the mission center.

Patty Jo remarked earlier that week how she was enjoying the last of spring, and after a long and punishing
winter, she eagerly anticipated the longer sun-filled days.
She showed a friend her Day-Timer and pointed to a
plethora of dates circled in red and starred.

"I have so much to do at the church in the next few
months," she said, "I'm not sure how I'm going to get it
all done."

For the Campus Harvest event, Patty Jo had solicited
the help of church administrator Richard Gardner and
they had worked hand in hand organizing the conference. The two of them had a number of conversations
that week, and on Thursday, May 13, they spoke for about
an hour in the church parking lot as they nailed down
the final preparations for the conference. At the close of
their conversation, Rick and Pastor Randy Sudduth drove
up in Rick's red truck, a vehicle he had recently acquired
from his friend Albert at a discounted price.

"See you later, Richard," Patty Jo said as she sort of
bounced over to the driver's side of her husband's vehicle and leaned into the window.

Gardner waited until Pastor Sudduth got out of the
passenger side of the vehicle. He then stood in the parking lot and chatted with Sudduth for a moment before
walking back to his church office. He didn't see any
more of Patty Jo or Rick that day. They had primarily discussed business and the upcoming conference at the
mission center, and there was never any indication of
Patty Jo being afraid, anxious, or amiss. She and Rick appeared as they always had, a loving and caring couple.

But everyone knows that suspicion often begins with
people who become preoccupied with petty details and
find fault about small matters. The remarkable thing is
that simple, daily activities of living, which are routinely
characterized as "normal," are often perceived as decep-
tive and suddenly interpreted as revelations of "abnormal" behavior. In light of a tragedy, these simple acts are

transformed into strange episodes from a person's past, thus concluding this is where he/she must have gotten "off the beaten path." A lot of those misperceptions occurred on the day after Patty Jo disappeared.

On the surface, nothing seemingly dramatic in Patty Jo Pulley's life on Friday, May 14, 1999, would have caused any real concern. According to Rick, he and Patty Jo began that day like every other day: they got up and got ready for work.

For the past two years, Patty Jo had routinely driven the six miles into Danville on every other Friday and cleaned the home of Dr. Robert and Glenda Honea. The Honeas had six children and lived in a large home. With all her duties as a wife and mother of six children, Glenda Honea found it impossible to clean and maintain their home without domestic help. Patty Jo would arrive at the Honeas' home at 9:00 A.M. and spend the day cleaning until about 5:00 P.M. Glenda was normally at home, but would routinely be taking care of her kids. It was a big house, but she and Patty Jo would cross paths with one another.

When Patty Jo went to get in her van early Friday morning, she noticed the tire was almost flat. For several days, the van had a slow leak and the tire had gone slack.

"Would you mind if I drove your truck into work?" Patty Jo asked.

Rick was getting ready to go to the church office. He had a few chores to do before he and church administrator Richard Gardner were scheduled to meet and complete a few last-minute details for the weekend conferences. Rick was going to help him transport some beds and set them up in the mission center. They had planned on going into Danville together, where they would pick up extra beds from the house of church member Tom Aberdeny and rent a few extra ones at the rental store.

Why Patty Jo didn't drive to work that day would forever remain a question. She could have driven the van, stopped at the nearest station, and had the tire repaired just as easily as Rick. Or she could have driven his truck. But, according to Rick, she assumed he was going to use the truck to transport beds at the church. That is why he offered to take her into work that day and drop her off.

"My plan was to get the tire fixed and then meet Richard at Aberdeny's house. We would load up his van with beds, then go back to the church and unload them."

Glenda Honea remembered that Patty Jo didn't drive herself that particular day. She assumed Patty Jo must have had car trouble, for in the two years she had worked for the Honeas, Patty Jo had always driven to work.

"I had never met Rick," Glenda recalled. "He might have driven her to work before, but I don't recall it."

Rick said after he dropped Patty Jo off at the Honeas' home in Danville, he drove to a couple of service stations to get the tire fixed. But no one seemed to have the time to help him. He then called Richard Gardner and told him the problem he was having.

"Why don't you stop at the Goodyear store on Highway 58, just coming out of Danville," Gardner suggested. "I will drive on to Tom's and he can help me load up the beds and mattresses."

Rick drove to the Goodyear store, but said he still couldn't get the tire fixed. He then drove back to the office and met Richard at the church, where they unloaded the beds from Richard's vehicle.

"Why don't we drive to the Milton Shell Station and get your tire fixed?" Gardner then suggested. He'd been living in the area for almost twenty years and knew this was the place where most everyone went to get their tires repaired.

"Okay with me," Rick agreed.

Rick drove the van the few miles south, across the North Carolina border, into Milton. Gardner planned on following him, but at the last moment was delayed.

"Go ahead of me, Rick," Gardner told him. "I'll meet you at the tire store and pick you up there, then bring you back to the church. We'll get our work done, have lunch together, and I'll take you back to the tire store so you can get your van."

Gardner finished his job at the church and was on his way to Milton when he saw Rick crossing the Dan River Bridge. Rick was driving toward him, waving him down.

"I went to the tire store," Rick said, looking a bit frustrated, "but they couldn't fix it."

"Then why didn't you just leave it and let them fix it later?" Gardner asked.

Rick paused. "Uh, they said they had several vehicles ahead of me." He had a little catch in his voice, but was able to squeeze out why he couldn't get his tire repaired. "They said because it was Friday, and they were too busy, they wouldn't be able to get to it today."

Gardner thought that was odd. In all the years he had dealt with this particular tire company, he had never known them to turn business away. He had never heard them say they were too busy that they couldn't take fifteen minutes to fix a flat.

Nevertheless, Gardner turned around and followed Rick back to the church. After working for a few hours, they drove into Cane Creek Shopping Center and had lunch at an Italian restaurant. They drove Rick's van so that he could get his tire fixed, but for whatever reason, he still didn't get it repaired.

Finally, after lunch, Rick walked into the Family Dollar Store and asked if they had anything in their store to stop a tire leak. While Richard stood outside the store and talked with church member Rick Petefish, he watched Rick leave the store, put one can of Stop-Leak in the tire, and the other can in the back of the van.

"Are you sure this will stop the leak?" Gardner asked curiously.

Rick assured him it would. But for Gardner, the leaking tire remained a small but continuing source of annoyance. He would later question Rick's motive for not getting it fixed and wonder if he ever intended to get it fixed.

Around 1:00 P.M., Rick and Gardner returned to the office. Rick was busy making phone calls and working on several different church projects. Later in the afternoon, Patty Jo called him at the office.

"I talked with Patty Jo," Rick said. "This morning, we thought that she was having some problems with her sinuses. She has allergies and her allergies have been kicking in a little bit after she left. I asked her how she was doing. She said she thought she had caught a cold, and I told her I was sorry she felt bad. She told me that she'd be ready to leave in about an hour."

Glenda Honea remembered she and Patty Jo chatted that particular day, but not about anything in particular. Glenda always had a list on the refrigerator, and if she was running out of supplies, Patty Jo would write down what she needed. That day, Patty Jo had written down she needed some cleaning supplies and gloves. She even wrote down her glove size.

"But I don't remember her complaining of being ill," Glenda said. "She didn't say anything about her being sick or feeling bad. She wasn't coughing or sneezing. She just was her normal self and did her normal job."

Chapter 20

Rick remembered doing a couple of things to tie up some loose ends at the office that day and then he walked across the parking lot and went home. He could never say exactly what he did at home, but just that he did a couple of things. While he was there, Bethany Sudduth called and asked if Rick and Patty Jo were going to the school play.

When Bethany rode the school bus home that Friday, there was talk of the evening play at Dan River High School. A number of Bethany's classmates and friends were performing that night in *South Pacific,* and she desperately wanted to see them perform.

Sixteen-year-old Bethany was a junior at Dan River High School, while her younger sister, Lauren, eleven, was enrolled at Dan River Middle School. Their eighteen-year-old sister, Megan, was still being homeschooled by their father, as well as their eight-year-old brother Jason.

When Bethany's mother, Judy, taught art in the Pittsylvania County schools, her father would take over at home, provide instruction for the children, and see to it they did their homework and completed their chores. Randy's office was at the church, only ninety steps away from their parsonage, but had long ago been converted to their home. While he studied and prepared himself for Sunday's worship, the Sudduth children helped out around the house and took care of Jason and their youngest brother, Caleb, until their mother arrived from school.

Because Judy had too many household chores to finish after she arrived home from school, she told Bethany she could not drive her to the play, nor could her father, who was working a second job at Domino's Pizza. When Bethany told her mother how many of their church youth were in the play, Judy suggested she call their neighbors, Rick and Patty Jo, and ask if they were going.

"The Pulleys usually go to any of the activities where our youth are involved," Judy reminded Bethany. "Maybe you should think about calling them first."

Bethany saw no harm in asking, so somewhere between 4:00 and 4:30 P.M., she picked up the phone and dialed the Pulleys' number. When Rick answered, she asked him if she could ride with them to the play.

"I'm not sure if we are even going to the play," Rick said, rolling off a list of reasons why. "I also know that Patty Jo has had a cold, and probably won't feel like it."

"Oh, okay," Bethany responded, certain she could probably find a ride with one of her friends.

"But I will let you know," Rick assured her. "I'll call you back and we'll stay in touch with each other."

Years later, Rick would recall that he was already certain when he spoke with Bethany at 4:00 P.M. that Patty Jo would not be attending the play. And although Bethany was his neighbor's child and in his church youth group, he felt somewhat uncomfortable about driving and attending the play with her—a young and attractive female—and that was why he did not offer her a ride.

At 4:45 P.M., Rick said, he drove from the church parsonage, picked Patty Jo up from work in Danville, and helped her load up the cleaning supplies she carried. They loaded a vacuum attachment and mop into the van, then drove to a gas station for gas. Rick never mentioned checking the tire or putting additional air in the tire at the service station, so apparently the Stop-Leak he had used to patch the leaky tire had done the trick.

"What would you like to do tonight?" Rick said he had asked his wife.

"Well, I know Richard Gardner and I were supposed to meet with two men from Danville at the mission center tonight," Patty Jo supposedly had said, "but I don't think we're going to be back home in time to meet with him. Would you mind asking Richard to take care of that?"

Nevertheless, according to Judy, he did call the Sudduths' home somewhere around 5:00 P.M. and asked if Bethany had secured another ride.

"Yes, she has," Judy informed him. "She's going to ride with one of her friends."

Rick was happy to hear Bethany had found another ride. According to Judy's testimony, he then asked her if she had seen Patty Jo or if she had been by her house.

"Why, no, Rick," Judy answered. "I haven't seen her all day."

Rick told Judy he had already picked Patty Jo up from work and she expressed a need to drive into Danville and purchase something for the weekend mission conference. He said Patty Jo had chosen to go shopping rather than attend the high-school play.

Rick's recollection of the events differed from Judy's. Rick said he remembered clearly it was around 5:30 P.M. or so before he and Patty Jo ever got home. She then took a long bath and they were trying to decide what they were going to do, when she came out of the bathroom, saying, "I've decided I'm just not going to go to the play tonight. I'm going to go in to town and I'm going to pick up some things for the conference. I want to do some shopping for myself. I want to do this so that we're not so busy tomorrow—that way, we can have the morning off on Saturday and not have to spend the day working."

Rick also said that it was Patty Jo who made the decision to do all those things, despite the fact she had just gotten off work and was still nursing a cold. He stated at that point they had also discussed whether he would go shopping or he would go to the play.

"It was very unusual for me and Patty Jo to go our separate ways. It was rare, even though Patty Jo liked to shop and I didn't. She even liked it better when I wasn't with her when she was shopping, because she could take her time, especially if she was looking for clothes or something like that.

"I used to complain to her a little bit because I said, 'You'll walk a half mile when you shop, but I'm walking five or six miles when I shop.' I would go to the sporting-goods section, while she was in one spot. I'd then go to electronics and about a dozen other places, while she stayed in that one spot. She just liked shopping better when I wasn't there."

Rick said he and Patty Jo had discussed the possibility of them meeting up again later, depending on how she felt after her shopping venture. He said they had discussed the possibility of her coming to the play and meeting him there.

"She had a cold, but it didn't mean it stopped her from functioning. She was able to function pretty well, even though she had sinus problems and infection. She would do what she had to do. She took the truck—I don't remember if it was on the way home or if it was after we got home, she asked me if I had gotten the tire fixed. And I told her I wasn't able to find anybody at a service place that could actually plug the tire, but I told her I put Stop-Leak in it, and I thought it might be fixed. We'd wait and see how that did and I would try later and get it fixed.

"Patty Jo didn't drive the truck often and neither did I. The days that she would clean or the days that she would teach piano in town, that would be my vehicle to drive if I needed to go anywhere, if I had left the office.

We needed a second vehicle at times, but I drove the truck probably slightly more than she did. We didn't drive it that much. We used it, we put our trash in there. We put the church trash in there. There was a lady that cleaned the church occasionally, and she asked if she could put the church trash in there. It was pretty typical for the back of our truck to be covered in trash."

Rick said while he was on the phone with Richard Gardner, Patty Jo asked if she could drive the truck to Danville.

"What do you think, Richard, about PJ driving the truck?" Rick laughed. The two men had a good working relationship and enjoyed joking around. "Should I let her drive the truck?"

Rick said that Patty Jo had been issued a check from Glenda Honea, but he had already cashed his paycheck and offered to give her $75 for shopping. She planned on going to Big Lots, Value City, and to Hill's for some candles and other items for the conference. She also planned on buying a new pair of jeans and a new shirt.

Chapter 21

Rick would recall later that when Patty Jo left for Danville, it was around 6:15 P.M., and there were no harsh words between them. That he had finished up with his phone call with Gardner and turned on the TV for a moment. Then he said he walked down to the missions center where two ladies were staying in the church's guesthouse. He said Patty Jo had asked him to check on them.

Rick said the purpose of checking on the two ladies was because it had been raining a lot and the basement flooded when it rained. He swore he went down to the center, knocked on the door, and introduced himself to the two ladies, then asked them if he could check the basement and make sure it wasn't flooding. It wasn't.

However, Judy Sudduth recalled that it was 6:00 P.M.—not 6:15—when Rick called her home a second time. He had asked Judy if she would watch out for his dog, Grace, that she had just gotten loose.

"She was chasing a squirrel," Rick said, "So if you happen to see her, try to catch her and put her in my house."

Judy didn't recall if Rick told her during that phone call if he was going to the play or not. She wasn't sure even if he said where he was going, but she did get the feeling he was leaving his house. And that was why he wanted her to watch for Grace.

Actually, it was Judy who had found the pup several years ago on Highway 58, and had asked Rick and Patty Jo if they wanted to adopt her. A collie-mixed breed, Grace was pampered and treated like a child by the Pulleys. They took excellent care of the dog. They brushed her coat, had lots of pet toys for her, and even brushed the dog's teeth with a toothbrush so she would have nice breath.

When the Pulleys went away on trips, the Sudduths would step in and "babysit" Grace. They knew how careful and particular the Pulleys were about their dog. She was never allowed to roam freely. In fact, the only time Judy remembered Rick saying he let her run loose was when she had gotten loose one night and he tried to teach her not to do that again. The other times she remembered the Pulleys being so very careful about her running away that they had put her on a clothesline lead outside the home. That was the only time Judy remembered Grace being out, other than the times the dog was free to roam in their house.

Even though Judy thought it was odd that Rick would be asking her if she had seen Grace, she assured him she would try and catch the dog, then put her back in the Pulleys' house. After she hung up with Rick, her husband called her from Domino's Pizza to let her know how busy he was. Randy was delivering pizzas, making extra money to help support his family, and by the number of deliveries he had already taken that night, it was going to be a long one.

"When you come tonight, make sure you keep an eye out for Grace," Judy informed him. "Rick just called me to say she had gotten out and was loose."

Around 6:15 P.M., Judy was talking on their portable phone to her husband and walked over near the front window. When she looked out, she saw Rick walking around outside and heard him calling for Grace. He was dressed in khaki pants and was wearing an olive green shirt. She told her husband she needed to go out and help Rick find her before Patty Jo got home; otherwise, he would be in hot water.

Judy hung up the phone and walked out the front door of their parsonage toward Rick, who was about twenty-five yards from her. He was near the pool area, calling, and looking for his dog. At first, Judy was kind of hesitant to go outside because it had started raining and she wasn't dressed in the proper attire. Edging her way out into the weather, she suddenly heard a crash—something like a fall—near the left of the church property. There was an embankment near the volleyball court adjacent to the parsonage, and she assumed Rick had fallen and slid down the embankment.

Slowly Rick began making his way back up the embankment.

"Am I bleeding, Judy?" he asked as he came walking toward her.

Rick had a scratch on the left side of his face which was bleeding, but it wasn't dripping blood. To Judy, it just looked red, like he had been hurt. She described it as something like when you might have a place that has been freshly wounded and it has blood on it that may be clotted just a little bit, but it was not oozing blood. It wasn't like blood was coming out from the wound in his face.

"Well, yes, there is blood," she told him. "You are bleeding."

The scratches and blood on Rick's face didn't seem to discourage him from looking for Grace. He and Judy talked a few minutes, and then she went back inside her house. She assumed Rick went back to his house, but wasn't certain if he went inside or not. She did remember when she walked inside her house, Rick stayed outside and continued looking for Grace.

Rick said he then remembered going home, washing, dressing, and getting ready for the play. He changed clothes and put on his black jeans and a long-sleeved, crew-neck black shirt. He thought it was best to take his dog, Grace, outside and let her go to the bathroom.

"I don't remember how many rabbits," Rick said, "but she saw a couple of rabbits and took after them. She would always come back with no problems, but this time she didn't. I walked toward her a little bit and I was yelling for her to come, calling her name, before I realized that she had gone, that she was chasing the rabbit. She was distracted and wasn't going to come back."

Rick would tell police at a later date that he had gone back into his house and called next door to the Sudduths' home. He wasn't sure if he should leave Grace out for the night or not, but he told Judy Sudduth to just put the dog inside if she happened to see her.

Rick said he thought twice about leaving Grace outside. Deciding he was going to go look for her, he changed into a pair of tan khaki-colored jeans and a long-sleeved olive green T-shirt. He searched for the dog on the wooded area on the left side of the Sudduths' home, assuming this was where the rabbit and the dog would have gone.

"I couldn't see the dog," Rick said. "I couldn't even hear her. But I just followed the path that I thought she would go. I walked around the Sudduths' house and saw Judy. I don't remember what I told her, actually."

Rick said he walked down to the wide line around the Sudduth's home, where he heard Grace running through the woods. He walked down into the edge of the woods, calling her by name, and that was when he tripped and fell.

"I nose-dived into the brambles and the brush," Rick said. "I landed on my face. I would assume I tried to shield myself, but I don't remember. I got up. I felt rather foolish and I know I looked rather silly. I had a hard time getting up. I was kind of tangled a little bit with my legs, but I got up—kind of rolled up—and finally stood on my feet.

"I saw Judy was standing there, and I knew that I had hurt myself. My face was stinging. My arm was stinging and my leg was hurting also, where I had fallen. I went toward Judy and I said something like, 'That was dumb,' or 'I must have looked stupid,' or something like that. And I just remarked how foolish I must have looked, and asked Judy if I was bleeding."

"Yes," she said, "you're bleeding."

"At that point, I continued to try to look for Grace. I don't remember what I asked Judy at that time. I think I asked her, if she saw Grace to let me know."

Rick said he later found and captured his dog, then took her home. After he gave Grace a bath and dried her, it was almost 7:00 P.M. After rinsing off a second time, he said he changed back into the clothes he had been wearing earlier and headed out toward Dan River High School for the school play.

Judy Sudduth never saw Grace again that night. Nor did she ever see Patty Jo Pulley again. And it would be a long time before she learned if either of them had been found.

Chapter 22

The old Broadway musical *South Pacific* has been a favorite of high-school drama clubs for nearly fifty years. The story was one of love, laughter, and ultimate tragedy. Pure Americana, it cast World War II American soldiers caught up in the South Pacific islands, experiencing customs and mores totally foreign to them.

The Dan River High School drama club had been rehearsing for weeks and were ready for their maiden performance. A large number of youth from the Ringgold church were involved in the performance. Patty Jo had taught music to several of the teens who had been given solo performances. Patty Jo was as excited as they were about the opportunities for them to display their musical talents.

Rick said he had found his dog that night, and she was dirty. Well, at least dirty enough that he had to wash her feet before he put her back in the house. Rick cleaned himself up, changed into a clean pair of black trousers and a black shirt, then left his dog inside his house and drove to the Dan River High School.

By the time Rick arrived at the Dan River High School auditorium, the musical had already started. He estimated he had arrived shortly after 7:00 P.M. Because the play had already started, he went into the front lobby, offered to pay for admission, then went inside the auditorium and sat in the back row.

"I thought there was the possibility that Patty Jo was going to join me at the play," Rick said. "I wanted to be where she could see me. There was a pay phone there at the entrance into the auditorium area. I called her cell phone, but there was no answer. I used the restroom and went back in and sat down and watched the rest of the first half of the play."

Rick said he remembered seeing Bethany Sudduth already seated and enjoying the play with one of her friends. Alone, he walked to the back of the auditorium and sat down in one of the rear seats.

Rick sat through the play, but by intermission he was thirsty and decided to get a drink. He stated he left the building, drove to a convenience store, and bought a Mountain Dew soda; then he drove back to the play and actually sat in the parking lot and finished his soda. He said he was only gone a few minutes, that he came back shortly before the close of the play, walked back inside, sat down, and watched it.

Rick also said he had wanted to beat the crowd, so he left before the end.

"I left a little bit early. I was tired that day. It had been a long day and I wanted to get home. So I left a little bit early. I'm not exactly sure what time it was, but I left shortly before the play ended and went home."

Rick stated as he went to get into his car in the parking lot, he saw an associate of theirs, Jamie Shackleford. He assumed Jamie had been chaperoning the group of kids who had been in the play. He remembered Jamie from some work in the schools called Little Life, which he and Patty Jo had led. The Pulleys had gone into the classroom and presented material relating to a family life curriculum, and Jamie's children were there.

"I saw Jamie coming from an exit at the back of the

stage, so I thought I would go out of my way and stop by to say hello," he recalled. "There was no real traffic in the parking lot at the time, so I decided to go and say hello to Jamie and the kids. I wanted to see if it was any of our kids that were in the play. I spoke to Jamie and commented on how well her daughter had done in the play."

Rick said before leaving the school play, he had called his house to speak with Patty Jo. He said he had also called her cell phone, just checking on her, like he normally did, but she did not answer their home phone, nor did she answer her cell phone.

Chapter 23

Dale Purvis would remember the evening of May 14, 1999, for the rest of his life. Purvis worked as a self-employed estimator for contractors, and for most of his adult life, he had labored from daylight to dark at his job. Hustling from job to job, making certain all his figures and numbers matched up exactly as he predicted—there were people in the construction industry who relied on his calculations and trusted his accuracy.

But on this particular Friday, Purvis had chosen not to work. It was a "special" day for him, for he was busy preparing for his fortieth birthday. As part of his celebration, Purvis had rented space for the weekend at the Pittsylvania County Fairgrounds, located just across Highway 62, north in Milton, and had invited his friends to join him in the festivities. All day Friday, he had been running from store to store, picking up drinks, ice, cups and plates, napkins, plastic silverware, etc., making certain everything was in order. After lunch, he had driven down to the Old Dutch Time meat market in Milton and picked up his order of a hundred pounds of Boston butts.

For most of his youth, Purvis had lived on the outskirts of the Cherokee Indian Reservation in western North Carolina, and because of that relationship, a number of his friends and acquaintances referred to him as "Cherokee." Retaining many of those old habits growing up in the mountainous terrain near the reservation, Cherokee was familiar with and had explored the general terrain, rivers, and road location in the area around his Milton, North Carolina, residence. In addition, his daily excursion to work as a contractor estimator normally began at his house on the River Bend Road, just below the River of Live Community Church, onto Route 62, and then crossed over the line into Virginia via US-58. That evening, he had scheduled a ten-minute trip from his house to the fairgrounds, which should have been like all the others taken previously.

Cherokee was planning on cooking the Boston butts up at the Pittsylvania County Fairgrounds. It was part of the preparation for his party on Saturday night. They were having a cookout; they had a band coming; they were going to have a big celebration. To make certain there would be plenty of food for everyone, he needed to transport his cooker up to the site so he could barbeque the Boston butts.

Somewhere between eight and eight-thirty that Friday evening, Cherokee engaged the services of his brother-in-law, Robert Dean Rowland (nicknamed "Jap"), and together they attached a cooker mounted on a trailer behind his four-wheel drive 1979 Chevrolet pickup truck. They drove straight to the fairgrounds, where they planned on leaving the cooker there until the next morning. At the first break of day, they would return to the fairgrounds, start the cooking process of several fine Boston butts, and have them sliced and sizzling on the grill by the time their party guests arrived the following afternoon.

It was a short ten miles in distance from Cherokee's house to the fairgrounds. A blinking turn signal on the back of the truck stated they would turn left at the intersection of River Bend Road and NC-75 or VA-62 (it's kind of left up to the driver to choose whichever name you

want to call the road at this point, Cherokee would say),
then travel north for about fifty feet until one reached the
stop sign and the Virginia border. As the two men traveled
up VA-62 toward the fairgrounds, they glanced back casually just to make certain the cooker was still in tow. It had
been raining earlier that day and the roads were still wet.
There were no other cars on the road, nor were there any
pedestrians walking alongside the road, yet the last thing
they needed was for the truck to slide around. With the
slightest bit of motion, the cooker could wiggle free, slip
off the trailer hitch, then go crashing across the road and
into the woods. Just to be on the safe side, Cherokee and
Jap drove a little slower than usual.

Turning to his brother-in-law, Cherokee grinned, then
related, "Hey, I heard something on the radio today
about the temperature dropping to sixty-five degrees."
All day long, they had been fretting over the weather,
afraid the party might have to be canceled due to in-
clement weather. "Do you think this rain is going to hold
off through the weekend?"

Jap turned toward the passenger side window, then
bobbed and weaved his head until he could get a better
look at the dark clouds in the western sky.

"Can't say for sure"—Jap shook his head—"but those
dark clouds appear to be moving away from us."

Cherokee breathed a sigh of relief, confident his
brother-in-law had spotted notable signs of good weather.

It took about five minutes or so for the two men to deliver the cooker from Cherokee's home to the rented site
at the fairgrounds. The day Cherokee had stopped by and
reserved the site at the fairground's office, he had been
given a key to the locked front gate. It took them about
ten or fifteen minutes to get the gate open, back the
cooker into the garage bay, drop the cooker off the truck
at the site, and relock the gate. They pulled away from the
fairgrounds and headed back home on 62 South.

Just as the truck passed the River of Life Church

entrance, which was about a tenth of a mile or so on the road up on the hill from Cherokee's house, they noticed something unusual. The light of day was fading and quickly transitioning into the dark of night, just enough so that Cherokee had turned on his headlights, but it was still light enough for him to see a red truck pulled over on the side of the River Bend Road.

"Uh-oh," Cherokee said under his breath, as it was rare to find vehicles parked along this portion of the road. "Somebody must have broken down."

Jap sat up in the passenger seat and nodded in agreement. He pointed to a figure walking ahead and away from the truck. *Must be the truck's owner,* he quietly assumed.

The two men continued in their truck slowly past the parked red truck and toward the figure walking on the side of the road. A quick visual examination led them to believe the figure was a large man, dressed in slacks and a white T-shirt. Or at least he looked like he was wearing some kind of white shirt that had been pulled out and stretched down over his belt and pants like a T-shirt.

As the truck pulled closer, the man kept walking away, with his back turned toward the two men. From where they were sitting inside the truck, the man appeared to have long, dark hair. At least Cherokee noticed the man's hair was as long as his shoulder-length hair. The only difference was the man's hair looked as if it was wet and flat on top. Cherokee figured because it had rained a bit that evening, the man had probably got caught in the rain and that was why his hair was wet and flat to his head. An even closer look at the man told them he was a stocky, heavyset man, probably tipping the scales at a good 220 pounds or better.

Leaning forward against the truck dash to take a closer look, Jap pointed toward the man and shouted, "Hey, that kind of looks like 'Too-Slow,' doesn't it?"

The two men shared a common acquaintance that somewhat resembled this person, in size and shape. Their

friend Too-Slow was also a big man, with dark hair and
weighed a good 220 pounds or more. He was so big that
he routinely rode a four-wheeler to get him where he
needed to go.

Cherokee tapped on the brakes and slowed down.
Whether it was Too-Slow or not, Cherokee had already
decided he was going to turn around and pick the
person up. Just as he was about to roll down the window
and ask the man if he needed a lift, Jap placed his hand
on his arm and motioned for Cherokee to drive on by.

"It looks like Too-Slow, but I don't think it is," Jap said.
He lived up above his brother-in-law and his sister in a
rented trailer they owned. It was about one hundred feet
above where Cherokee lived. "Why don't you just go on
to the house. I got to leave as soon as we get there, so I'll
stop and pick him up on my way out."

Although Cherokee hadn't realized it at the time, he
had committed to memory the exact spot where he first
saw the truck and the stranger walking away from the
truck. For some strange and bizarre reason, he remembered turning onto River Bend Road from VA-62, where
he first saw the truck parked on the left-hand side of the
road, opposite the driver's side of the truck, and about
halfway between his driveway and the end of the road. It
was on the river side, or the North Carolina side of the
road—as people like to refer to it—toward his house.

Cherokee remembered this distinct spot because of a
little clearing on the opposite side of the road where a
posted sign advertised SEVEN LOTS FOR SALE. He was familiar with that sign; had seen it a thousand times as he
came into the curve and turned onto River Bend Road,
heading home and toward his driveway.

Cherokee had a watch on, but the funny thing was that
he hadn't noted the time he spotted the truck or the
stranger walking away from the truck. At that precise
moment, he had no need to record the time. Although
he was positive that the truck was not parked on the side

of the road, nor did he see the man walking on the side of the road when he and his brother-in-law had driven with the cooker in tow toward the fairgrounds—this was somewhere between 8:15 and 8:30 P.M.—he estimated it was probably about 8:45 P.M. before he got back to his house.

"It all went by so quickly, like in a couple of seconds," Cherokee would recall years later. "But I still remember it like it was yesterday."

Chapter 24

Robert "Jap" Rowland said he would always remember that same Friday, May 14, when he and his brother-in-law spotted the parked truck and the stranger walking alongside River Bend Road. All that week, Jap had helped Cherokee with planning his birthday party. In fact, he had already moved his camper to the fairgrounds and invited his three children to spend the weekend with him there. The way Jap figured it, the birthday party would begin at noon, but in all likelihood it would probably continue throughout the day and even into the wee hours of the night. After all, this was a party and most likely there would be some drinking going on and a number of people getting in a festive mood. He thought the best situation for him and his children would be to spend the night at the campground.

That Friday evening on the way back from the fairgrounds, after riding with Cherokee to deliver his cooker, Jap remembered the time they spotted the parked truck and stranger was around 8:30 P.M. It hadn't gotten completely dark, when he saw the truck approaching on his right-hand side, the passenger side. If the truck was broken down, he didn't know it, as there was no white flag or lifted hood. There was no indication that anyone needed or was seeking any kind of help.

Jap estimated the truck was traveling around forty-five to fifty miles per hour, when Cherokee let up off the gas. He remembered the conversation about the man looking like Too-Slow, and when Cherokee asked if he should pick him up, Jap thought about it. Then Jap told him they were going up to his house, and there was no sense in the man riding up there just for him to get out again and get in his car.

"We're going to my house," Jap remembered saying to Cherokee. "I got to go out and get something to eat. I'll just stop on my way and pick the guy up, then carry him wherever he needs to go."

Immediately, after getting out of Cherokee's truck, Jap did exactly as he promised. He hopped into his Nissan and drove back onto River Bend Road, toward the parked truck. The stranger in the white T-shirt had gained some distance up the road, but was still traveling and walking on the same side of the road.

Jap drove toward the stranger, then slowed. Stopping his car a bit over the middle white line, to where the man stood only ten to twelve feet away from the driver's side of his car, he opened the door and spoke.

"Howdy." Jap nodded.

The stranger took a few steps backward, then grunted.

It was getting darker and Jap Rowland couldn't make out a lot of the man's features, other than he was a white male. Large and chunky. Long, dark hair. "Do you need a ride?" he asked in a friendly tone.

The stranger shook his head. "No, I'm all right. You go on."

"Are you sure?" Jap asked. The rain was beginning to fall again, and he didn't see any reason for the man to be getting all wet, when he could easily ride with him.

"Oh, I'm all right," the man insisted. "I don't have far to go."

Rowland pointed toward his truck. "Are you broke down?"

The man didn't look back at the truck, nor did he answer Jap's question.

Jap continued his inquiry. "You know, I am a mechanic and work on farm machinery and such. If you need some help, really, I don't mind. I'll be more than happy to help you."

The stranger turned his face away from Jap, then mumbled what sounded like an obligatory response. "No thanks," he said in a low voice.

Jap came from a long line of good old Southern boys, who were quick to offer hospitality and a helping hand. In fact, he thought it would be downright rude of him if he didn't insist the stranger take his help.

"Listen, it's beginning to rain harder and I'll be glad to help you," he insisted. The man's long, dark hair was wet and flat across the top. *Must have been from the misty rain.* He was a big man, wearing dark pants and what now looked like a white bedsheet or something like a T-shirt hanging over the top of his body. One more time, Jap asked, "Are you sure you don't need my help? No sense in turning down a free ride."

No response this time from the stranger, who kept turning his back toward Jap and trying to hide his face.

Jap Rowland narrowed his eyes, looked hard at the man standing directly across from him, then wondered, *Why is he turning away from me? Is he trying to hide? Is he afraid I am going to harm him?* For the next few minutes, Jap sat there in his car, offering the man help or at the very least a ride. But the man refused any and every offer.

Now studying the T-shirt, the bedsheet, or whatever the hell it was that hung out and over the man's belt, Jap noticed it was torn, and that got him to wondering if there just wasn't something quite right about this guy.

Besides, what person in his right mind would choose to walk in the rain, away from a broken-down truck, and refuse any offer of help or a free ride?

The stranger gave no explanation as to why he didn't need Jap's help. Still keeping his back turned toward him, the stranger continued motioning and saying, "Go ahead, I'm all right. I don't need your help."

Jap thought it was even stranger the way this guy was acting: his refusing to turn around and look at him directly. In Jap Rowland's neck of the woods, when another guy wouldn't look someone straight in the eyes, that was a sure sign somebody was trying to hide something.

After a minute of complete silence, the stranger walked away and left Jap sitting in his car, watching him walk away. By now, Jap figured if that was what the man wanted to do, to walk away in the rain, then more power to him. After all, it was a free country and everyone had the right to do whatever the hell he wanted.

Jap Rowland closed his car door and drove away. He was too hungry to waste his time on a guy who didn't want to be helped.

Chapter 25

Rick Pulley said he didn't remember exactly what happened when he got home from the school play, but he thought he had arrived somewhere between 10:15 and 10:30 P.M. When Rick pulled into the church parking lot, he said, he noticed immediately that his red truck wasn't there.

"I didn't panic or anything, I didn't even have any real alarms then, because I knew that Patty Jo could go shopping and get lost in the process of shopping. So I really wasn't alarmed at the moment. I definitely noticed it, but I just pulled up and parked and went inside."

Rick said he had forgotten exactly what happened from that point. He believed he had taken his dog for a walk, that she had been cooped up and she hadn't had the opportunity to go out while he was at the play.

"I went back inside, turned on the television for a little bit, and was just unwinding. Then, at some point, I began to get a little alarmed. And I decided to call Wal-Mart because that was, I had deducted, going to be the last place that she went. I knew the mall closed earlier, and Value City and the others closed earlier, but Wal-Mart stayed open twenty-four hours and that would be the last place that she went shopping."

Rick said he had called Wal-Mart and asked them to page her. He said he didn't remember much of what happened next, but he did remember seeing a group of teenagers between his house and a smaller guesthouse at the church. He said the teenagers were gathered under the streetlight, and mulling around several cars that were in the church parking lot. Ironically, Rick said, he noticed the teenagers were some of the same ones he had seen at the play, but they were making a lot of noise. And because the church had the two ladies staying in the guesthouse that were there for a prayer retreat, Rick said, he didn't want the noise to interrupt them.

"So I walked down—I don't remember if I had Grace with me or not—and I just asked them to keep the noise down a little bit. I then went back, up to the house, and waited for just a few minutes. I just don't know how long, but I just waited to see if Patty Jo was coming home. I mean, I just did normal activities. I was getting a little concerned, but I wasn't panicking."

Rick said he began to worry and started calling around and looking for her. He then phoned several of Patty Jo's friends and asked nervously, "Have you seen my wife?"

No one had seen Patty Jo. No one had talked to Patty Jo since early that morning. And no one knew where Patty Jo was.

Rick said he didn't remember if he called Patty Jo's cell phone or not, because at some point he finally realized her cell phone was either in the van or was on the charger. It was then he decided he was going to drive to Wal-Mart in Danville.

"I just thought she just didn't hear the page, but it was possible that they didn't maybe even page her—that they just said they had paged her. So I thought I would go and see if I saw the truck in the parking lot."

Rick said he believed he wrote a note and told Patty Jo to call his cell phone if she came home while he was out.

At 11:15 P.M., Rick called Judy Sudduth again and

asked if she had heard from Patty Jo. He then asked Judy if she would keep an eye out for her too, just in case she came home.

"I may have called Judy from my cell phone, but I don't remember which, but I called her and said, 'Judy, I'm worried and I'm going to look for her. Would you mind watching out for her? If she comes home, tell her to call me on my cell phone.'"

At that time, Judy believed Rick was intentionally trying not to worry her. He had said he wanted to go meet Patty Jo in Danville and drive her back home, but told Judy not to worry about her because she had a lot of errands to run and a lot of things to pick up.

Rick said he left to go to Wal-Mart and look for his wife. When he got on Highway 58, he called Wal-Mart again and asked them to page her again. It was somewhere around 11:00 or 11:30 P.M. when, Rick said, he arrived at Wal-Mart.

"I pulled in the parking lot, and I don't remember if I pulled all the way in and went all around, but the lot was relatively empty at that hour. I'm not sure exactly what time it was, but I scanned the parking lot. I didn't see the truck at all. I don't believe at that time I went into the parking lot, I may have just sort of went into the fringes of the parking lot and scanned it. But I didn't see our vehicle. I then decided I would go to the mall and the other places I expected Patty Jo to go shopping and I went to those other areas."

All the stores Rick went to were closed, so, he said, he started scanning the parking lots. He remembered going in the parking lots behind a few stores to see if the truck was parked there. He said he drove around the mall, then went to a couple of locations in Danville where he thought she might have stopped over at a friend's house.

"It was getting late, and I didn't want to call people and wake them up. I didn't want to panic people, so I decided just to drive to some friends' house that lived in

Danville just to see if maybe she stopped to see them and just lost track of time. So I drove by those houses and didn't see the truck. I left Danville and went back to Wal-Mart again, because I was thinking at that time that it was open twenty-four hours. I tried to call, but I didn't see the truck there, and at that time, I think I tried to call 911, but it didn't work. I don't remember that exactly, but I stopped at an Express Mart or one of the stores there on Highway 58, across from the airport, and called 911 at that time. I told them that my wife had not returned from shopping, that she had gone out between six and six-thirty that evening and hadn't returned home. I gave a description of the truck. I gave the year and the model of the truck, and told them what it looked like. I gave a description of Patty Jo. I think they asked me where she could have possibly gone, and did she have family? I told [them], I believe, her family lived in northeastern Carolina and were far away from our area. I may have told them the places that I had gone looking for her. I don't remember exactly what time it was, but it was after midnight."

At approximately 12:40 A.M., Rick Pulley's call was received by a 911 dispatcher and the information immediately relayed to the Pittsylvania County Sheriff's Office (PCSO). After receiving all the information from Rick, the dispatcher informed him, "I'm sorry, sir, it's probably a little too early for a missing person's report. But please contact us if your wife doesn't return home by morning."

Chapter 26

This just isn't a normal situation, Rick remembered thinking. *This isn't a normal situation at all.*

Rick said he felt worse after he talked with the PCSO and decided to go back to Wal-Mart. He still was doubtful they had paged her and wanted to go into the store and look for her.

"By now, I was getting a little bit borderline frantic at one point, really getting nervous. So I walked into the store and I was kind of numb, I was getting emotional, getting a little frantic, and I was walking around in the store in almost a daze. I didn't even know where to go or what to look for. I was trying to think of what to do, and Wal-Mart was the only place that I could think to begin. So I walked around the store briefly and prayed as I was walking about what to do and try to calm myself.

"I believe I talked to a security guard. I don't remember if it was entering Wal-Mart or leaving, but, just in an attempt to calm my nerves and try to get in a normal mode of thinking, I just stopped for a moment. I think I took a shirt off a rack and just grabbed a shirt that I thought would fit and went through the line and I asked the lady, because I went through the line, that was the cashier if she had seen anybody that looked like Patty Jo."

Rick said no one in the store remembered Patty Jo even being there. On his way out, he stopped and talked to a security guard and described both Patty Jo and the red truck to him. He then left Wal-Mart and drove to some other stores across town.

"I don't remember where I went. I looked on Riverside, and I may have gone up Piney Forest. I don't know. I was just driving, thinking where she may go. I may have gone over to Averett College just to see if I saw her truck there. There were so many places in my mind. I don't remember where I went.

"At some point, I remembered that Randy Sudduth, my pastor, was working at Domino's that night. I didn't know what time he got off, but I knew I had to go there. When I pulled up in the parking lot, I saw him inside, mopping the floor. I banged on the door and got his attention. He came to the door, and I remember I just broke down at that point. I just broke down and cried."

Chapter 27

The night Patty Jo was believed to be missing, Randy Sudduth was supplementing his income with a part-time job at Domino's Pizza in Danville. Earlier that day, he had left the church office around three-fifteen that afternoon, and remembered that before he left, he was standing between the church administrator's office and Rick's office. On the way out, Randy stuck his head in the door and waved good-bye to Rick. Hearing the phone ring in the church office, Randy hesitated and waited for the caller to identify himself. He knew there was a more than average chance the call was for him.

"Rick, it's Patty Jo on line one," church administrator Richard Gardner announced from inside his office.

Randy stood between the two offices and watched as Rick took his wife's call. He noticed a look of concern on Rick's face and heard him say he was so sorry. Randy waited to find out if something was wrong with Patty Jo.

After Rick hung up the phone, Randy stepped forward and asked, "Is something wrong?"

"Well, we thought Patty Jo was just having some allergy problems, but it seems like it's become a full-blown cold." Rick stood up and felt around the papers on his desk for his car keys. "I'm gonna go and pick her up."

Randy knew Patty Jo was employed, but didn't know

exactly what she was doing. He had heard she was trying to make some extra money by cleaning someone's home. That wasn't unusual these days for the church's ministers. The church was going through some lean times, financially, and everyone was trying to help ease that burden.

On the night of May 14, 1999, Randy had the responsibility of closing the Domino store and working alongside the manager. Shortly before 1:00 A.M., he was mopping the floor and had his back turned to the front window when he heard a rap at the door. Like any normal pizza delivery person, he immediately froze, suddenly feeling gravely concerned about his safety. After his heart rate dropped and his adrenaline returned to normal, Randy turned and saw Rick standing at the door.

It was after midnight, and because Domino's no longer served customers in their restaurant, their lobby door was locked. Randy unlocked the door and let Rick into the lobby. Rick told him about Patty Jo being missing and that no one had seen her since that evening.

"I am going to try and find her," Rick said, openly sobbing.

The two spiritual brothers knelt together in the lobby and prayed, asking God for guidance and seeking protection for Patty Jo. Randy recognized how distraught and confused Rick was and instructed him what to do.

"You need to go home, Rick," Randy told him, slipping an arm around his shoulder. "Go home, and wait for her phone call. I'll tell my manager what is taking place, finish my responsibilities here as quickly as I can, then meet you at your house."

Rick wiped the tears away from his eyes on the back of his shirtsleeve. He was still wearing the black pants and black shirt he had worn earlier to the high-school play. On his way out of the lobby, he turned and looked, as if he still weren't clear on what to do.

Randy noticed the scratches on Rick's face and asked him what had happened. Why the scratches? Why was there blood on his face?

At first, Rick blew it off, like it was no big deal, but

later told him what had happened. "Oh, I was chasing Grace in the woods down below the volleyball court," Rick stated, "and fell in a briar patch."

Initially Randy was more concerned with Patty Jo's disappearance than he was with scratches on Rick's face. But later as he thought about it, he remembered playing on that volleyball court down below the front of his house. Because they were not very good volleyball players, he and other church members had made frequent trips to the woods next to the volleyball court to retrieve the ball from the woods. He was very familiar with that area because he had retrieved the ball more times than he could count, but he wasn't familiar with any briars in that area. He had personally never gotten scratched when he retrieved the ball out of the woods.

"Just go home and stay by the phone," Randy advised Rick. "I will get there as soon as I can."

Randy completed the last of his tasks at Domino's, clocked out, and drove straight to Rick's house. He arrived shortly after 2:00 A.M. and was relieved to see Patty Jo's Dodge van parked out front in the church parking lot. As long as he had known the Pulleys, she had driven the van. It was only on rare occasions, like taking the trash to the county dump, that she drove Rick's red truck. But if the van was there, where was the red truck? Had Rick gone out looking for Patty Jo, rather than going home as he suggested?

When Randy knocked on the door, he was surprised to find Rick inside the house, alone, nervously pacing across the living-room floor.

"I guess you've heard from Patty Jo?" Randy asked, thumbing toward the van parked outside.

Rick looked up at Randy and shook his head. He hadn't heard anything.

"Then who is driving Patty Jo's van?" Randy asked with a perplexed look on his face.

"I am," Rick answered nonchalantly. "She's driving my truck." He explained in detail how they had switched

vehicles earlier in the day when Patty Jo discovered one
of her tires was leaking air.

Randy sat and stared at Rick. He was as helpless as a
lapdog. "Then, what do you think we can do?" he asked
quietly.

Rick didn't know. All he knew to do was wait until
Patty Jo or someone contacted him. The thought of contacting the hospital never occurred to him.

But Randy was getting impatient. He put himself in
Rick's place, then decided if it was his wife missing, he
would be out looking for her.

"If it is okay with you, I'd like to retrace possible routes
that Patty Jo may have taken," Randy suggested. "Maybe
start with her shopping route, if that is what she did, and
drive along that route, then drive back to where the play
was held at Dan River High School. There's a possibility
she might have finished shopping early and drove to the
high school to look for you."

Rick nodded. He trusted Randy as a friend and agreed
to whatever he believed was best.

Randy walked next door, fifty feet away, to his own home
and woke his wife, Judy. He explained to her what was
going on, that Rick had called the police and reported
Patty Jo missing, and how he was helping him look for her.

Judy was shocked. She had never remembered Patty Jo
staying out this late. She was always so punctual. Looking
up at her husband, she asked for an answer to the question that would keep her awake for the next eight hours.
"Do you mean to say Patty Jo still hasn't come home?"

"Yes," Randy said in a single word.

Randy quickly changed clothes and walked outside to
where his car was parked. As he thought about it, he
couldn't remember if he had told Judy to go and spend
time with Rick until he got back, but it probably was a
good idea. He didn't think Rick was in any condition to
be left alone.

Chapter 28

"I don't remember exactly what Randy said," Rick Pulley would say later, "but I do remember he prayed with me and gave me some instructions of what he thought I should do. Based on his advice, I went home and went to the house. I believe I then went over to the church and got my guitar and brought it back to the house. The only place I knew to find comfort was in prayer or was in worship. So my mind-set was to just find some encouragement or find some sort of sense of direction. That's when I went to the church, grabbed my guitar, and brought it to the house.

"Judy came over. I don't have any idea of what time it was. I think it was during that time when Randy told me to go home and wait by the phone, and she came over and sat with me. I think we prayed and I think we just talked and brainstormed, and then at some point, Randy came over to the house. I don't remember exactly the sequence of the events, but at some point, her and I went out looking. We went out searching.

"Randy suggested that we go to the Sonshine South Development, which was the development PJ and I had once lived in. We had friends in that area, people from the church, and I think his reasoning was that maybe she went out to visit somebody and just lost track of time.

That maybe she saw somebody while she was shopping and went to their house. We just drove through the neighborhood and went by the people's homes that we knew, but we never saw any signs of her.

"We searched a long time. We may have gone back to Danville. It was at some point—but I don't remember exactly—that we went into Danville several times with different people.

"At one time, when me and Randy thought we had found the truck, we were coming back and leaving Danville. We were coming back to our house, and as we drove past Cane Creek, between where the airport is— I don't know who spotted it first—but we spotted a red truck in the parking lot of Advance Auto Parts. I think you had to go past the parking lot entrance of the direction we were going and turn around, and we went back in and drove the parking lot to check out the truck. It wasn't our truck, but another truck parked there.

"We also drove the route back into Danville into the county where the Dan River High School was. We then drove through Milton to go to Sonshine South. We didn't think the River Bend Road was an option, so we didn't go that route. It wasn't a route she would normally travel.

"I don't remember exactly what happened after that— the sequence of events is kind of fuzzy, but I remember coming home at some point, and it was getting light and we went back to my house and we called some of the leaders of the church and some of our friends and let them know what was happening. I believe when I called 911, they had told me that in order for a missing person's report to actually be filed, they said it took eighteen, twenty-four, maybe even forty-eight hours. It was some figure of time before the police can start looking for her. I don't remember the exact time I called 911. I don't know if it was 911 I called, or if it was the sheriff's department that I called, but I did call somebody."

Chapter 29

After hearing the search for Patty Jo had been fruit-less, Judy Sudduth could not go back to sleep. Randy had told her he was going to go out and look for her, that he was going to leave Rick there at home to answer the phone in case she was to call.

Judy thought about the situation for about fifteen minutes before making the decision that she should go over and stay with Rick. *By now,* she thought, *he's bound to be distraught, worried out of his wits, and needs somebody there to be with him.* She quickly dressed and was almost out the door when through her window she saw Rick walking across the parking lot. Apparently, he was walk-ing from the church, back over to his house, but he had his guitar case slung over his back.

"Now, that is so strange," Judy mumbled.

The idea of Rick walking from the church and carry-ing his guitar wasn't strange, but why now? And at three in the morning? She thought about it, but didn't re-member any other worship team members coming to the church and playing music when they were upset. Was this a quirk of Rick's? And why hadn't she noticed this before? Because she and Rick lived within fifty yards of each other, she knew just about all of Rick's habits, but she had never observed him doing that in the eighteen years or so they had been neighbors. Of course, in all honesty, Rick's wife had never been missing in the eighteen years they had been neighbors too.

Meanwhile, Randy Sudduth had driven up Highway 62 and headed toward the Dan River High School. His first thought was that Patty Jo Pulley had finished shopping in Danville, driven back to the school to meet Rick, and maybe arrived after the play was over, where she then couldn't get her car started. He drove around the parking lot several times at the high school, then returned home down the Kentuck Road to Highway 58 east and back to 62.

While Randy searched for Patty Jo, Judy comforted Rick. As she later thought about their conversation that night, two things Rick had said to her stuck out clearly in her mind. First, Rick had asked Judy, "You don't think Patty Jo has left me, do you?" And second, when Randy arrived an hour or so later, they both urged him to call the police, but Rick kept saying something about having to wait twenty-four hours before calling the police.

Above all else, Judy and Randy Sudduth were both trying to keep Rick calm and positive. If he had called the police and reported Patty Jo missing, they were not aware of it.

Randy Sudduth was relieved to see his wife comforting Rick when he arrived at Rick's home. The look on both their faces told him all he needed to know—there was still no word from Patty Jo. Randy still believed Patty Jo was probably stranded somewhere along the highway.

"I have an idea that we should go back out and look in other areas," he said to his wife and Rick. Another set of eyes would have been helpful, so he asked Rick if he would like to ride with him this time.

Rick jumped up from the couch and volunteered to drive his van. He and Randy drove toward the town of Milton, North Carolina, and into an area called Sonshine

South. He and Patty Jo had once rented a home in this area and there were still a large number of congregational members that lived there. In particular, there were two ladies who lived in this area and were good friends with Patty Jo. Perhaps she had found something nice at the store that she wanted to show them and was en route to their house, when maybe she had an accident. It was a long shot, but that was their way of thinking.

Regardless, Rick and Randy were trying to retrace every possible route and all the places they suspected she would have visited. They followed Route 57 and continued on their way to Sunshine South. Only once did Rick veer off the main road, and that was to turn in and circle the boat ramp on the Virginia side of the Dan River. When they saw no sign of the Pulleys' red truck, they swung back up the highway, crossed the bridge, and drove through Milton and into the Sonshine South neighborhood.

Again, no sign of Patty Jo. No sign of the red truck. No sign of her stranded vehicle.

Rick and Randy decided to drive back to the Pulleys' home before they went out again. Judy was still at Rick's home, and who knew? Maybe Patty Jo had called in by now.

Judy Sudduth was waiting on the porch at the Pulleys' home with a portable phone in her hand. When she saw Rick's van pulling into the parking lot, she ran out and gave them the news.

"Still no word from Patty Jo," Judy said quickly when Rick rolled down his window. Both men looked tired and desperate.

"We're going to drive into Danville," Rick told her. "Maybe she's still there at Wal-Mart."

My God, it's three in the morning, Judy thought. *I don't think Patty Jo is going to be out shopping this late without calling someone.*

Judy looked down at her feet, then back at Rick. "I

know it is a stupid question to ask, but don't you guys have a cell phone?"

Rick grimaced. He reached inside the pocket on the driver's door and pulled out a cell phone, then held it out in front of Judy.

Judy took a deep breath. "That explains that," she said, letting go of all the air she had been holding.

"Rick, don't you think we need to call the police?" Randy suggested, leaning toward the driver's seat. From the very beginning, he had encouraged him to call the police and insist they get involved in the search. It just wasn't like Patty Jo to go out alone and not call *someone* to let Rick know where she was.

"I've called the police," Rick kept saying, "but they keep telling me we have to wait twenty-four hours before we can report her missing."

Randy was careful not to tell Rick what to do, but he could not help but believe the police could at least alert their patrol cars in the area that Patty Jo was missing. They could at least keep an eye out for the Pulleys' missing red truck. Surely, with one phone call, the police could cover more territory in an hour than they could all night.

"You might want to try calling the Pittsylvania Sheriff's Office again," Randy continued urging Rick. "It wouldn't hurt matters any."

Rick agreed, but decided he would drive across the border and into Danville, before calling the police again. Randy sat on the passenger side of Rick's van and kept an eye out for the red truck. They drove into Danville, circled all the parking lots and the major department stores, and went as far west on Highway 58 as they could go before giving up their search. They had checked almost every single parking lot in Danville, along the route they believed Patty Jo would have taken from her home, but still no sign of her or the red truck.

Randy looked at his watch, then noticed that it was almost time for morning. Before they could make it back

Albert and Elva Mae Riddick were simple, God-fearing people. All they ever wanted was to be happy and to love God, their children, and their grandchildren. *(Photos courtesy of Pauline Riddick)*

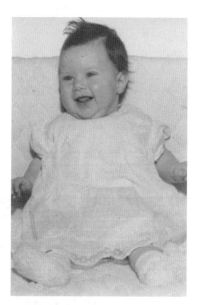

Born July 31, 1961, Patty Jo was showered with affection.
She was always a bright and fun-loving child.
(Top photo taken by Pauline Riddick; school photo at bottom)

Patty Jo blossomed into a beautiful woman. By the time she graduated
from high school, she was certain her calling was to serve God and
others through music. *(School photos)*

Athletics were also a big part of Patty Jo's childhood. She particularly enjoyed playing softball for her high school team. *(Photo taken by Pauline Riddick)*

In college, Patty Jo traveled with the school's ministerial team. *(Photo taken by Elva Mae Riddick)*

After Patty Jo taught Rick how to sing and play the guitar, they quickly recognized how effective they could be as a team.
(Photo taken by Elva Mae Riddick)

Underneath this photo, Patty Jo wrote in her scrapbook: "Once upon a time, there was this precious young couple. Music was one of the things they enjoyed together." *(Photo taken by Elva Mae Riddick)*

After getting married, Rick and Patty Jo immediately began a career in music ministry. *(Photo taken by William G. Riddick)*

Rick worked in a grocery store, while Patty Jo majored in music at Meredith College. *(Photo taken by Pauline Riddick)*

Always clowning around, Rick changed into Patty Jo's cap and gown. He said he had worked just as hard as Patty Jo for her degree, so he should be receiving one as well. *(Photos taken by Elva Mae Riddick)*

Excited about the opportunities in their music ministry, Patty Jo began writing songs for her and Rick to sing while on tour. They even recorded their own album and sold it to help fund their ministry.
(Photos taken by Michael Corprew)

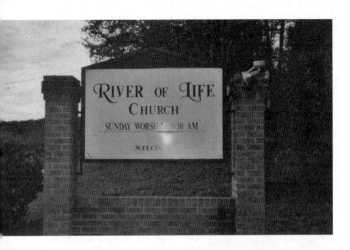

When their music ministry didn't make enough to pay the bills, Patty Jo and Rick decided to accept employment with the River of Life Church in Ringgold, Virginia. *(Photo taken by Jo Clayton)*

Rick was hired as the minister of youth and placed in charge of church worship. Although not paid, Patty Jo served as the visiting host committee and was a big part of the church's music ministry. As part of Rick's salary, the Pulleys were allowed to live in the parsonage next to the church shown above. *(Photo taken by Jo Clayton)*

Patty Jo was very talented and transformed the parsonage into a
real home. *(Photos taken by Elva Mae Riddick)*

While working at the River of Life Church, Patty Jo and Rick were allowed to continue their music ministry. *(Photo courtesy of Connie Winslow)*

Rick's new interest became missionary work. He organized and led several missionary trips to such places as Haiti and Romania. *(Photos taken by Patty Jo Pulley, courtesy of Elva Mae Riddick)*

When Rick confessed to Patty Jo he had been unfaithful, she was crushed. But she forgave him and tried to act as if they were still happily married. *(Photo taken by Elva Mae Riddick)*

The Pulleys named their dog Grace, for that is what Patty Jo demonstrated to Rick. *(Photo taken by Bobby Corprew)*

Patty's brother and sister and their spouses had no idea what was going on between her and Rick. *(Photo taken by Elva Mae Riddick)*

On May 14, 1999, Rick reported Patty Jo missing. Her truck was found the next day, but she went missing for three years. *(Photo taken by Jo Clayton)*

The next day, after Patty Jo was reported missing, an eyewitness described a person he saw walking away from Patty Jo's truck. He would later identify this person as Rick. *(Photo courtesy of Connie Winslow)*

The remains of Patty Jo Pulley were discovered three years later in this ravine. *(Photo taken by Jo Clayton)*

Patty Jo's casket was adorned with roses, but there was no body inside. Her remains were placed inside a box and set at the foot of the casket. *(Photo taken by Elva Mae Riddick)*

A memorial was also placed by Patty Jo's family at the site where her body was found. *(Photo taken by Jo Clayton)*

Patty Jo's siblings and father purchased her piano, which Rick had sold after she disappeared, and presented it to her mother as a surprise gift.
(Photo taken by Elva Mae Riddick)

Three years after his wife disappeared, Rick Pulley was arrested and tried for murder in the courthouse at Caswell County, North Carolina, the same county where Patty Jo's remains had been found. *(Photo taken by Jo Clayton)*

Caswell County District Attorney Joel Brewer was the man who prosecuted Rick Pulley. *(Photo taken by Kera Satterwhite)*

Rick, looking twenty years older, alongside his feisty lawyer, Theresa Pressley. *(Photo taken by Brian Clayton of the Danville Register & Bee)*

home, the sun would appear and begin a new day. He was about to give up all hope when he spotted a red truck in the Advance Auto parking lot off Highway 58.

"Look, Rick," Randy shouted. "There it is. There's the truck."

Rick got very excited and immediately pulled off the road and into the parking lot. But the truck was not only a newer model, it had a different license tag number.

When the two men arrived back at the Pulleys' home, Judy Sudduth was there to greet them, along with two other church members, Cathy and Gene Smith. The Smiths were also former neighbors of the Pulleys when they had lived in the Sonshine South Community.

The sun was just coming out. While the Smiths embraced Rick and comforted him, Randy bowed his head and prayed. Without God's help, he knew it was going to be impossible to locate Patty Jo Pulley.

Chapter 30

By nature, Judy Sudduth had always been an organized person. Years of teaching in the public school, working alongside her husband in the church, and rearing a large family had convinced her that planning and documentation were the keys to success. It was her way of keeping herself, her family, and her world organized. Even after Patty Jo disappeared, it wasn't out of the ordinary for Judy to take some time and make some notes in an attempt to document all that had happened.

The appreciation for organization and use of note taking was one of the things Judy and Patty Jo had in common. She did know that Patty Jo was a very efficient and very organized person and kept a date book. Every day, she would write down what she was doing in her Day-Timer and check it off as she completed the task. Patty Jo always kept her Day-Timer with her and would not go anyplace without it.

At three that morning, while Randy Sudduth was looking for Patty Jo, and Judy was comforting Rick in his home, Judy noticed nothing abnormal in the Pulleys' home. However, she did remember seeing Patty Jo's date book. She wasn't exactly sure where she saw it, if it had been lying on the dining-room table, but she was positive she had seen it there in the home that morning. Immediately she was concerned and wondered why it wasn't with Patty Jo. In all the years she had known her, she had made multiple lists in her Day-Timer: shopping lists, grocery lists, and to-do lists. Call it a woman's intuition, but Judy was so concerned that Patty Jo didn't have her Day-Timer that it started making her ask questions in her head about where she really was.

It wasn't that Judy was playing detective or trying to be a hero and solve the missing puzzle as to what had really happened to Patty Jo. But as she thought about it, there were a lot of things happening, and she was documenting everything just so she wouldn't have to rely on her memory. Rick was already beginning to tell a somewhat slightly different version of what had transpired the night before. She had overheard him say to the Smiths that Grace had been chasing a rabbit, when he clearly had told her it had been a squirrel the dog had been chasing.

These weren't huge contradictions in Rick's story, and that was what was so disturbing to Judy. For certain, he knew the difference between a dog chasing a rabbit and a dog chasing a squirrel. It was the minor details in Rick's story that were leading her to think Patty Jo's disappearance might become a major problem. So there was justification, Judy was convinced, to try and keep up with all the information, and, at the very least, have some sort of timeline to give the police when they came to talk with her.

The last time anyone besides Rick had heard from Patty Jo was when she had phoned Rick at the church and Associate Pastor Richard Gardner had answered the phone. Gardner remembered that he had become so disturbed by Patty Jo's disappearance that he got up early that Saturday morning and drove around the area, searching for her.

Around 7:30 A.M., Gardner decided to retrace what he thought would have been a reasonable route that she might have taken the evening she disappeared. He began in the church parking lot and drove to the end of Sonshine Drive, turned left, and headed toward Milton. Checking all the shopping center, motel, and business parking lots, he combed the major arteries in Milton, and as far as Danville, looking for any signs of the Pulleys' red pickup truck.

Two hours later, Gardner returned to the church and was disappointed that the red truck and Patty Jo Pulley had not found their way home. He stopped in and visited with Rick for a few moments. Rick was very distraught, and because there were some other people there, Gardner did not linger, but drove home, changed clothes, and had a little breakfast.

Later in the morning, as word got out about Patty Jo's disappearance, members from Rick's church and other people in the community who knew the Pulleys started arriving at Rick's home and at the church. Some people came to pray for her safe return. Others came just to offer comfort to Rick and one another. And still others came, bearing food and beverages, and asking how could they be of help in the search for Patty Jo.

The Dan River floods easily, especially during the heavy rains. The water runs off the land and into the waters faster when there is not enough vegetation to absorb the precipitation. The harder it rains, the more water runs off the land and the Dan River rises faster.

Gardner remembered someone had mentioned to him that because of all the rain they had had on Thursday evening and Friday, that the Dan River was rising rather rapidly. It then dawned upon him that on occasions in the past, the River Bend Road had been flooded to the point where it had been impassible. There was a slim chance that Patty Jo's truck had gotten stuck in the road and prevented her from passing beyond that point.

Richard Gardner would never have believed he would be the person God used to answer those many prayers.

Gardner had almost given up hope in finding any signs of Patty Jo, but he couldn't just sit there and let the thoughts about her being stuck at the River Bend Road pass by. Around 2:00 P.M., he decided it was worth a shot to check that area, especially before the river did rise and make the road impassible.

Driving to the end of Sonshine Drive, Gardner turned left onto Highway 62, traveled down to the intersection of River Bend Road, and took a right. To his surprise, he spotted the Pulleys' red truck, approximately a half mile down the road and parked on the left side.

Gardner parked his car some twenty-five yards behind the red truck. Fearing the worst had happened to Patty Jo, he ran to the truck and looked in the windows.

Patty Jo Pulley was not inside the truck.

Gardner checked the doors of the truck. They were locked. Careful not to touch anything, he leaned toward the truck and looked inside again. He noticed an empty Mello Yello bottle and a wrapper from a candy bar on the floor of the truck.

Had a Mello Yello and a chocolate candy bar served as Patty Jo's last meal? Gardner posed the question.

Just to make certain he had not missed anything, Gardner circled the vehicle, looking for any obvious signs or clues that would shed light on Patty Jo's whereabouts, but he saw nothing.

Gardner believed the closest place to a phone and to Rick Pulley was back at the church. He felt like Rick should be the first to know his truck had been found. After all, she was his wife.

Also, while Gardner was at Rick's, he could phone the Pittsylvania County Sheriff's Office and inform them the truck had been located on River Bend Road. After he made the call to 911, the dispatcher instructed him to return to the vehicle and wait for law enforcement to arrive. Just in case there were any problems, Gardner asked a church elder, David Wilson, to accompany him back to the truck.

Before the police could arrive, Gardner saw Rick Pulley's van approaching him on River Bend Road. Rick was driving and stopped some distance away from the truck, got out of his vehicle, and walked toward the truck. He and Wilson met Rick and tried to stop him from approaching the car.

"Don't do it, Rick," Gardner admonished him. "Leave it for the police."

Rick was a large man. He was bawling and insisting that he look inside the truck for Patty Jo. "I want to see my wife," he kept repeating, over and over. "I want to know she is okay."

Richard Gardner and David Wilson were able to hold Rick back until the police arrived. Uniformed officers from the Pittsylvania County Sheriff's Office ordered everyone to stand back and move away from the truck.

"We have an ongoing investigation here, people," one officer shouted out to the crowd. "I suggest you either step toward the north shoulder of the road or return back to your vehicles."

The small group of spectators backed up and moved away from the vehicle. A few minutes later, several church members persuaded Rick to return home and let the police continue their investigation. There was nothing there for him that the police wouldn't share with him later, they assured him.

Chapter 31

A tenth of a mile up River Bend Road, Dale "Cherokee" Purvis was still packing last-minute items for his birthday party. When he walked out to his truck, he noticed a lot of activity around the red pickup truck that he and his brother-in-law had seen parked on the side of the road the night before.

Curious as to what was happening, Cherokee walked from his house down River Bend Road and approached the law enforcement officers standing around the truck.

"Good afternoon, Officers," Cherokee said with a smile. "What's going on?"

"We're looking for a woman," one of the officers said. "Her name is Patty Jo Pulley." He pointed toward the truck and mentioned that she was last seen driving this vehicle.

"Well, maybe I can help you fellows out here."

The officer stepped away from the other officers and pulled Cherokee to the side. He was told that Cherokee had seen this same Ford red truck parked on the side of River Bend Road the night before. Around seven this morning, when Cherokee drove down that road again on his way to the fairgrounds, he saw the truck again.

"Yep, we had to drive up to the fairgrounds and put on some Boston butts about seven this morning so they'd be ready by twelve today," Cherokee told the officer. "That truck was still sitting there. It's the same truck, as far as I know. It was still in the same spot and the same position when we saw it this morning."

"And you say there was a guy walking up the road from this direction of the truck," the officer asked.

Cherokee nodded his head. "Yeah, me and a buddy of mine saw him last night walking down the road. I got a good look at him from the back. He was a white guy, with long, dark hair, and he wore a white T-shirt."

The officer listened as Cherokee described in detail the man he and Jap had tried to give a ride to the night before, and where they had last seen him. He found Cherokee's description of the large man, with long, dark hair, very helpful.

Later, Cherokee would receive a visit from Officer Keith Isom, but would tell Isom he couldn't really say much about this person because he only saw him for a few seconds. And in those few seconds, Cherokee really didn't see him well at all.

"Who you really need to talk to is my brother-in-law, Robert Rowland," Cherokee suggested to the officer. "I know he went back and tried to offer him a ride, so he probably got a better look at him than I did."

Chapter 32

The Pulleys' home had gotten so crowded with church members, and there were so many different people coming in and out to comfort Rick and help out, that Pastor Randy Sudduth politely excused himself. He then walked over to his house, crawled into bed, and started a brief nap. Just as he closed his eyes, Judy awakened him with further news about the truck being located.

"Randy," Judy said, standing over her husband and lightly shaking his arm. "Someone just called our home and said the police had found the Pulleys' red truck."

Randy sat up in bed and rubbed his eyes. He then asked Judy if anyone was with Rick.

"Well, there is a large number of people who are still at the church, praying and supporting one another," Judy replied. "They're asking us what they can do to help. Besides bringing food and drinks to Rick's house, there are a few groups of people who are taking turns going out and looking for Patty Jo."

Randy was comforted. The parishioners at his church were always eager to respond in a crisis.

"How about at the place where they found the truck," he asked further, "is anyone there from our church yet?"

Judy paused, thinking hard before she answered that question.

"I don't know for sure who from our church is there, but I was told a crowd of people have already gathered down at the place where they found her truck."

Randy slipped his shoes back on and headed for the door. He had a premonition that Rick would be needing him soon. Just as he predicted, a Pittsylvania County sheriff's deputy, Keith Isom, arrived and took a statement from Rick, Judy, and Randy. Seated at Rick's dining-room table, they answered all the questions asked of them by the uniformed officer. Randy confirmed the afternoon phone call Associate Pastor Richard Gardner had received from PJ, who then handed the phone over to Rick.

In short, Rick told Isom he had gone and picked her up from work an hour after that phone call; then she later decided to go shopping in Danville for a new dress and that was the last he had heard from her. He said that Patty Jo was five-seven, weighed 135 pounds, and that her maiden name was Riddick.

"Mr. and Mrs. Albert Riddick are her parents," Rick said in a matter-of-fact tone.

When Isom asked Rick if Patty Jo was taking any medications, he shrugged, then answered. "No, not really. She was taking birth control pills, but stopped taking them. She took some type of nonprescribed sinus medication, and an eczema medication. Otherwise, nothing of any great quantity or strong dosage."

Keith Isom had been the officer on call when Rick called the Pittsylvania County Sheriff's Office and reported his wife missing on May 14. Now that he was sitting face-to-face with Rick, the first thing he noticed was three predominant marks across his face. Hopefully, Patty Jo Pulley would arrive home soon and all of Isom's suspicions would be for nothing. At least that was what he and hordes of other people were hoping and praying for.

Chapter 33

In times of great grief and trauma, the mind seems to slip into neutral, and the mouth into high gear. Due to the high level of stress, a lot of what is said and done is sometimes forgotten.

"I don't remember exactly if Randy and Judy encouraged me to call the police the night Patty Jo disappeared," Rick said in response to why he hadn't called the police when the Sudduths suggested it. "But I don't remember being resistant to calling either. You see, I had already called the police. I don't remember when I called them, but it was in the morning. I know it was before Randy called the Riddicks.

"I didn't call the Riddicks because I was just very emotional at the time and I was having a hard time talking to anyone, let alone talking to the Riddicks. I knew they were gonna be beside themselves with worry, so I didn't want to make it any worse on them than it already was. I thought Randy would have had a more even tone. He could just do it in a way that wouldn't alarm them any greater than they would be already. I mean, at that point, I was just having a difficult time communicating with anybody.

"I talked to the police a couple of times. I remember talking to two people when I called—whether this was a second or third time, I don't remember. But when I called, I remember talking to a lady and I asked the lady if she could expedite it. I asked her if she could somehow get things moving and get somebody out to help with an investigation and see if we could find Patty Jo. This is when she put me in touch with the sheriff's department.

"She put me on hold for a moment. I don't remember how long, but it was a length of time. It wasn't just for a few seconds, and then she came back on the phone and said it was an officer that was going to be coming. I didn't recognize the officer's name, but when he arrived, he took a statement from me. It was a brief statement. It wasn't like an interview or anything like that.

"The officer asked me about the scratches and about how that had happened. I told him that I had been out looking for my dog, that I went to retrieve her and I fell when I was doing that. I don't believe I offered much more. I don't think he even inquired any more than that as far as an explanation.

"There were people already at my house when the officer arrived. I believe Gene Smith was already there when he came. I'm not certain about that, but somebody was at the house. The officer talked to me and Gene, or whoever was there, came back inside, and we tried to develop a plan again. I just sort of felt like I needed to be doing something to find Patty Jo.

"I had not slept at all. I believe Gene and I were in my van. We went looking in several neighborhoods and drove to several locations, but I don't remember where. I just know through that period of time we looked in many different locations. But I don't remember exactly where we went. This would have been between noon and two that Saturday afternoon.

"It was then that I realized my cell phone was running low on minutes and that I needed to stop and purchase some from the cell phone company. I believe we had gone to Wal-Mart again to look for the truck in that parking lot.

I was in the cell phone office near Wal-Mart, where I ran in and purchased some additional minutes for the phone. I don't remember if Gene came into the office or not, but when I came out, he was talking on his cell phone to Richard Gardner. Richard told Gene that he had found the truck, so we drove directly to the area where Richard said the truck had been found.

"We drove as fast as we could without breaking the speed limit. At a certain point, we turned down the River Bend Road and saw the truck, then saw Richard, and there may have been a couple of other people out there at the time too. I remember seeing several people there that day standing near the truck, but I don't remember the sequence actually when I saw it.

"I wanted to look in the truck. I wanted to look around. I tried to do that as I walked up to the truck and looked inside. I didn't touch anything. Somebody yelled out and told me not to. I wasn't planning on touching anything, but I went and looked in the truck. I didn't observe anything that was out of the ordinary. There was nothing that I noticed at that time that was strange or unusual.

"I stood there for a moment, looked around, and just scanned the area where the truck was. I walked down the road with Michael Wilson, David Wilson's son (a youth at the church), and we talked, and I believe we prayed. I don't remember what we talked about, and I don't remember what we said. I was pretty numb at that point. I just don't remember what I talked about.

"I was aware of the officers arriving some time later. They came and they asked everybody to move away and I think they eventually asked us to leave. We left at some point—again, the sequence is fuzzy—but as we were driving back home, we stopped along the road. We got out of the car and walked on the side of the road between River Bend and where our house at the church was.

"We went back to the house and I think at some time

I know I contacted the Riddicks several times that day. I don't remember if I called them at that point to let them know that the truck had been found or if I called them some time later. But I did call them at some point and let them know the truck had been found."

Chapter 34

At the age of nineteen, Keith Isom began his career with the Danville, Virginia, Police Department (DPD). Since 1981, Isom had been working with the Pittsylvania County Sheriff's Office and attended numerous homicide schools to further his ability as an investigator. A friendly, happy-go-lucky fellow who loves to talk, he was on call the night Rick Pulley called 911 and reported his wife missing. The next morning, he was the first person to meet and interview Rick and the others at the church.

At approximately two-thirty that Saturday afternoon, Isom drove to the location where the Pulleys' truck had been found on River Bend Road. Sergeant Robert Bailer and several other deputies were there when he arrived, but there were no civilians present. The truck was locked and sitting off on the side of the road. It had been parked in the grass and on the shoulder of the road. There was a (North Carolina) Caswell County sergeant there, several (Virginia) Pittsylvania County deputies, and another officer from Caswell County.

"Have you guys found out anything from this scene?" Isom asked.

The officers stated they had found nothing significant around the general area that indicated foul play or where

Patty Jo Pulley might be. After looking over the car for about five minutes, Isom decided he probably needed to speak with Rick Pulley again. "I'm going to ride up there to the church and interview the husband a second time," he informed the deputies.

The parsonage was an attractive mobile home with gray siding and wooden porches. Isom stood at the glass-paned back door and knocked. He was greeted by a gentleman who introduced himself as Gene Smith and led him into the dining room, where Rick sat at the table.

The rooms inside the Pulleys' home were brightly painted and decorated with a number of pictures. Handcrafted items and a number of vases with colorful artificial flowers sat on tables and countertops. An intricate multicolored and framed needlepoint tapestry, with the words "Home Sweet Home," emblazoned in red, hung on the wall in the dining room.

Someone who lives here is very talented, Isom observed.

Isom glanced in Gene Smith's direction, then mumbled, "I need to speak with Mr. Pulley in private about his wife's disappearance."

Smith nodded, excused himself, and walked outside.

Isom intended to speak briefly with Rick, give him his calling card, and then leave. He would offer Rick the opportunity to call him at any time, if his situation changed or if his wife returned home. Until the police had any further leads, Isom would drive back down to the scene where the truck had been found and see if he could help them in any way.

But all of that changed when Isom saw Rick's face. There were three deep marks on his face, all across his left cheek. Under his right eye, there appeared to be a little plug of skin missing. Not wanting to alarm Rick, Isom tried to ignore what he had seen, but he knew he needed to take a statement from him.

"Hello, I'm Officer Keith Isom." The stocky, balding officer stuck out his hand when Rick stood up at the table.

"Mr. Pulley, do you mind if I talk with you for a few seconds?" Isom asked in a polite voice. He diverted his eyes, making certain he was looking anywhere but at the scratches on Rick's face.

Rick looked back at Isom, as if to say, "Is this really necessary?"

But Isom didn't give Rick any time to protest. "Well, anytime a person's wife is missing, I like to talk to her husband. I want to see if he might remember something that would help us locate her, or maybe you might remember somewhere she was going."

Isom grabbed a mini tape recorder that he kept with him at all times. He sat down at the table with Rick; then, as if it were no big deal, he turned the recorder on. "Now, why don't you tell me all you know about your wife's disappearance."

Rick related his story to the officer. He started at the beginning of the day, when Patty Jo saw the rear tire on her van was almost flat. He told how he had taken her into work and taken the van to get the tire fixed. The pastor claimed he had last seen his wife at 6:00 P.M., and that he had spent the rest of the night at the local high school. When he got to the point where he started talking about the high-school play, Isom sat up in his seat and cocked his head.

"What time did you get there at the play?" Isom asked.

"About seven-fifteen, seven-twenty, I think."

"Had the play already started?"

"Yes, it had already started."

Isom sat back and considered the matter. It just so happened that he had attended that same play. Although he had never heard of the musical *South Pacific* before that night, he was familiar with the songs, "Some Enchanted Evening" and "Bali Ha'i." He had enjoyed every minute of the lively and funny musical.

But Rick was never told that Isom was at the same play. Maybe it was coincidence or luck, or perhaps a bit of both, but Isom's son was one of the actors that night and the investigator had been in the audience enjoying the whole show. As if fate had deemed it so, Isom quizzed Rick about the musical, then asked, "Do you remember what was the last scene?"

Rick shook his head. "I don't remember. You mean the name of it?"

"No, what happened. What happened up onstage during the last act?"

There was a long pause before Rick spoke. "Um," he started fumbling his way through the answer, "the last . . . the last act was . . . was the, uh, the lovers uh, they finally come together and everything is consummated with their relationship." He paused again, then added as a post-script, "And it ends with that. It's happy ever after."

Isom knew by the way Rick had answered the question that he hadn't been at the play. So he asked, "Do you remember how the play ended?"

Rick nodded, looking confident and proud of himself. He was sure he had given the officer enough information to pass the test. Rick's final answer was that both couples came together and lived happily ever after.

Isom knew that wasn't true. Near the end of the play, two of the main characters went on a dangerous mission behind Japanese lines, successfully sending back reports on the strength of enemy forces. The Americans use this information to intercept and destroy Japanese convoys. But in the end, one of those characters, Cable, is killed. So it didn't end "happy ever after."

That SOB is lying, Isom thought. *If he doesn't know what happened, then he wasn't there that night. But why is he lying?*

Isom had learned that things aren't always what they appear. Everyone has problems, and when you start looking behind the scenes, one finds out there are two sides to every story. He knew it was time to press down on this bereaved husband.

"Do you mind if I get a photograph of you?" Isom asked, watching him closely for a response to his request.

Rick didn't protest. He smiled, said okay, then posed nervously for the camera.

Isom's father was a Pentecostal Holiness minister. He had been brought up around preachers all his life. He knew the other side—the human side—of the minister that the public didn't see. He had seen it firsthand, and just because someone says they are religious or a minister didn't make it so. No more than saying a cop makes you a cop, or guarantees you are a cop. Isom wasn't intimidated by Rick to the point where he couldn't go a little further.

Rick waited patiently while Isom took photos of his face.

"Rick, tell me again what happened to your face?" Isom asked, only this time his words had a certain bite to them.

Like a sporty old gentleman who coolly explains his ruddy face as a sunburn, Rick nonchalantly said, "Briars. I fell in some briars."

Isom was familiar with briars and the scratches they left when in contact with skin, but the scratches on Rick's face just didn't match. These were not the same. He started mapping out his strategy.

Okay, no more Mr. Nice Guy. No more promises of finding your wife and she's going to be okay. There are things here that I need to get from you. If I don't get them now, then I am never going to get them. And that is going to be crucial down the road.

Isom desperately wanted to see what was under Rick's shirt. That small, still voice he had entrusted all these years asked him to do that. He normally didn't ask a man to take his shirt off, but after he saw the marks on Rick's face, he had a hunch there was more to the story than Rick was telling him.

"Mr. Pulley, would you mind taking your shirt off?"

Rick unbuttoned and pulled his long-sleeved shirt away from his upper torso. He had a few scratches on his arm that looked consistent with scratches that could have been the result of briars, but what really stood out to Isom were the scratch marks on his chest and four elongated bruises on his right bicep.

As Isom studied the scratches and bruises on Rick's face, his arms, and across his chest, he envisioned Patty Jo fighting Rick off; grabbing him with her left hand on his right bicep and trying to hold him back, while defending herself with her right hand—all the time scratching him on his chest and his left cheek. It was as clear as any picture he had ever seen.

Both Isom's voice and his demeanor had changed, because he believed Rick was not where he said he was—at the school play—when his wife disappeared. Because he saw the marks on Rick's face and body, which were consistent with someone trying to fight him off—and because he believed Rick was strong enough to kill his wife—Isom knew he had to go deeper into the investigation. What started out as a courtesy call to a concerned husband had now turned into a Q&A with a possible suspect.

Rick cooperated all the time, acting as if he couldn't do enough to help the police. And that was what deepened Isom's suspicion. Rick was humble—too humble. The odd thing was that he was acting a part, or at least trying to pass himself off as a wounded spirit. Isom decided to take advantage of that.

"Would you mind giving us permission to search your house?" Isom then asked Rick, who willingly agreed and signed a Consent to Search form, at 4:20 P.M. The signed form allowed the police to search his home, take photographs, and remove anything from the Pulleys' premises they deemed necessary. It was an open invitation to a thorough investigation.

As Isom began searching the Pulleys' residence, the first thing he noticed was that everything that supposedly belonged to Patty Jo was very neat and tidy. Both the bedrooms and two bathrooms in the front of the house were in the same order, but the bathroom off the master bedroom—the one that Rick identified as his—was just the opposite. His area was disorganized and unkempt.

Inside Rick's bathroom closet, there was an area built

for a washer and a dryer, where his dirty clothes were kept. Isom looked through the pile of clothes stacked high, but he didn't see signs of any kind of struggle, any blood, or any evidence pointing to a crime that had been committed. There was no reason for him to dig through all the clothes, so he asked Rick to help him sort the clothes.

"Are the clothes you were wearing the night your wife disappeared in this same pile?" he asked.

Rick nodded and pointed toward a stack of clothing. "They're in there somewhere," he said, walking toward the pile.

After briefly searching the pile of clothing in the bathroom, Rick handed the detective two pairs of pants, two shirts, and one pair of socks. He said he had worn one particular pair of khaki pants and olive-colored shirt to look for his dog, and then another pair of black pants and shirt he had changed into after he had come back inside. These black pants and black shirt were the same items he had worn to the school play.

Isom set the clothes aside, then walked outside to his car and retrieved several paper bags. He put on latex gloves, then took each pair of pants, folded them up, and placed them in a bag, which he then sealed and labeled each bag separately.

What surprised Isom about the Pulleys' house was that they really didn't have closets. The storage areas were more like wardrobes than closets, but what he was looking for, more or less, was not Rick's clothing, but Patty Jo's belongings. He wanted to see where they were stored. Isom was more interested in how things were set out on her makeup dresser and other items that were part of her everyday normal life. A simple toothbrush, a comb, a few pieces of jewelry, and some makeup could almost paint a picture of a person's temperament in the last hours before they disappeared.

Isom did not do a thorough search of the Pulley home. Because he didn't know what belonged to Patty

Jo or if anything of hers was missing, he did not note any-thing particular about her clothing or any of the items that looked out of place. Of course, even if he had noted that, he would only have Rick's word to go on for what was missing or out of place.

Isom photographed several areas in the house, including the dining room and bathroom. He also made good use of the tape recorder, being very careful to capture Rick's exact words and descriptions of items in the house. What he noticed that struck him as odd were two sets of keys.

"On the dining-room table"—Isom pointed the keys out to Rick—"there are two sets of keys. Whose keys are those?"

Rick spoke causally and without any difficulty. "Those keys on the table there belong to Patty Jo," he told Isom. "I know it is her keys because it has a clip on it, and the clip is where you see the truck keys are attached."

One by one, Rick went through the keys, identifying the ones to unlock the church, the red truck, and their house. There was a second set of keys on the table, which Isom found odd, but nothing more significant. Still, he wondered why Rick would have Patty Jo's keys, if she had been driving the truck that night.

In addition to the keys, Isom photographed the bed-room to the right of the dining room. Immediately to the right and in the bedroom, he saw what looked like a makeup dresser. There was a mirror on the dresser, a hair dryer, and several of Patty Jo's hair bows. Surely, if Patty Jo was planning on leaving anytime soon, wouldn't she have taken a hair dryer with her?

Another item Isom found very interesting was a check made out to Patty Jo from Glenda Honea. When he asked Rick about the check, he said it was the check she had earned for housecleaning the day she disappeared. It had never been cashed. And on the right-hand side of the dressing table, Isom also photographed a pocket-book that had belonged to Patty Jo, another item Patty Jo would have probably needed to take with her.

It was getting late in the evening and there were a lot of other people gathered in the parking lot that Isom had hoped he could speak with. He thanked Rick for his time and gave him his calling card.

"If anything changes, Rick, please give me a call."

Rick promised he would.

Isom walked outside and strolled around in the parking lot. He noticed everyone was still talking about Patty Jo's disappearance and their eyes were red from crying.

Patty Jo must have had a lot of people who loved her, he thought.

Standing in the parking lot, Isom listened and tried to get a general idea of what people were saying from the conversations around him. He wanted to know what they were saying about Rick and wanted to see if they had the same feeling about Rick as he did.

Isom spoke with Randy Sudduth again. He joined him and a number of congregational members in the parking lot for prayer. After leaving the church, he called into headquarters and checked with dispatch to see if they had put out an all-points bulletin (APB) on Patty Jo Pulley. He wanted everyone in the community to be aware that a lady was missing under suspicious circumstances.

Finally the night fell. Isom watched as the groups of people in the parking lot broke up into smaller groups, then finally dispersed and either went inside to be with Rick or went home.

I wonder what Rick Pulley is going to do now? Isom turned over in his mind. *Who will he call? Will he tell them his wife is missing? And will he tell them what really happened to her?*

Chapter 35

Rick said he had deliberately postponed calling Patty Jo's family until he was positive she was missing. He said he didn't want to upset them, until he had to. It was a phone call he dreaded to make, however.

After discussing the situation with Randy Sudduth, Rick changed his mind about making the phone call. He asked, instead, if Randy would call the Riddicks and break the news for him.

Seventy-seven-year-old Albert Riddick answered the phone on the second ring. He was told by Randy Sudduth that his daughter Patty Jo was missing.

"Well, can you tell me what happened to her?" Albert asked with grave concern.

Randy was sympathetic, but tried to be optimistic as well.

"All we know at this point is that she left home last evening to go shopping in Danville and she hasn't returned."

Shopping? Albert immediately thought. *That doesn't make any sense. Why would she go shopping and not return home?*

Randy paused and waited for Albert to process his thoughts, then explained, "I'm sorry, Mr. Riddick. I wish I could tell you more, but that's the only information we have. The police are here now and they are probably the best qualified to provide the correct information. I think it is best that you speak with them."

"Do you know if she is . . ." Albert's voice broke in mid-sentence. He had stopped short of asking the dreaded question. Normally, the calm and solid one in the family, he felt as if someone had just driven a wooden stake through his heart. Everyone in the family had always turned to him when there was a problem, but this time he had a feeling he would need all the help he could get to make it through this. His greatest concern at the moment was breaking the news to Patty Jo's mom.

Albert hung up the phone and turned toward the bedroom where his wife was still getting ready for the day. He thought about the last time they had talked with Rick and Patty Jo on Mother's Day. That had only been a few weeks ago.

"I wanted to hold on to my daughter for as long as I could," Elva Mae Riddick would recall. "At that moment, I didn't know when I would ever see her again, and that is what bothered me the most. Every mother has the right to be with her child, to love her, and hold on to her for as long as she can. That is all I ever wanted."

On a Sunday, two weeks prior, the Riddicks had played horseshoes and baseball, then enjoyed watching all the mothers and grandmothers open their Mother's Day gifts. Every present was presented to the mothers as gifts of love and in appreciation for all that they had given to the family. Albert especially remembered Patty Jo's gifts for her mother and grandmother, but it was her remarks afterward that touched his heart.

"I am fortunate enough to have two wonderful mothers," Patty Jo said, her voice breaking. "I have never known the privilege of what it felt like to be a mother, but I can assure you I do know how wonderful it is to have a mother."

Patty Jo had then walked over to her mother,

wrapped her arms around her, and told her how much she loved her.

Albert took a deep breath, then tapped on the door of the bedroom.

"Elva Mae," he said evenly, trying not to alarm her, "it seems we have a situation with Rick and Patty Jo that needs tending to."

The first thought that came to Elva Mae's mind was that Rick and Patty Jo needed some kind of financial assistance. It was not unusual for them to ask for help when they were in a bind. They lived in Ringgold, Virginia, nearly four hours away and were ministers in a contemporary church. They had never made a lot of money and there were many challenges they had to overcome in the last few years, especially while traveling up and down the East Coast and spreading the Gospel.

Elva Mae sat on the side of the bed. *What is it that Patty Jo needs?* she wondered. *I just talked with her last week and she seemed so happy. She has such great neighbors, lots of good friends, and a good, kind pastor. I know she enjoys her work, so what could it be?* She kept racking her brain, until finally she narrowed it down to: *I know, it has to be that she and Rick need money for their mission trip to Romania.*

Elva Mae asked Albert if Patty Jo's problem was related to the church.

"No, this is not about Rick and Patty Jo's church work." Albert's tone was solemn. "This is about Patty Jo."

Elva Mae looked at her husband. She had never seen him look this way. There was pure fright in his eyes. "What is it Albert?" she said, motioning for him to come and sit down on the bed beside her. "Please tell me what has happened to our daughter?"

Albert tried to speak, but the words were lodged in his throat. He took a deep breath, but still the words wouldn't come. Finally he was able to tell Elva Mae what had happened to Patty Jo.

"I just got off the phone . . . talked with Rick's pastor,"

Albert said in broken sentences. His lips were trembling and his body shook. "He says to me . . . He told me Patty Jo didn't come home last night. . . . He says she is missing."

"Missing?" Elva Mae exclaimed. "What do you mean 'missing'?"

Albert buried his head in his hands. "I don't know" was all he could tell her. "Pastor Randy, he said to me . . . He said that she just went out shopping . . . then she never came home."

Tears quickly formed at the bottom of Elva Mae's eyes. How could her daughter be missing? Did something happen at the church Pastor Randy didn't tell them about? Had something happened between Patty Jo and Rick?

"I don't know, Elva Mae," Albert said in a low voice.

"How about Rick? Is he okay?"

"I don't know," Albert acknowledged. "I just don't know all the answers to your questions."

Elva started wringing her hands, acting as if she hadn't heard her husband, and continuing a long string of questions.

Finally Albert stopped and grabbed her by the hands. "All I know is our little girl is missing," he said, looking at her troubled face. "The only way we are going to find out what has happened is to get in the car and drive up to Ringgold and talk with Rick and the police. That is the only way either of us is going to find out what is going on."

The disturbing news about Patty Jo suggested to Elva Mae that there were maybe some things in her daughter's life that she had not told her about. They had to drive to Ringgold and talk to the police, but they had to do everything they could until then to help the police try and find her. Perhaps, then, they could talk with Patty Jo and help sort out the secrets of her life.

Chapter 36

As early as 3:00 P.M., Saturday, May 15, 1999, Rick Pulley had already emerged as a suspect in his wife's disappearance. Although Pittsylvania County officer Keith Isom couldn't prove it, he did have the gnawing suspicion that Mary Jo Pulley was already dead.

"Yes, Isom came to the house and interviewed me," Rick recalled. "He took a statement and we went into some depth and some detail about Patty Jo. He just took what seemed to be an ordinary statement in the beginning. He asked me about my face, and then he asked me to take my shirt off and he took pictures of my chest and arms. No pictures of my legs.

"He asked if he could search the house. I believe that's when I signed or gave him permission to search the house. I believe he asked about a few things that were around the house. Patty Jo's date book was someplace in the dining room and he asked about that. I believe he looked through it. I don't remember if he did.

"He also asked about the keys that were on the table. Patty Jo had two key rings. We both had two key rings. We each had a key ring that had the ring or the keys to the church. The church had several buildings and we had keys to those. Then, I had a key ring that had my truck key and the house key, the necessary keys, and my van key, and then, she had a key of a similar nature that was, I think, one of the college students had given her a little ID pouch, and it had a key ring. She had her license in it and maybe a birth certificate.

"The officer took a few pictures. He then asked about the clothes that I was wearing that day. I don't remember where they were. They were someplace in our utility room. . . . I don't remember if those clothes were thrown on the floor, which would have been pretty normal for me, or if they were actually in a pile in the closet, where the dirty clothes were, but he asked about the clothes that I wore and he took those. He asked permission to take them, but he did not ask for any belongings of Patty Jo's.

"He did ask to see her purse. She had a couple of different things that she would use. She just had multiple bags that she used. She had a backpack that she used frequently if she was going to someplace that needed to have books in it. If she was going to some church, she had a backpack that she put her Bible in. She would put her worship notes and all the songs in it that we played. She had had a large pocketbook that was a denim material pocketbook, and within that, she had a small black wallet that had other things in it—money, checkbook, and things like that.

"Everything I mentioned was at the house except for the little black wallet-type thing that would have been like an informal clutch purse."

Rick said as soon as Isom left his house, Rick and his friends went out looking for Patty Jo again.

"We just started driving to different places, trying to think of anyplace that we might be able to go to. I wanted to be active. I wanted to do something.

"I didn't sleep that night very much. I think I may have dozed off briefly, but I don't think I got any sleep. On Sunday morning, I went over to the church and typed out an e-mail to all people that I could think of who would pray, who may have even possibly had some information. I don't remember my particular state of mind at the time. I just sent a mass e-mail to maybe fifty or seventy-five people—friends and acquaintances that we had met on the road, that we had met traveling—and I just asked them to pray.

"I don't remember the exact time, but that was relatively early that morning, and then later that morning, Robert Mearns, who had kind of a pastoral function within our church, came and talked to me. In a relational kind of way, he is almost a kind of father figure—in a real sense—to the church.

"I believe it was that Sunday morning he walked with me at church and prayed with me. We talked and he told me how he had contacted other churches—international churches, like the Macedonia Church in Germany—people who he believed to have some sort of spiritual insight as to what may have occurred. As we were walking around, he told me there was a consensus that possibly Patty Jo had just gotten tired or gotten frustrated and had decided to take a break. I believe those were his words.

"I didn't believe it was true. I just told him it wasn't true, that I didn't believe that had happened. I couldn't believe that would ever happen. Yet, when he asked me if Patty Jo and I were having any problems that could have caused this, I told him about my inability to have an erection.

"Robert encouraged me at that point. As we were going over to the church, I believe he shared Scripture with me about the importance of not giving over to speculation that would produce panic—the kind that would produce an emotional response. I thought that was pretty much impossible, but after thinking about it, I agreed that that panic would feed an emotional response that could potentially cloud any kind of ability to think in a way that might help.

"Sometime after church was over, I went over briefly

to the church and I think some people prayed for me. I know I didn't stay for the whole service, but sometime that afternoon, there were constant comings and goings between my house and the church. I think there had been some flyers provided, and at some time during that afternoon, I and some other individuals started going out and handing out flyers at different locations.

"The flyers had been printed up at the church and was a plea to the community for anyone who had any knowledge of Patty Jo's disappearance to help us bring her home safely."

Chapter 37

The trip from Gates County, North Carolina, to Ringgold, Virginia, was a four-hour drive. Under the circumstances, Albert and Elva Mae would not be able to drive the trip alone. They both agreed they would want one of their children to drive them. After calling Billy and Rita, Albert then called granddaughter Connie Winslow.

Connie was in college now and majoring in criminology. She planned on being an officer of the law. After explaining what was going on with Patty Jo, Albert agreed he would feel better about the situation if she was there. She would know what to do and know what questions to ask, especially when they went to talk to the police.

"Don't worry, Grandma," Connie said as she greeted Elva Mae and Albert at the door. "It's going to be okay, Grandma. We'll find out what happened to Patty Jo when we get there."

Elva Mae grabbed her granddaughter around the waist and held on tight. There was no way she could have ever prepared herself for such a tragedy as this.

Connie held on to her grandmother longer than usual, just to assure her she was there for her. Choking back her own tears, she felt more anger than she did fear. She had heard enough and seen enough already in class to know how easily these things can happen.

Some psycho maniac with nothing better to do has kidnapped my aunt, Connie imagined. *I just hope she's not dead.* She said a silent prayer. *O God, I pray Patty Jo is not dead. Stuff like this is in the news all the time, but I pray this can't be happening to my family—it just can't be.*

News traveled fast in the small town of Gates County. The telephone had already started to ring with friends and family who had heard about Patty Jo and were asking what they could do to help her.

"Grandma, if you stop to answer all these phone calls," Connie cautioned, "we'll never get to Ringgold. We have to think about Patty Jo and her safety now. We can't worry about everyone else. We have to take care of Patty Jo."

Connie and her grandparents sat in the den and waited for the other family members to arrive. The hands of the old grandfather clock boomed out louder than ever before. Every second that ticked off reminded them of how fleeting life was, and, like Patty Jo, how easily it could be lost.

"I wonder how Rick is doing," Connie said to no one in particular. She felt as if she were in a dream and no one had stopped to wake her. "Rick must really be going through a lot by now. I know he wishes we were there, and is feeling lost and alone without us."

Rick was Patty Jo's husband, the other half of her that they loved so dearly. Other than Rick's mom, who lived in Raleigh, the Riddicks were the only family Rick had.

As fast as Elva Mae hung up the phone, it would ring again with another call about Patty Jo. She told many of the callers she had planned on riding to Virginia, but if Patty Jo was missing, then maybe she should stay home, just in case she called.

"I just know if Patty Jo had any way to call home, she would," Elva Mae said nervously to her callers. "I don't think I could ever live with myself if she was in trouble and I found out later that she had called me to help her and I wasn't there to take her phone call."

Connie paced awkwardly from the den to the dining room. Every few minutes, she looked at her watch.

"This is more than nerve-racking," she mumbled under her breath, "this is pure agony."

Her grandparents agreed. The greatest fear of their lives had come true.

"Every minute seemed like an hour," Connie would remember later. "Every tick of the clock reminded us of why were there and what we had to face. Every chime moved us further into this nightmare. Our greatest fears grew worse with every passing second."

Yet, in all of the Riddicks' troubled moments, they still thought of Rick and considered how much he needed their support.

The phone rang again and Albert jumped, then motioned for Elva to take the call. "Maybe it's Patty Jo or Rick calling," he said under his breath.

Albert and Connie waited—for what seemed forever—on Elva Mae to pick up the phone and answer it. Shortly after she said hello, she let the phone fall from her hands and started crying.

Albert jumped up and stepped toward his wife. He grabbed the phone and talked to the other person on the line, then hung up.

"That was Randy Sudduth again," Albert said softly. "The red truck Patty Jo was driving has been found about a mile from their house."

Before Albert had a chance to speak, Connie came out of her seat, asking, "Did he say if Patty Jo was in it?"

Albert shook his head. "No, they didn't find her, just the truck." Seeing a ray of hope, he added with some sense of relief, "I reckon that is a good sign, isn't it?"

Connie shrugged. She honestly didn't know—only God and Patty Jo knew if it was a good sign.

Once Elva Mae Riddick received the news that her

daughter was missing, she could not stop crying. In between her sobs, she shared what Patty Jo had told her on Mother's Day.

"She told me she and Rick were struggling financially. She had taken on a couple of part-time jobs, in addition to all that she was doing at the church. I told her that was why she looked so weak and tired, that she had been doing too much and taking on too much responsibility."

Albert walked from the kitchen and handed his wife a cup of coffee. She sipped slowly from the cup, trying to settle her nerves and regain her composure. But just as quick as one thought was resolved, another one rose to take its place.

Elva Mae's lips began to quiver again. "What if she is lost somewhere and has amnesia?" She dabbed at her eyes with a tissue and nervously twisted her rings on her fingers. She was not holding up well under the strain and pressure.

Connie picked up the phone and dialed Rick's house number, then asked to speak with Randy Sudduth. Randy told her the truck had been found on River Bend Road.

"It's not too far from where Rick and Patty Jo live," Randy said in a tired voice. "It was found neatly parked on the shoulder of the road, in the opposite direction of the route she had traveled to Danville. It looked as if someone had picked her up and would drop her off again at that same spot."

Now, that is a bit strange, Connie thought, trying to keep her concerns to herself. She didn't want her grandparents to worry any more than they already were.

"All I want to know is why Patty Jo was driving the red truck?" Elva Mae couldn't seem to shake the notion she should have been driving her van. "She's always driven the van, but I can never remember her driving the red truck." She seemed to be obsessed with the thought that the red truck was somehow connected to her disappearance and it was causing her great grief.

Elva Mae reached out and grabbed Albert by his arm. "I wish now we'd never helped Rick and Patty Jo buy that truck," she mumbled. "Now look at what has happened."

After Albert sold the truck and signed the title over to Rick, he then gave Rick both sets of keys, and accepted Rick's promise to make an equal number of payments until the truck was paid off. There were no legal papers drawn up, but as part of Rick's gentleman's agreement, he wrote Albert a check for $350 and posted it as a down payment.

Since it was the weekend, Albert didn't think about the check. He trusted Rick enough to know he wouldn't write him a bogus check. But on Monday, when he went to the bank to deposit Rick's check, he opened his wallet and discovered the check was missing. Although Albert never said anything to Rick or Patty Jo about it, he told Elva Mae he suspected Rick had somehow gone in his wallet and removed the check.

"What makes you think that about Rick?" Elva Mae had challenged him at the time.

"Well, I put it in my wallet and it's not there," Albert said, opening his wallet to her. "Why would anyone but Rick have a reason to get that check?"

As if the thought about that check suddenly resurfaced in Elva Mae's mind, she looked up at Albert and asked, "Did Rick ever send you one payment for that truck?"

"Not the first payment," Albert responded in disgust. He looked away from Elva Mae and shook his head, as if to clear that thought about Rick. "But what does that matter now? Helping them to buy that truck hasn't got nothing to do with this, Elva Mae."

The Riddicks had been lending Rick and Patty Jo money for some time. They had promised to spend more time together as a couple, but their financial problems always kept their noses to the grindstone. Rick's salary was very low, and even though Patty Jo was helping out with a couple of extra jobs, they still weren't making enough money to even pay their bills.

Connie picked up the phone and dialed Rick's number again, hoping she would get a chance to speak with him. Rick answered, but he was so upset and distraught that he couldn't stop crying.

"Just hang in there, Rick," she encouraged him. "We're going to drive up and see you, so you won't have to go through this alone."

Rick suddenly found the voice he had lost earlier. "Oh, don't worry about me, I'm fine," he said in a clear, but flat, tone. "I have my friends and my church family here. I don't want you driving up here, 'cause there's really nothing you can do. The sheriff's department is in charge and everyone is out looking for Patty Jo. So why don't you just stay there with Patty Jo's mom and dad? I will call you with updates."

Connie stiffened. This definitely didn't sound like the old Rick Pulley she knew, or at least the Rick Pulley she thought she knew. At a time like this, she thought, he would want to be around Patty Jo's family, if nothing else but to draw strength from one another and comfort each other.

"So how's Rick?" Connie's grandparents asked after Connie hung up the phone.

"Well, when I first talked to him, he was crying. But by the end of the conversation, he was saying we should stay here and wait for his updates." Connie locked her bottom jaw and bit down on her lower lip to keep from saying something she didn't want her grandparents to hear. "According to Rick, there is nothing we can do to help him there."

Albert jumped up from his chair and threw his hands into the air. "That's exactly what he told us this morning after the pastor told us Patty Jo was missing," he said, glaring at Connie. "I guess it has been his pastor who has helped him calm down."

"Well, I think we can do a lot to help him," Connie chimed in. "We're family and family sticks together. He's probably putting on a brave face and trying not to burden us further. But he doesn't have any family there, and I really believe he'd feel better if we were with him."

Albert nodded. "Oh, I definitely agree with you," he shouted. "Once we get to Ringgold, then we can talk to his neighbors and ask them to help us figure out a way to find Patty Jo. If we stick together, somehow, we'll get through all this confusion."

Meanwhile, back in Ringgold, Virginia, the Pulleys' red pickup truck had been towed from River Bend Road by Nick's Towing and taken to the Pittsylvania County Sheriff's Office. About the same time Officer Isom was leaving the church on Saturday evening, he saw the wrecker driving by with the truck being transported.

Early the next morning, Isom checked in with his office, then called Sergeant Tommy Nicholson. Nicholson was the supervisor over the Pittsylvania County's deputy units. Even though the officers were officially listed as "deputies," they were more like a specialized unit and were available to Isom whenever he needed them. Nicholson was gracious enough to loan out a half-dozen of his men who drove out to the River Bend Road location and assisted Isom in the search. The deputies did a general canvass of the area, knocking on resident doors, and speaking to people who believed they had something valid to aid in their investigation.

In addition to the Pittsylvania County Sheriff's Office's canvassing along River Bend Road, other deputies were stopping anyone in the area and asking if anyone knew anything, had seen anything, or had heard anything.

The Caswell County Sheriff's Office (CCSO) were also there with their men working the roadblocks, helping Isom, and assisting in the search.

As investigative leads began to come in, Officer Isom made it a point to follow up each lead as quickly as possible. He met with Investigator Dallas Stephens, of the Caswell County Sheriff's Office, and brought him up to speed as to what information he had with regard to the suspicious disappearance of Patty Jo Pulley.

"I really think we should go back and search the Pulley home again," Isom said to Stephens, suggesting they join forces.

The longer the two seasoned officers discussed the case, the more convinced they were that they had to return to the Pulley home. Just so nothing was overlooked, they both agreed to return together and search the home.

Isom told Stephens they should talk with Rick as soon as possible.

"I want to speak with Rick while he feels comfortable about speaking freely," Isom said. "Once he catches wind he is a suspect, then he is going to be all lawyered up and shut down on me. I got a feeling, by now, he knows he is a suspect. But I am just curious to see if he will still be that same, old wounded soul he was when he talked with me yesterday."

Chapter 38

The Riddicks decided it was best to get up early Sunday morning and drive to Ringgold. Albert and Elva Mae Riddick didn't think they could make that long trip, so Connie and her mother, Rita, and her uncle Billy agreed to take it for them. Of course, everyone believed Patty Jo would be home by then, and, most likely, she would be cuddled up next to Rick when they got there, all safe and sound.

Driving Connie's dark blue Blazer for the four-hour drive, the Riddicks made the last leg of their journey and turned toward the turnoff that led them to Ringgold. They still wondered if Patty Jo had been injured and was lying in the grass at the bottom of one of those hills. Maybe she had gotten hurt and wandered off somewhere aimlessly. Maybe she had gotten lost in the woods or— God forbid— had fallen into the Dan River.

In times like these, one's mind wreaks havoc upon a person's thoughts. The eerie feelings and visions of Patty Jo's mangled body lying exposed somewhere were unsettling.

Think positive thoughts, girl, Connie reminded herself. *Positive thoughts are what you need, not negative. Your criminal justice classes and television crime shows are messing with your mind again.*

The Riddicks were truly unprepared for the world they were about to enter. Sheriff's deputies were everywhere in the church parking lot and at Rick's house. A helicopter was hovering above the Dan River and River Bend Road, where the red truck had been found. There were hundreds of people walking the miles of hillside and along the waterside of the Dan River. All were looking and searching for Patty Jo.

A new dose of reality was thrust upon the Riddick family as they prepared themselves for what they saw was going on before them. As they walked from their vehicle in the church parking lot to Rick's house, they saw a group of people huddled around the front of the church as if they were forming a protective human shield. Connie and her entourage walked over to the group and introduced themselves as "Rick and Patty Jo's family."

The introduction didn't seem to get the Riddicks any special notice or favor, until Connie demanded to speak with Rick. The church members pointed toward Rick's house, but watched them warily—some even stared—as they made their way up the small hill and to the parsonage.

When the Riddicks entered Rick's home, the people standing outside and near the front door were even more reluctant to talk. All they could say was that the police were questioning Rick and pointed to another small farmhouse across the road.

While waiting on Rick, the Riddicks walked the premises, observing and looking for anything helpful or suspicious in nature. The cold and unfriendly ambiance made them feel as if they were not welcome there and gave them a creepy, uneasy feeling.

Keep a good perspective, Connie reminded herself as she kept looking around.

The Riddicks learned that the River of Life Church was located on a fifty-acre tract in a private community called the Sonshine Farm. It was surrounded by homes owned by members of the church, many of whom lived within walking distance. They found it strange that the women of the church wore little or no makeup and adorned simple clothing. They appeared to be quiet and subservient to the men, yet seemed comfortable with that arrangement. It was obvious that the men of the church clearly were in charge.

Connie felt out of place immediately. The church's lack of response and initiative to make them feel welcome was a complete turnoff. She wondered how Patty Jo, who was friendly, gracious, and always the perfect hostess, ever got along with these women. Later, she would learn that Patty Jo had adapted to this kind of life. Her talents of sewing, crafting, and painting had helped her blend in easily with the other ladies in the church. And because she was so dedicated to her marriage and to Rick, that made an easy transition as well.

Connie sensed everyone was staring at them. "What's wrong with us? Why does everyone keep staring at us?" she whispered to her mother.

"I don't know, but I find it hard to believe Patty Jo fit in this group of people we see here today. Their behavior scares me."

"Maybe we stepped into a time warp or something," Connie said sarcastically, noting the dress and presentation of those around her. "These folks look like they had gotten stuck in the 1970s and had never got off the train."

Connie pointed out that many of the men in the parking lot had long beards, which in itself wasn't strange. However, they also wore dark sunglasses, the kind she remembered seeing in the old FBI meetings, where all the agents wore black suits, white shirts, skinny black ties, lace-up shoes, and dark sunglasses. And what was even stranger, neither man nor woman ever made eye contact with any of them.

Finally a few men sporting a hippie-type look walked over to Billy Riddick and started talking with him. They were even suspicious of Billy, who was by nature and birth a mild-mannered and calm person. The men seemed a bit disturbed by the Riddicks' presence, wary that Patty Jo's family might find out something they already knew.

"Do you think it's true what they are saying about Patty Jo?" one of the men asked in a low voice.

"I don't know," Billy answered. "What is it they are saying about my sister?"

The man leaned toward Billy, turned his head slightly, then revealed, "Do you think Patty Jo ran away to Florida with another man?"

Billy was completely caught off guard by such a bizarre thought. That would be the last thing he believed Patty Jo would do. She would never give up her ministry, her church, her marriage, and her family for another man. So as not to look surprised, he recovered, then shot back, "No, Patty Jo would never act like this and not tell anyone where she was. Especially her family."

The color drained from the man's face and he took two steps backward and away from Billy. His eyes widened and his jaw dropped.

But Billy wasn't through with the man. In fact, he was just getting started. He told him, in no uncertain terms, "Nor would she ever run off with another man. And I don't appreciate you going around, talking about my baby sister like that. Do you understand me?"

The man nodded and slipped back into the fold of the crowd. And to no one in particular, Billy said loud enough for everyone to hear, "You're not going to talk about Patty Jo in that manner. I tell you, I won't allow it."

Chapter 39

When officers Isom and Stephens arrived at Rick Pulley's home, they immediately requested time alone with him. It seemed as if the wait for Rick to complete his interview with the police was taking forever. In the interim, the Riddicks thought that some of the church members would want to call on them and pray with them for Patty Jo's safe return, but no such offer ever materialized. The Riddicks stood alone on the farmhouse side of the road and waited in the shade of elm trees, without even the offer of a cup of water.

Across the street on the other side of the road, members from the River of Life Church gathered out front of the brown metal church building and ominously stared back at them. The air was thick with tension, or something that had not yet been identified.

Inside Rick's house, where the police were conducting another taped interview and taking additional pictures of Rick, the air was also thick with tension.

"Something happened to our pictures we took yesterday," Isom made the excuse to Rick. "So I brought a thirty-five-millimeter camera just in case."

Rick didn't seem to be worried about talking with the police officers again.

"They came and they left. I don't remember exactly what I did after they left, but I do know we were going to go out and pass out flyers. We were praying a lot. And I know I called Patty Jo's family again. Some of the family came that afternoon, but I don't know exactly when they came."

Several minutes later, Officer Keith Isom and a patrol officer walked outside and updated the Riddicks on Patty Jo's disappearance. They carefully explained what little progress they had made in locating Patty Jo, and that they were still interviewing people, trying to find out whether anyone had seen or heard anything.

Connie stood up and introduced herself to Isom. They shook hands and she then inquired, "Can I ask you why you talked with Rick for such a long time?"

"It's just procedure," Isom said without a hitch in his voice.

Isom was straightforward and candid with the Riddicks. They found him to be a knowledgeable, patient, and observant officer of the law. One noticeable quirk was that when Isom talked seriously, he leaned back and closed his eyes, as if he were picturing the story as it unfolded.

"Unfortunately, due to the recent rainfall in the area, a search of the Dan River is almost out of the picture," Isom said, leaning back on his heels again. "The river runs adjacent to where the truck was found, and we would like to look in that area, but we're going to have to wait until the waters recede.

"Meanwhile, the truck is being processed in a secure area adjacent to the jail. We hope to find out something more, but as of this minute, I have nothing left to share with you."

Isom's kind words and matter-of-fact manner assured the Riddicks they were hearing the truth, and nothing but the truth, without a lot of candy-coated promises.

"Thank you," the Riddicks responded in unison.

Isom asked if there were any additional questions, then handed the Riddicks a business card.

"We'll keep you posted," he assured them.

The Riddicks walked toward the house, hoping to see and talk with Rick. They wanted to know if he was okay and how he was holding up emotionally under this terrible strain. As they approached Rick's house, they saw a young man, Michael Wilson, sitting on the steps, holding a cordless phone. Rick and Patty Jo had once mentioned a young man had been living with them while he attended college and worked part-time.

"Can I help you with something?" the young man asked, standing to block the doorway.

"Yes, we're here to see Rick," Connie announced bluntly.

"Well, who are you and what do you want?"

Connie was in no mood to be played with. She and her family had driven four hours, stood in the hot sun for another two and waited on Rick, been exposed to rude people—and now this? Oh, no, it wasn't going to happen.

Connie gave the young boy one of her "don't mess with me, asshole, I'm in no mood for it today" looks. Although she was usually very polite and talkative, on top of being worried about Patty Jo, she was hot and tired. In no mood to be foolishly dealt with, Connie had to bite her tongue so as not to bite his head off.

"I'm Patty Jo's niece, so move out of my way," she said strongly.

The young boy swallowed hard and stepped aside.

The Riddicks followed Connie past the young man and into the house. Rick saw them down the hall, walked out of the bedroom, and began sobbing. They all grabbed each other and held on tightly, as if they would break apart if they let go of one another.

Connie finally broke the silence. "What can we do to help?" she said, patting Rick on the shoulder.

As Rick stepped away, Connie noticed he was wearing denim jeans and a long-sleeved shirt. It was very warm outside, and most of the people around him were wearing shorts and T-shirts. Why was he dressed for a winter day? she wondered.

"Aren't you hot in these clothes, Rick?" Connie asked, fingering the long-sleeved shirt.

Rick shrugged, but didn't respond.

Connie saw how much Rick was perspiring, then commented, "You're sweating, Rick. Do you have a fever?"

"No, I just threw on some clothes, not really paying attention," he offered. "I don't think I have a fever. I've just been shivering on and off all day. I guess it is just the shock and the fact that I am so upset over Patty Jo."

"That's understandable, especially after all the bad weather I've heard you-all had yesterday. Have you rested at all? Have you eaten?"

Rick turned and faced Connie. "Not really."

For the first time, Connie noticed there were some scratches on Rick's left cheek. Her first thought was that maybe he had gotten the scratches somehow while searching in the woods for Patty Jo. "Oh, no, Rick, what happened to your face?"

The color drained from Rick's face. "Well, you know Grace and how she likes to run off. She got away from me again the other evening—running after rabbits, I think—right before I had to leave for the school play. Some of our youth group members were in it, you know."

Connie stared at Rick. His story somehow sounded rigid. Rehearsed. Fake. Why? She didn't know, but she waited for him to finish.

"I had to chase Grace into the woods, across the road. I fell down and got all scratched up in the briars." Rick shook his head. "Must have looked like an idiot. Finally I got her back, though. That dog! If she won't be the end of me, I don't know what will. I'm still glad Patty Jo let me have her, though."

Rick then chuckled weakly.

The Riddicks stared at each other sadly. Rick was either on medication or had lost a lot of sleep. He wasn't the same person they knew and loved. He was so evasive and distant that he seemed like a total stranger.

"Can I speak to you in private?" Rick motioned with a curled finger and asked them to follow him.

The Riddicks followed Rick into the bedroom, where he confessed to them that he believed Patty Jo had eloped to Florida with another man.

Connie rolled her eyes.

"That's preposterous, Rick," she said angrily. "What is it with all these strange questions? It is as if, after seventeen years, you don't even know Patty Jo at all."

Rick lowered his head and stared at an imaginary object on the carpet while Connie admonished him further.

"I know you're probably just scared and grasping at straws, but what's up with you and your bizarre friends? First they stare at us like we're from another planet, then they try and keep us away from you, like we have the plague or something. We're your family, Rick. We're Patty Jo's family. We have more of a right than anyone to be here."

Rick rubbed his eyes and kept looking downward. Connie put aside his lack of eye contact and continued her admonishment.

"And now you want us to think that Patty Jo ran off with another man? Come on, Rick, anyone in their right mind would know that Patty Jo would never do anything like that."

Connie was so angry that she threw up her hands in frustration and headed for the door. Rick never looked up.

"Come on, let's get out of here for a while," she suggested. "Let's get in the car and go find the spot where the truck was found and Patty Jo was probably last seen. At least maybe then we can do something constructive from there, rather than stand around talking this nonsense about Patty Jo having an affair."

Perhaps as an apologetic gesture for having asked such a ridiculous question, Rick followed them outside and offered to drive the Riddicks in his van. Although he never apologized, he was amicable and began to perk up during the drive. As they crossed over the hills and drove through curvy roads, he spoke as if he were their tour guide.

Connie softened. She was willing to let bygones be bygones and put their ill will behind them. After all, this whole trip was about comforting Rick and helping him cope with the loss of Patty Jo. And she was willing to do almost anything to help.

Chapter 40

After talking with the Riddick family, the officers went back and interviewed Judy Sudduth—a second time—and a number of other people there. All total, the two detectives completed nearly fifteen interviews, asking questions of anyone that had any knowledge of the Pulleys or their habits.

Up until that point, Officer Isom was the only one that had conducted any interviews. CCSO's officer Stephens was a tremendous help in that while the cop units were gathering information, the two of them could be conducting interviews.

Isom and Stephens made themselves available to anyone who could provide them with information about the Pulleys. Making notes all the time, the detectives kept a list of addresses and phone numbers and how best to get in touch with witnesses. That Sunday afternoon, Isom started assembling all the information he had collected in two days. He had garnered quite a stack of notes. His policy was when someone was interviewed to have them sign off on a form and give the detectives a copy. That way, the detectives could go back and read everything that was being said. If they discovered they needed to go back and talk to someone, then they had all the information they needed on their copies.

On Sunday night, Isom spoke with Investigator Jimmy Lipscomb. He had spoken to Lipscomb earlier that day about how much help Sergeant Nicholson and his officers had been. Lipscomb then decided to step away from the cops unit and give Isom a hand. The following day, he started riding with Isom, working with him on the case, and assisting him in the interviews.

"What I really need you to do," Isom told Lipscomb later that night, "is to take another look at the Pulleys' red truck."

"I'm sure it is still secured," Lipscomb said. "And I'll be glad to set up a time and place to look at it."

Isom looked like he had just been smacked in the face with a two-by-four. "You know, it just dawned on me that we do not have a set of keys to that truck. We have no way of getting inside the truck. Rick Pulley has both sets of keys, so we need to go back and ask him for a set of keys."

Lipscomb agreed with Isom's suggestion, and at 6:30 P.M. that Sunday, they drove over to the Pulley home and asked Rick for a set of truck keys. The officers talked with a few people, mostly family, who were still there, and then left.

By now, Patty Jo's family, friends, and church members had gone to great efforts to get the media involved so they could get the word out. The church voluntarily printed up flyers, and by Saturday evening, they had the flyers printed and posted throughout the community. All areas within a one-hundred-mile radius were notified that Patty Jo Pulley, the youth pastor's wife at the River of Life Church, was missing and was desperately needed to be found. Overnight, the church and community had become as busy as an anthill filled with ants. That was all everyone talked about, and by the weekend, the message had caught on with the media.

In the circumstances of a disappearance, the sheriff's

department always notifies all media agencies. The radio and television stations were aware of Patty Jo's disappearance. The newspapers were aware of it, for the community was plastered with flyers and pictures of Patty Jo. They were posted everywhere.

Three days had passed since the search for Patty Jo had started, and still there were no signs of her. Members of the Ringgold community offered a $10,000 reward for her safe return and any information leading to her whereabouts.

Rick was moved, especially knowing how difficult things had been financially for the church and the community.

"Pastor Sudduth had mentioned the possibility of a reward, but there was no offer at that point or any direct amount of money. I knew there was no way the church could afford that. [I'd] considered hiring a private investigator and even asked about fees."

Later in the week, an anonymous donor would donate an additional $50,000 to Patty Jo's fund. The reward money of $60,000 should have been more than enough to get concerned citizens motivated and involved in her case.

On Monday morning, May 17, Isom met with Officer Lipscomb to search the vehicle. They met at the gas pumps right inside of Danville, a place referred to as the "City Farm." It was like a detention center where the police could be safe to gas up their vehicles.

Isom handed Lipscomb the keys to the truck, but realized they had failed to get Rick's signature on a Consent to Search form. The signed form gave them permission to actually look in the truck and see what was in the truck. Even though Isom had the keys, they could not legally search the vehicle without Rick's permission. Isom then called Rick Pulley, getting in touch with him on his cell phone.

Rick informed Isom he wasn't in Ringgold, but that he and a friend were driving down I-95 toward Burlington, North Carolina. Their plans were to drive over to

Greensboro and then all the way up to Winston-Salem. Rick said he had only slept a few hours and didn't think he would be of much help to the police officers.

"What are you guys doing?" Isom asked curiously.

Rick explained that they were going to stop at all the motels and hotels along I-95, present a missing person flyer with Patty Jo's picture on it, and ask if anyone had reported seeing her.

"Then how about you meeting with me and Sergeant Nicholson in Yanceyville," Isom asked Rick. "It's right off I-95, not far from the other places you have mentioned. I just need you to sign a paper, giving us permission to search your truck."

Rick agreed, ultimately meeting Isom and Nicholson at a Hardee's fast-food restaurant, where he signed the Consent to Search form, giving the detectives permission to search his vehicle. Isom asked Rick a second time, why he and his buddy were riding up and down I-95, and what they hoped to accomplish?

"Maybe someone along this way could have seen her," Rick explained. "We've stopped at about thirty places so far and plan on doing more tonight."

The Consent to Search form had been signed both by Rick and Sergeant Nicholson. At the bottom of the form, Nicholson listed the time it was signed. There was nothing unusual about the form, just the same type of form they had used and Rick had signed the day before.

As the investigation continued, the police kept interviewing witnesses, hoping one of those would turn up some kind of lead. A call came in that Patty Jo had possibly been spotted at a Hardee's in Danville. Isom hopped in his car and immediately went there. He kept a picture of Patty Jo in his car, and when someone called in and said they had seen her, he would hustle to the area with a photograph and either confirm it was or was not her. Every time a call came in that said someone had spotted her, Isom would respond. And each and every time a witness would look at the photograph and say no, that it was not her, a piece of him would die as well.

Patty Jo's flyers were everywhere, all over the Milton and Danville area and region, and they were getting a lot of response to those. The PCSO had Isom and Lipscomb primarily working on the case, canvassing, and conducting the interviews, but there were other officers also out searching and gathering information. They would take their notes and pass them on to Isom and Lipscomb, who would then follow up on the leads and the information that the sheriff's department was getting.

On May 18, the detectives decided to pay Rick Pulley another visit and went back to the Pulley house both that morning and that evening. When they first arrived, they spoke to Rick in his home, and Reverend Sudduth, sort of in between his and Rick's home on the walkway and driveway. They asked Rick if he would mind accompanying them to the Chatham County Sheriff's Office and answer a few more questions. Rick agreed, but asked if Randy Sudduth, his neighbor and his pastor, could accompany him.

For seven hours, Isom and Nicholson grilled Rick on the details of May 14. Where was he all that time? What was he doing? Did he have an alibi? What kind of relationship did he and Patty Jo have? How did he get those scratches on his face, and where did those bruises on his arm come from?

In another taped interview with Isom, Rick swore there was no bone of contention between him and his wife the day she disappeared. She simply had gone into Danville to purchase some things she needed for the church conference, and never returned.

During the interview, Rick clarified an incident where Patty Jo had gone into the Winn-Dixie grocery on Thursday, the night before she disappeared, at the Cambridge Shopping Center. Patty Jo had already gathered some things she needed for the church conference, placed them in a buggy, written a check, and stood at the checkout counter, when the store manager informed her the check would not be honored.

"Yes, they refused the check," Rick admitted. "That is why she had to go back to Danville the next night. Evidently, we had written a check or multiple checks to Winn-Dixie in the past that had been returned for insufficient funds. We had failed to take care of those, so they refused to accept her check."

It suddenly dawned upon Isom that he had seen Patty Jo's paycheck still in her home the day after she disappeared. If Winn-Dixie had refused to cash her check and she had to go back to Danville the next night to purchase those same items she needed for the church conference, then why wouldn't she have cashed her paycheck that same day?

"Not a clue." Rick tried to sound bored, but he wasn't too convincing.

Continuing his statement, Rick said Patty Jo was embarrassed when Winn-Dixie refused to honor her check, but she was used to it. Things like this had been going on for a long time. Rick said when they were in Romania and together all the time, they talked about their finances and how they needed to get that taken care of. There were other outstanding bills in the past that they had had to deal with, so the Winn-Dixie episode wasn't something that was unexpected or something that hadn't happened before.

"But she was angry at me when she got home that Thursday night," Rick said. "We discussed it and we agreed that we were going to take care of everything. We were doing what we could to get our finances in order and everything looked like it was going to work out. When we went to bed Thursday night, everything was settled between me and Patty Jo."

Isom got that gnawing feeling in the pit of his stomach again. Just maybe, he began to formulate another theory in his head, Patty Jo was embarrassed and hurt enough that she and Rick had gotten into an argument over the matter. Maybe she was bold enough to tell Rick she had had enough and if things didn't change, then she would be leaving. Then an argument would have followed, the couple would have fought, and one thing led to another until Patty Jo was left lying dead somewhere. Isom had seen it happen all too many times before, so just maybe this was a case of domestic violence, after all.

"Can you tell me again about the bruising on your arm?" Isom asked, unwittingly opening up another rambling monologue from Rick about his unloading mattresses at the church.

"I don't know how I got them," Rick said as he gestured toward his right bicep. "I had thought I may have gotten them while I was moving stuff with Richard Gardner. We had been moving beds that day, bed frames, mattresses—things like that—and I possibly could have gotten them when we were moving those." He lifted his arm again and looked down at it. "I hadn't noticed the bruises, actually, until you said something about them, whenever that was. I think just in carrying those things that day, I possibly could have bruised my arm. I remember I carried them in one arm and then reached back and opened the door, or I pushed open the door, and just in the movement of the back and forth, the tugging of the mattresses through the door, I probably bruised my arm. Between moving that and pushing the door open, I could have bruised it then, but I don't know for sure."

Isom asked a lot of questions about Rick and Patty Jo's personal life. Rick often became confused as he struggled to keep up with Isom's burdensome questions.

"Yes," Rick said, he and Patty Jo had carried life insurance on each other at one point, "but it had lapsed." He didn't remember the exact time, but it had been some time since they had life insurance.

"I think we had borrowed some money," Rick continued

again. "I don't know if it was borrowed, but whatever it was when you take money out of your life insurance policy, that was what had happened to us. We had gotten some money out on a couple of occasions and I think we just decided we were going to let it lapse. It was a benefit through Covenant Ministry, our music ministry, and we were kind of phasing out of that—we wanted to do something else. So I think the policies had lapsed at least a couple of years before she disappeared."

Isom asked Rick what he meant by calling his next-door neighbor Bethany Sudduth a liar about the conversation he had with her on the Friday night his wife disappeared. Rick said he didn't remember any of that conversation with Bethany. And he was sure that never happened—that he, at no time, had ever called that girl a liar.

Rick's answer had hit Isom like a rubber-tipped dart. He knew better, because he was standing there listening when Rick called Bethany a liar. Isom was leading Rick right into a minefield about his last moments of his life with Patty Jo. To Isom's surprise, Rick was still holding up pretty well and was still sticking by his story.

"I was tired and I just wanted to go home," Rick would recall. "I'd been there a long time and they kept on asking the same questions, over and over again. I was really frustrated. At that point, I just didn't think what they were doing was productive and had anything to do with finding Patty Jo."

After the interview at the police station, Rick signed another consent form, giving the investigating officers permission to search his home a second time, only this time he decided to put a limit of twenty minutes. He thought that was enough time for them to get what items they had overlooked the first time they had searched his home.

Detective Isom wasn't exactly sure why Rick had put them on a time limit of twenty minutes. The officers had no choice but to abide by Rick's wishes and remain within the time constraints.

Chapter 41

The search of Rick Pulley's home began at approximately 6:40 in the evening. Isom and Nicholson worked feverishly to complete their assignments in the time frame Rick had given them. While they were searching Rick's bedroom, they found Rick and Patty Jo's passports, the ones they had used on their missionary trips overseas. They were concerned and asked Rick, "You're not planning on taking any trips anytime soon, are you?"

Rick didn't answer.

The officers were looking for anything at that time to help solve the disappearance of Patty Jo. They were looking inside drawers, checking any crevices, examining the bathrooms, and investigating under the mattresses, the beds, and anything that was not nailed down. The officers were doing as thorough a job as they could within those time limits. They were able to complete as much as they could of the house in twenty minutes. It wasn't as thorough as they would have liked, but they had done the best they could with what they had to work with at that time.

After this search on May 18, Officer Isom still continued interviewing people along River Bend Road, talking with other people associated with the church and following up leads, and responding to sightings of Patty Jo that either confirmed what he had already known or provided information that proved to be bogus. Isom and his partner, Officer Jimmy Lipscomb, continued working this case, and they continued interviewing people, dispelling rumors and idle gossip that would come in, but they still could not find out what had happened to Patty Jo Pulley. Any lead that would come in, the officers would got out and investigate to its fullest and see if there was something there. Despite them putting in a sixteen-hour days, each and every day, they still were no better off than when they first started.

Even though the police had been allowed to search Rick Pulley's residence, they had found nothing of significance. He had spoken with them only once since that time, and that was in the parking lot right where he lived. The officers had spoken with him by phone only a few times during that period.

The officers were also staying in contact with Connie Winslow, Patty Jo's niece, who was very cooperative. They would speak to her or to her mother, Rita, about every other day, if not every day. They appreciated hearing from the family.

But a week passed, and still there were no clues as to what had happened to Patty Jo. The officers had also called in the Virginia State Police (VSP) to work this case. They were using their helicopter and had brought in a search and rescue team to search the riverbank and down at the boat ramp. They supplied the Pittsylvania police with an aerial view looking over bodies of water and several ponds around there. Finally a search-and-rescue team aided by divers and dogs met to scour eleven miles along the Dan River, near where the Pulleys' truck had been found.

Earlier in the week, Officer Tommy Nicholson had visited Rick and informed him a massive search was being organized. He wanted to know if Rick would participate and be part of the search.

When Rick agreed to be part of the search, he and
church member Gene Smith drove down to the boat
ramp area on the Dan River and waited for instructions.
Organized groups of volunteers were walking the banks
around the river and calling out Patty Jo's name. The
police had brought in all types of special equipment, all-
terrain vehicles (ATVs), helicopters, and boats to drag
the bottom of the river. They even had brought their
sniff dogs to see if the canines could find Patty Jo's body.
The dogs began at the Pulleys' house with the scent of
her clothing and searched in whatever direction the
scent led them. It seemed hundreds of people had
turned out at the church for the search, and when the
searchers weren't searching, they were standing in the
parking lot, gathering into smaller prayer groups, and
praying for guidance.

Several large, massive searches were also undertaken,
with the Caswell County Sheriff's Offices and Milton Fire
Department. The Pittsylvania sheriff's department was
also able to get the North Carolina Department of Cor-
rections (DOC) involved in the search. The VSP also had
cadaver dogs and they were brought out to help locate
Patty Jo. It was a huge coordinated event, and Sheriff
John Plaster and Major Tim Goodson had set this massive search up, without Isom's input. Isom knew when it
was going to happen, but they were the ones who had set
it up and organized it.

Isom was not a vain man. He didn't care who organized and ran the searches. All he was interested in was
finding Patty Jo Pulley, alive. From what he had heard,
Rick had been out every day since she disappeared, supposedly looking for her and passing out flyers. There
had been a few leads in the investigation, but it was
noted that none of them came from Rick.

Isom had heard the rumor that someone had been ab-
ducted from the Hyco Lake Campground, and was told
that Rick and his "bodyguards"—a couple of young guys

from the church who stayed with Rick, kept him company, and helped him search for Patty Jo—had seen some of that same information floating around on the Internet. Someone had spotted them driving around on the Blue Ridge Parkway, as far north as Martinsville, Virginia, where they had stopped at the campgrounds, passed out flyers, and asked the campers if they had seen Patty Jo.

There were a couple of other suspects that had developed over the month that Isom had investigated. A couple of days after Patty disappeared, Steven Keel, a neighbor of Rick's and former member at the Ringgold church, had contacted him. At first, Keel had told him about an incident where he had conducted his own private investigation into the disappearance of Patty Jo. He claimed he had taken a picture of Rick to Robert "Jap" Rowland and Jap had positively identified him as the person he had seen walking down the road near Patty Jo's truck the night she had disappeared. Isom investigated the incident and later warned Keel not to get involved in police business. Since Keel was not a trained police officer, he was actually hampering police efforts, not helping them.

After conducting his own investigation into the matter with Robert Rowland, Isom wasn't 100 percent certain Rowland could make a positive identification of Rick. Isom informed Keel to back off the investigation, but Keel continued to phone and write letters in regard to what he believed had happened. When Keel named another of his neighbors, Randy Glascot, as a suspect, Isom knew Keel was reaching for something other than his concern for the Pulleys. He figured it must have been the $60,000 reward money that kept Keel so hot to trot.

"I know Steven Keel," Rick would say later. "He and his family are sort of on the fringes of our church. Our relationship with the Keels is unusual in a lot of respects. His children were a part of our youth ministry. Some of them had even gone on mission trips with us. On occasions,

Steve and I had played basketball and volleyball together, but I wouldn't say we were good friends. During the years we've known each other, there has always been a bit of a strain on that relationship. There would always be a myriad of disagreements that would crop up from time to time, where Keel, for whatever reason, was either critical of Patty Jo or me, or critical of the church. I was just never really comfortable around him or with him, and I struggled with our relationship altogether.

"He came to me after Patty Jo disappeared, and things got a little heated. He asked me to go and see the men—Robert Rowland and Dale Purvis—who said they were driving on River Bend Road and had seen me there. I told him I would, but I never did. I just thought it was strange why Keel kept on insisting that I go see them and pushing this issue, like he did. I didn't know who these men were and I didn't know what connection they were making with me and seeing me on River Bend Road. I began to wonder that maybe they had something to do with Patty Jo's disappearance.

"The next thing I heard, Keel was pointing the finger not at me, but at my neighbor Randy Glascot. I knew Randy, he had two daughters that had taken piano lessons from Patty Jo over a period of time, so I knew him through his children. He and his family would come to special events at the church, like church picnics and things like that. His kids would come to youth groups on occasions, and his older son, Josh, was one of the kids that would skateboard and ride motorcycles through the church property. There was definitely a strain with my relationship with Randy and Josh. I guess Josh and his friends viewed me as some kind of spoil sport for running them off church property, but I knew some of them were dabbling into some things like occult and satanic worship, and other things like that."

While the police backed off Rick as a suspect—as other suspects were made known—Rick began asking some questions of his own. He and Richard Gardner had met a man at the church in early spring 1999. A couple of weeks before Patty Jo disappeared, a man drove up to the church and told them he was staying at the Hyco Lake Campground and was looking for a church to attend. A week or so later, this same man came back to the church and spoke with Rick. This time, he introduced himself as Newman Voss, and Rick invited him inside his home for dinner. Before Voss left, Rick said, he invited him to church the next Sunday, but never saw him again. Now, looking back on it, Rick wondered if maybe this man had something to do with Patty Jo's disappearance.

The massive searches for Patty Jo would continue through the spring and summer months of 1999. On each occasion, the searches would involve a hundred people or more. Trained emergency personnel and police officers would assign certain volunteers respective teams and lead them through a thorough search of particular grids in and around the Dan River. For hours upon hours, concerned volunteers would line up in rows, walk miles and miles of assigned areas, all the while crossing their grids slowly and observing every inch of the ground. Their instructions were to never touch anything they saw that looked important, but only to make a note of it and report it to their supervisors.

Just as he had been with the passing out of flyers and searching any place he could think of, Rick participated in the searches and thanked the authorities and volunteers for their help. During the searches, he would either be assigned to one of the search boats or he would be assigned to a group of volunteers to cover the riverbanks.

On weekends, Connie Winslow would drive the four-hour-long drive from Gates County to Ringgold and help look for her aunt. In 1999, she was working two jobs, attending college full-time, going through a separation from her husband, while at the same time taking care of her two sons. Finding the time to search for Patty Jo wasn't always easy. However, every chance she got, Connie would drive up to the Ringgold and Milton areas, walk around and search in odd places. She always carried a shovel in her car and a tool kit, just in case she saw anything that was suspicious or resembled a shallow grave. She searched in old abandoned houses, under bridges, in old tobacco barns, in graveyards, and in campgrounds. She combed secluded and isolated areas, anywhere and everywhere she thought she should look. When she talked with people in the community, at the church, or with anyone else who knew anything about Patty Jo, she wore a microphone and a tape recorder so she could accurately capture all that was said.

"I would walk and look for miles," Connie said. "I would start off praying, then I would cry, and finally I would get angry, just knowing someone had done something to Patty Jo. All the while I walked, I tried to figure out how I would handle finding Patty Jo in the condition I knew she would be in. I was beginning to realize deep down inside that I was not going to be the one to find her. God didn't want me to find her, because, the truth of the matter was, I could not have handled it. I would have never been able to get over finding her in the condition I knew she would be in."

For more than a year, Connie Winslow and others spent days and weekends looking for Patty Jo Pulley. Any information they had was then passed on to the police, hoping they would follow up on it. It was Patty Jo's family and friends who were trusting Patty Jo was still alive, and at the same time, they were keeping their hopes alive. But, at the same time, they were running out of ideas, were exhausted, and growing even more frustrated with every day that passed.

In mid-July 1999, Rick received a hand-addressed envelope in the mail just before his birthday. When he opened the envelope and looked inside, he was surprised to see it was a romantic birthday card. The card was not signed, but on the inside were two rows of block letters and the cutout message read: *Happy Birthday Sweetheart, the sweetest dreams of all come true when beautiful things are shared by two.*

Rick was shocked and confused. Someone was either playing a sick joke on him, or this card had been sent to him by Patty Jo. The card created a lot more questions for him than it did answers. He was already in a troubled state of mind and didn't want to think about this. Even if someone was trying to cheer him up, they had only made things harder for him.

Was Patty Jo Pulley still alive? If so, why didn't she contact anyone? Why weren't the police doing more? Why didn't they have any leads? And why hadn't they been able to solve this case? Who was sending him the cryptic message and what did it mean?

Chapter 42

In the summer of 1999, Rick Pulley's emotional state seemed to plummet. Rick was not only depressed, but he seemed to live in total confusion. Though distraught and still troubled by his wife's mysterious disappearance, Rick continued his job as an associate pastor and youth director at the River of Life Church. For almost twenty years, Patty Jo had stood faithfully at Rick's side. She worked tirelessly, always supporting him in every way and shouldering a lot of his responsibility—both in their church and their music ministry. She was not only his partner, but she was also a driving and stabilizing force in his life.

"I'll never find anyone to take her place," Rick had formed a pattern of saying, "but somehow I will manage. I just have to trust God and learn to make the best of a bad situation."

Without Patty Jo in his life, Rick's situation quickly went from bad to worse. Although he still lived in the church parsonage, drew the same salary from the church, and had a lot of his expenses paid by the church, he still struggled financially. So much so, he had resorted to paying most of his personal expenses with the church's credit cards.

"When Patty Jo and I were together, I think we probably used the credit cards for personal use on some occasions, when we would go out and buy necessary items for church functions. Then we used it sometimes to buy food for fund-raisers, dinners, or other activities that we were involved in at the church.

"I think Patty Jo and I did that a couple of times, where we would go in together and buy something, and then decide to get some stuff of our own as well. We would pay for those items separately, of course, or we would reimburse the church for those items. Then, when times got tough financially for us, we started doing that more frequently. Most of what we got was during the times we moved into the parsonages. We were remodeling the old farmhouse, and that took a lot of money out of our budget. And then we moved into the smaller parsonage, we had to turn around and remodel it. We always had a budget to work with that the church had given us, but we would inevitably purchase things for remodeling that we wanted personally. We always paid it back."

In June 1999, less than a month after Patty Jo disappeared, Rick went to Pastor Randy Sudduth and told him he needed help. "I just need some money," Rick said, clearly unnerved. "My finances are very bad, and I've got this huge phone bill I've got to pay or they are going to shut my phone off."

When Randy offered to help Rick with his phone bill, the pastor found out Rick's problems went much deeper than that. Rick told him he was also behind on his van payments and a few other things. Randy advised him the best thing for him to do was to take it up with the board of elders at the church.

In the past, when Rick and Patty Jo ran into financial difficulties, it was comforting to know her parents were always willing to help. When Rick needed another vehicle, the Riddicks practically gave him their 1991 F-150 four-wheel-drive truck. When Rick fell behind in his payments on the piano, the Riddicks pitched in and gave him the money to catch up. And when Rick or Patty Jo needed something they couldn't afford, the Riddicks always stepped in and helped out. Even though Rick was busy working at the church, and was handing out flyers and searching for Patty Jo every day, he took time out in June to visit the Riddicks and have lunch with them.

Rick's communications with the Riddicks, however, were more and more infrequent. He let them know that it was too hard for him to be around them without Patty Jo. They respected his wishes. He had always been her shadow, always leaned on her for support—not having Patty Jo may have been more difficult for him than it was for them. She was all he ever had.

Rick was so overwhelmed with his financial problems that he thought it would help his situation if he took some time off, drove to Boone, North Carolina, and visited his spiritual advisor Robert Mearns. Sometime during their meeting, Mearns suggested he and Rick drive to Georgia and attend a Destiny Quest spiritual conference. Although Rick knew he didn't have any money, he still went ahead and drove to Georgia, using the church's credit card to finance his trip.

"Shoes" was what Rick said he had charged to the church. "There were some other personal items—like, I didn't have a belt—that I also charged to the church as well. I didn't have a lot of money—so mostly, I used it to buy gas on that trip.

"In July, I went to Texas. I don't know if it was Randy's idea, Robert's idea, or the elders' idea for me to go to the conference there, but I did go. By then, I was just itching to do something. I wanted to do something productive. This was the second version of Destiny Quest and I knew it would be good for me to attend."

Rick said he felt refreshed and renewed in Texas, but something unusual started happening when he arrived home. After being warned by Detective Isom that he was going to get some strange phone calls and mysterious letters, Rick started taking stock of what was happening. He had gotten some strange cards in the mail, most of them saying they had seen Patty Jo at places, like lying out in the sun at an apartment complex pool in Raleigh. Rick showed the letters to a couple of people who were friends of his in the church, and asked them what they thought. His friends advised him to call Detective Isom and tell him about the letters.

Rick said this made him consider the fact that Patty Jo might still be alive somewhere, and he thought about hiring a private investigator. He remembered getting some information about hourly rates and fees from the Yellow Pages and the Internet, even calling Greensboro and inquiring there as well, but he knew he didn't have the funds to finance it.

"Randy Sudduth mentioned hiring a private investigator," Rick recalled, "but he didn't make an offer to contribute any money. I knew there was no way the church could afford it, so I didn't even ask them to help with those expenses. There was only one thing I could think of at the time to help me out, and that was to sell the piano."

Desperate situations call for desperate measures, and Rick was in a sticky situation. His quandary was that he and Patty Jo had discussed selling her piano before, but out of loyalty to her, he had never considered it. Since they had married in 1982, he and Patty Jo had moved at least ten different times, always having to move her piano, load and transport, then unload and move it again. Rick thought it might be time to sell the piano before it decreased in value.

"Because her piano didn't have wheels on it, it was both difficult and expensive to move. We didn't even like hiring piano movers because her piano always got dinged or scratched up somehow. There were already a few dings and scratches on it, so I started [to think] about selling it before it lost its value. It was about this same time that I had also considered the possibility of leaving the church and moving elsewhere."

In the fall of 1998, six months or so before Patty Jo disappeared, Rick had called Reverend Jeff Williams, pastor of the Lebanon Community Fellowship Church in Lebanon, Virginia, and discussed the possibility of them moving there. Williams knew the effects of lifelong vocations in the church, but wanted to hear it directly from Rick. "I don't want to get into your personal life or anything," he stated, then asked, "but why are you considering moving to another location?"

Rick and Patty Jo were drowning in an ocean of financial and marital problems. They still loved each other and were committed to their marriage, but were barely able to keep themselves above water. If they didn't make a change, and soon, they both feared their relationship and their ministry would be over forever.

Without incriminating himself, Rick told Williams, "We're just ready for a change." They had both been working at the Ringgold church for a long time, and they were now "ready for a different venue, ready for a different focus."

In August 1999, when Rick finally decided to move to Lebanon, he knew he couldn't afford a large house to rent, so he started selling off some of his excess furniture. There were some of Patty Jo's handmade decorations that they had attached to the walls that he would leave in the small parsonage. He sold their nicer refrigerator to the church and kept the smaller one for himself. What things he couldn't afford to keep or no longer needed, he donated to the church.

To help pay for the moving expense to Lebanon, Rick sold his guitar and most of his furnishings to his friend David Wilson. His handmade electric guitar was a quality item, one that he thought he would never be able to afford, but he had no choice but to sell it. Fortunately,

David said if Rick ever needed it or wanted to buy it back, it would always be there for the asking.

In the same month, Rick had gotten a call from a church member telling him the "piano man" was coming. Once a year, a piano tuner—a guy by the name of Andy, from Martinsville, Virginia—came to their neighborhood in Ringgold. Andy offered a reduced rate to anyone who would refer other customers to him while he was in the area. He always tuned Patty Jo's piano, her students' pianos, and the church's pianos at the same time. When he came by to visit Rick, Rick shared the unfortunate news about Patty Jo and asked if he wanted to buy her piano.

"I was disappointed in the amount I got for the piano." Rick didn't remember how much, but he thought he had received somewhere between $1,500 and $2,500. "I used it for moving expenses and as a deposit for travel expenses back and forth between Lebanon and Ringgold. Honestly, I don't remember if Mrs. Riddick called me and asked for the piano or not, but I do recall our having talked about the piano. When they came to visit me and pick up Patty Jo's things, that's when she brought it up. She was very distraught and upset, very disappointed that I had sold the piano."

The Riddicks were not too happy to hear that Rick was selling some of Patty Jo's possessions. For some reason, Rick would soon discover, he had not gotten the warm and fuzzy reception he had imagined. It all began with a statement about Rick not wearing his wedding ring.

On the day Rick was married in 1982, he and Patty Jo exchanged rings. They were both wide gold bands and had the date *1-2-82* engraved on the inside. Over the years, he had gained some weight and the wedding ring had started to cut into his finger. On Valentine's Day, 1996—a year to the date of Rick's confession of an adulterous relationship—Patty Jo surprised Rick with a second wedding band. On the inside of the ring the words *Committed to You* and the date *1-2-82* were engraved.

When the Riddicks arrived to pick up Patty Jo's belongings, they noticed Rick was not wearing his wedding band. They asked immediately, "Why don't you have your wedding ring on?" Rick explained that he was in the process of packing and moving some stuff around, and just didn't have it on. But the truth was, he had been slowly moving his things to Lebanon, and had put some trash and a few other things in his van. As was his habit, he always took off his wedding ring and put it on the turn signal—otherwise, he knew he would lose it.

Rick had been wearing his second wedding ring since 1996, and had no idea where his first wedding ring was. He assumed it was being stored in a little cedar box, jewelry chest, but he wasn't sure. Had Rick known the wedding rings were going to be such a sore spot for the Riddicks, he would have put a ring on both fingers. Rick said it was then their conversation turned into an assault.

"Our conversation was not pleasant. The Riddicks were very vocal, and downright accusatory. Not her whole family, mostly Connie and Rita. They were both so angry. When Connie and I walked down to the basketball courts near the church, she started accusing me of having something to do with Patty Jo's disappearance."

Rick claimed Connie was adamant about his involvement in a plot to do away with Patty Jo. He said she was almost abusive about it. Connie had brought a black man with her, who was supposed to be a police officer in training. While he and Connie talked, her friend walked and stood near the church and monitored their conversation. Rick felt very hurt and frustrated. He was uncomfortable talking about such matters with Connie in front of a total stranger.

"I asked Connie, could we go back inside and talk about it. Once we got inside, they started asking all kinds of questions again and making all kinds of accusations against me.

Finally I asked them to leave my house, and they did. As they were walking away, Connie said something—I don't remember exactly what it was she said—and then slapped me with an open hand, hard, on the left side of my face. The black man with her then said something to me like, 'Please don't commit suicide,' or 'Don't kill yourself,' something on that order, and then they got in their car and left."

A week later, Rick received two envelopes in the mail, both similar to the one he had gotten in July. Only this time, the first card spelled out, in cutout letters, *He watches over me,* while the second one spelled out, *I can continue the message for God in Jesus' name.*

Just like the first card he had received, there was no signature or return address. Rick was sure someone was playing with his mind and decided it was time for him to leave.

In October 1999, Rick resigned from the Ringgold church and moved to Lebanon. He took all his clothes, and the majority of Patty Jo's clothes he left with Jo Wilson. Wilson had agreed to box them up and store them until Rick had room for them. A few weeks later, Jo and her husband, David, transported them to Lebanon and helped Rick unload them in his spare bedroom. Another room in Rick's house was filled with small things that belonged to Patty Jo, their photo albums, and other household items he had not yet unpacked.

Although Keith Isom and the other detectives at the Pittsylvania County Sheriff's Office were keeping their cards close to their chests, they already fingered Rick Pulley as a suspect and believed he knew more about his wife's disappearance than he was telling. Throughout most of Isom's investigation, he had managed to stay out of Isom's way. Isom suspected there had been foul play, that Patty Jo was another domestic violence statistic, but until he had a body, he couldn't prove that Rick had killed her. Isom had even gone so far as to call Patty Jo's family and tell them he and his team had done everything they could, exhausted every lead they had, but were no closer to solving the case than when they began.

"I hate to say this," Isom had communicated to Connie Winslow, "but without a body, there isn't much more we can do."

Connie vowed she and her family would continue their own private investigation. She had been shocked when Isom had told her Rick had left the Ringgold church and moved to Lebanon. Even Connie's mother, Rita Corprew, had asked her, "How could Rick move at a time like this? What about Patty Jo? What if she's alive and tries to contact him?"

Rick seemed to be happy and content living in Lebanon. He was working as a Christian counselor for Dr. Dwight Bailey, a charismatic physician, who helped people with food, lodging, and medical care. Because the Catholic church in town was the only place that offered free lodging, Rick thought he might like to offer someone a place to stay that needed it, now that he had cleaned out his spare bedroom at his house.

Life had not been easy for Rick after May 14. His normal assumption was that the experience of losing his wife would have gotten easier by now, but it hadn't. He had tried to look past all the gossip, past all the innuendos, past all the staring eyes, but that date was always there. Like a black cloud, it continually hung over him. He'd see someone in town that he knew and the whispering behind his back would start all over again; then he'd know it was there. He'd try to start a conversation in the grocery store, and the person would cut him off in midsentence; then he'd know it was there. He'd try to begin a new relationship, and it was always the same: "Say, I heard about your wife. What ever happened to her?" It was there and then he'd wonder, *How much do they know? How much should I tell them?* A black cloud didn't always mean rain, but Rick was smart enough to know that it didn't rain without it.

While living alone in Lebanon, Rick had been spending a lot of his free time surfing the Internet. A friend of his had met some people on the Internet and suggested Rick give it a go. Rick had a lot of close friends in Lebanon, but for the most part, their relationship centered around those people taking care of him. All the while he had been in Lebanon, his friends had been there for him, and had helped him deal with Patty Jo's disappearance. It seemed lately as if that had become the focus of every relationship. Rick wanted something different. He wanted a friend: a casual relationship where he could talk about himself and what was going on in his life. Not that he was tired of talking about Patty Jo, but he wanted—no, he needed—something different in his life. Patty Jo was gone and he needed to move on. Rick's friend was more than happy to give him the Web site address for the online introduction service.

There were two parts of the Internet introduction service. One part was for people to meet and play golf, for people to do activities together, and for people of the opposite sex to meet. Rick's goal was to meet somebody who was looking for a casual acquaintance. He wasn't looking for a girlfriend—just someone he could do things with, like go to a movie or go out to dinner.

Rick first met Donna Dotson in August 2002. Their relationship started slowly: e-mail for a month or so, followed by phone conversations, and then, finally, they met at a restaurant and had dinner together. At first, Rick didn't tell Donna anything about Patty Jo. They weren't talking about their past relationships or anything like that. Neither he nor Donna wanted to discuss the past. They were interested more in getting to know each other in the here and now. Besides, Donna had gone through a divorce, an ugly divorce, and she didn't care to talk about it.

Never one to worry about rumors floating around, Rick let it be known that he and Donna had a lot in common; that he enjoyed her companionship and wanted to see more of her. It was obvious, Rick believed, that Donna wanted the same, and they could have a good relationship.

While the city of Lebanon buzzed during the Christmas holiday, Rick concerned himself with putting a Christmas tree in his living room. He wasn't sure if he wanted to go to all that trouble, especially with Grace running around in such a small house.

It was just before Christmas when Rick found another mysterious letter in his mailbox. Shocked to see that certain person had caught up with him, now that he had moved from Ringgold to Lebanon, he carefully ripped open the envelope and found a Christmas card. Again, there was no signature, just a Christmas message:

> *For my husband: In the rush of our everyday lives, what's really important sometimes gets set aside. And I may forget to say how much you mean to me, but I want you to know that, even though I don't always put it in words, I'll always love you. Merry Christmas.*

For the past two years, Rick had kept Patty Jo on his hospitalization insurance policy, just to be sure there was no lapse in her coverage. He also kept a photo of him and Patty Jo on his wall at his Lebanon home. The photo was framed and fixed into a calligraphy of a Scripture from Ecclesiastes: *A chord of three stands is not quickly broken.*

Underneath Rick and Patty Jo's picture and the Scripture verse was the imprinted date *1-2-82*. It was a grave reminder of all that had gone wrong in his past life and all he had to face in the future.

In the early spring of 2000, David Peters, a private eye

who had been hired by Patty Jo's family, visited Rick at his Lebanon home. When he walked up to the front door, he could hear a dog barking inside the house. Rick came to the door; Peters then introduced himself and handed him a business card.

"What can I do to help in the investigation?" Rick had asked.

Peters suggested Rick write a timeline of the day Patty Jo disappeared. A few days later, he received Rick's handwritten fax, detailing dates, times, and places from May 14, 1999. It was right after that when Peters drove back up to Lebanon and talked with Rick again.

"Nathan Zackery called me today and told me that some hunters had found a body in the woods not too far from here, on Friday," Peters volunteered.

"Where were they found?" Rick asked without any emotion.

"I really don't know," Peters admitted honestly. "All I know is that they had found somebody."

Rick was quiet for a few moments, before saying, "I wish it was Patty Jo." He looked away from Peters, then swallowed hard and hung his head. "I'd like for it to be over."

The air Peters breathed suddenly grew dense. Not sure of how to respond to Rick's macabre comment, he said, "Are you gonna come up here, since the body has been found?"

Rick's head snapped back. "I think I will just wait and see."

"Well, if I find out where the body was found, I'll come back and tell you," Peters promised.

"You do that," Rick said with a good-bye wave.

Two days later, Peters returned and spoke with Rick again, on a Monday evening. "I found out that was a body they found near here last week."

Rick's eyes widened. "Well, that can't be Patty Jo!" he exclaimed. "That's not the right area."

Rick would argue to police at a later date that he never

said anything remotely like that to Peters. "That's not what I said," he told police. "When he told me they had found some bones, I then asked him, where the remains were found. Then he said, I believe, Randolph County. I asked him, where was Randolph County? But I never said, 'I hope it is Patty Jo' or 'That's not the right place.'"

When David Peters relayed to Nathan Zackery, the Riddicks' contact person, all Rick had said, Zackery asked him if he would beat Rick up.

Peters was appalled at such a request. "I don't do that," he said with contempt. "That's not part of my work."

Chapter 43

Dana Goodnight was a geologist employed with Trigon Engineering Consultants, who did subsurface investigations for new buildings and/or bridges—in particular, for the North Carolina Department of Transportation (DOT). Goodnight lived in Hillsborough, North Carolina, but since 2001 he had traveled extensively, doing subsurface investigation. He had earned an M.S. in geology from North Carolina State University.

For approximately two weeks in December 2002, Goodnight and several of his crew members had been working at the bridge over Hyco Creek, off Highway 158. They had been drilling to discover the geotechnical situation at the bridge in preparation for building a new one. On one side of the bridge, the traffic would be moving in the direction of Roxboro. On the opposite side of the bridge, traffic would be back toward Yanceyville, where the floodplain area showed the scour hole filled with water. That was the area where Goodnight would make a gruesome discovery.

During the course of the investigation, the Trigon crews had drilled in a number of locations in the floodplain area, on both sides of the bridge and up on the end vents near the scour hole, or the erosion hole. A scour

hole is basically when there was a flood event and water
starts flowing over the floodplain. The existing columns,
or existing vents, produce vortices in the water, and they
scour around or form a depression, where sediment is removed. So there is a depression left where that movement has taken place around the column, and then that
fills in with water. Those depression areas are important
for the design of a future bridge, and that's why Goodnight and the Trigon crews were investigating that.

There had been a few other people working with
Goodnight that week, but on this particular December
day, in 2002, he was by himself, wrapping things up, and
completing the last of the job. He said he had an occasion to go up against something, which was unusual in
his day-to-day work. As he was performing his work of
mapping out the scour hole, he stepped on something
and heard a crack, so he looked down and noticed that
there were some bones. That was not uncommon in the
places where he worked, for they often saw animals that
had died. But the thing that struck Goodnight was when
he noticed there appeared to be a bra stretched across
the bones.

At that point, Goodnight began to think that this was
something much different, and he probably was going
to need to go and report this. There was a possibility that
something in the floodplain could have floated down
and gotten hung up on it, but he just wanted to make
sure. That would have been an incredible coincidence
to see a bra across the bones in that position.

Goodnight remembered leaving and driving to the
nearest police station to report it, the Roxboro Police
Department (RPD). He had already been there to turn
in a wallet he had found under the bridge. It was on the
other side of the bridge near a stream gauge device,
which measures the water level, and it turned out to be
an old lady's. It had a license in it and it was maybe seven
or eight years old. Who knew how long it had been down

in the river? But it was there, in the sand, and Goodnight just wanted to turn it in, not knowing if it was important or not, but knowing it needed to be in the hands of the authorities.

Goodnight explained to the Roxboro police that in a floodplain—which is the area when the water goes out of its bank and flows over the flat portion—around a river, obviously, things can float down in the floodplain. When water is moving, anything can float that's being carried by swift water, and from his experience, there was always trash, articles of clothing, balls, and all kinds of things that could be carried and deposited there.

It is typically after there's been a flood event, that there may be something that floated down and was deposited there. Typically, no one is in a floodplain when it's being flooded, but afterward, one sees the effects of what was brought down or deposited, or trash that's been carried down into this area.

Goodnight knew where the RPD was. He had no cell phone coverage down at the bridge and needed to call his supervisor and let him know he was going to be delayed at his next appointment. Approximately fifteen minutes after his gruesome discovery, Goodnight arrived at the police station, spoke to an officer, and gave a signed statement. The police asked him to return to the site with them, and he did so and showed them what he had discovered. Other people were contacted, and Goodnight moved on to his next appointment.

From the discovery of the bones, until Goodnight returned with the Roxboro officers, it had taken about thirty minutes. In no time, multiple people arrived on the scene from Person County and Caswell County. Goodnight assumed they were forensic people. There were lots of people that were coming to the site when he left. He saw no one disturb the bones.

At 10:00 A.M., Caswell County's sheriff Michael Welch, who had just taken office on December 2, received communication from the Person County's sheriff, Dennis Oakley, to attend to a location in their jurisdiction. The thirty-eight-year-old Welch had started his police career at the age of eighteen in the military police at Fort Bragg. Prior to serving in Caswell County, he had served as criminal investigator supervisor for the city of Roxboro and supervisor for both the criminal investigations and narcotics investigations. He had been a lieutenant in the Roxboro police, third in the department out of approximately thirty-five sworn law enforcement officers. Welch was now over twenty-eight sworn positions, a full-service sheriff's office, including a 911 communications center and a detention facility. In addition to earning his bachelor's degree in criminal justice at UNC-Charlotte, Welch completed some graduate work at North Carolina Central in law enforcement administration.

"I'm en route on 158 east, to the Hyco Creek Bridge in Caswell County," the sheriff communicated to Captain Henry Fleetwood. "Why don't you meet me there with the possibility of locating human skeletal remains." They were to meet up with Sheriff Oakley and Captain Calvin Clayton, who was the supervisor over investigators for the sheriff's department.

Welch arrived at 10:30 A.M., had a brief conversation with Fleetwood, and then gave him the okay to go ahead and secure the crime scene. Fleetwood was also told to start a crime scene log, which was an exit and entry log for the crime scene. Welch remained on the scene, providing instructions and monitoring the steps the Caswell County Sheriff's Office were taking in the investigative process.

It was also Sheriff Welch's duty to contact the North Carolina State Bureau of Investigation (SBI) and request assistance. Because there was no cell signal in that area, he had to leave the scene and drive to Leasburg Grocery, where he utilized his cell phone and made contact with the SBI. He requested the SBI's crime scene lab meet with him at the location at the bridge. The SBI stated they would arrive on the scene later that day.

Welch surveyed the area under the bridge, then walked down and looked around. He saw the bones and some clothing, but didn't see any weapons. He quickly designated Investigator Michael Adkins as the case agent for this particular investigation. Adkins was a seasoned investigator and Welch would rely on him for his expertise. The crime scene technician was Pat Daly.

For the past two years, Clayton Myers had been working as an investigator with the criminal investigation division of the Caswell County Sheriff's Office. Myers had been a deputy for five years, and had attended numerous criminal investigations schools. On that day, December 18, he was the patrol deputy and had been called out to the bridge area at eleven that morning by Captain Henry Fleetwood. Myers had been asked to respond to the scene and fill out a report. Fleetwood didn't give any details over the radio or tell him what it was about. He said he just wanted Myers to meet with him.

Myers responded and parked on the shoulder of the road. There was already a Person County unmarked vehicle, a burgundy Ford explorer, driven by Captain Fleetwood, and there was some type of maintenance vehicle down in the area as well. Myers immediately went to see Captain Fleetwood, who asked him to speak to Dana Goodnight and take his statement.

At 11:49 A.M., while Myers took Goodnight's statement, Captain Fleetwood started securing the crime scene area. He first took a roll of yellow barrier tape and surrounded the area where the discovery was located. He then took the tape from the corner of the bridge to the embankment so nobody could come down the opposite side. Myers then joined him and ran some more crime scene tape from the pillar at the roadway all the way back into the woods to prevent anybody from coming through the woods and into the crime scene.

Once Mr. Goodnight was released, Myers hunkered down and began an in-and-out log as a security measure for the crime scene. He was the law enforcement now—the big cheese—and nobody was to go in or come out unless they came through him first.

The crime scene barricade tape has always been standard equipment for the deputies and investigators to secure or rope off a particular area so as to prevent any unwanted entry into that area, in addition to preserving everything that is within that area. It is basic protocol in every forensic investigative department.

Myers would stay at his post until he was relieved at eight-thirty that evening. He'd be there for almost 9½ hours and would make sure that during this entire time the crime scene area remained intact until the investigation was ready to begin. Sergeant Steven Williamson finally came on duty and relieved Myers.

Sheriff Welch also stayed at the crime scene, along with Captain Fleetwood and the two officers from Person County, who made the initial contact with the Caswell County agency to let Welch know it was in his county. The call had already gone out to the SBI for assistance, and other officers were beginning to report to the scene. Kelly Cummings, Agent J. R. Bowman, and Agent Scott Williams all trickled in at about the same time.

Michael Adkins had been designated the main investigator of the case, and immediately upon his arrival, he had met with Sheriff Welch and Deputy Clayton Myers. They described to him the area where Mr. Goodnight found the skeletal remains. Adkins started taking pictures of the upper ground of Hyco Creek Bridge from the road area and stood by until the agents from North Carolina SBI arrived. Once they entered the scene and started processing it, he watched them uncover the skeleton. They collected each bone meticulously, measured, and photographed all the skeletal remains they had uncovered there.

It took the SBI's forensic crew quite a long time to uncover and collect all the remains. They started processing the crime scene around 2:30 P.M., but did not finish until late in the evening hours. Earlier in the day, it was dark under the bridge where the remains were located because of the shadows overcasting from the bridge. But when night began to fall, floodlights had to be brought in from the Leasburg Fire Department (LFD) to illuminate the area.

Adkins stood by and watched the SBI's skilled team of technicians process the crime scene. He assisted Agent Pat Daly and Agent Kelly Cummings as they worked through the day and after dark, into late evening. The remains were collected and items that were located were also collected. Adkins then left the crime scene and met back at the sheriff's office with Agent Pat Daly, who turned everything over to him.

The SBI had uncovered quite a bit at the crime scene: several pieces of jewelry (two rings—a small ruby ring, a small gold pinky ring—and one gold loop earring); clothing, such as what appeared to be a horizontal multistriped shirt, and a pocket section from a pair of khaki pants with a black belt; three plastic two-hole buttons; an orange hair clip; a hair band; a spring-loaded hair band; plastic hair clips; red-colored metal hairpins, the kind larger than a bobby pin that women use to hold their hair in place. Also found at the crime scene was a piece of a single fingernail.

One of the most significant discoveries by the SBI forensic team was a rope—a nylon cord—that was looped twice, with a standard square knot. The loop had a circumference of 3½ to four inches in diameter. It had been found under the earth, underneath the victim's back. The victim's hands, however, were located several feet away in both directions. One hand was located approximately one foot away from the torso, and the other hand was located approximately four feet away from the torso.

There were a number of bones missing. Short, numerous bones from both feet were missing and not recovered. A lot of the smaller bones, the metacarpals and the carpals of the hands and the feet, were also missing. Some bones were found as far as three to five feet from the body.

A woman's bra had been found, along with the arm bone and the mass of rib cage and ribs. It would be impossible to determine if these remains had been disturbed before the authorities got there. There had to have been a number of disturbances, due to water, wind, heat—not to mention the possibility of animal infestation that could have moved articles from one area to another. The pieces of jewelry were bagged in a clear plastic bag.

After some excavation and some cleaning up with the use of a paintbrush, which is the procedure in skeletal remains recovery, the remains began to take shape. The technicians cleaned off the area for better photographic purposes, so the skull and teeth area could be depicted appropriately.

There were no weapons or animal remains inside the grid. If this indeed was the missing body of Patty Jo Pulley, they didn't know it. No hair as well. They had no way of knowing if the body had been dumped there on May 14, 1999. The bones were not found in their original spot, so there could be a hundred different explanations as to how the victim died, or how the remains even got there.

It was twenty-seven feet from the top of the bridge to the floodplain below. And based on the fact that the remains were not found in their natural state, Adkins was of the opinion the victim did not get there of her own accord. His testimony would be that the remains were put there by somebody, and that they had not been taken there by their own free will and natural state.

The fingernail, which the SBI lab analyzed, was found

to have no tissue that could be derived from the nail. The SBI lab in Raleigh would do specific tests, but basically only if there were large visual clumps of tissue. There was certain chemical procedures that could have been done to determine if there was any blood on the nail, but it would not distinguish between animal or human. The fingernail did have the elements of blood, and the lab analysis sheet failed to reveal the presence of any blood or tissues. And without that blood or tissue, there was no way to tell to whom the fingernail belonged.

When the SBI forensic team found the nylon rope, it was more at the top of the rib cage area, very close in proximity to the clavicle and around the neck area, but intertwined within the bones of the rib cage area. The hands were at some distance, so there was no evidence at the crime scene to suggest the victim's hands had been tied behind her back.

As Adkins would later determine in his investigation, the closest route by motor vehicle from Rick Pulley's residence to the Hyco Creek Bridge would have been Highway 57, toward Roxboro, toward Milton, and then right onto 119 going southbound. At the intersections of 119 and 158, all he had to do was take a left on 158 and the Hyco Creek Bridge was approximately a mile from the intersection. It was a distance of approximately nineteen miles to the Sonshine Community, where Rick lived, approximately thirteen miles from Milton to 62 North. As soon as he crossed the state line, he came to 62 North and to 58; he then crossed the intersection toward this area, known as Kentuck. The distance then from the Sonshine Community, where Patty Jo lived, to the Dan River High School was only thirteen miles, just close enough to Rick for convenience, yet still far enough away to distance himself from the crime.

Of all the places Akdins could think about hiding a body, this was one of the best. First of all, the bridge was so isolated at night that it would be easy for someone to do a quick stop-and-toss without being spotted. Secondly, the bridge was so steep, it would be almost impossible for a victim to fall off the bridge and not sustain serious injury or death. Third, the vegetation around the bridge was so thick that a body could easily be concealed and disposed of. And lastly, the bridge was so high above the ground that the smell of a dead body would likely not be noticed by anyone driving with his windows up and air conditioner on during the month of May.

When all was said and done, was it possible that Rick and Patty Jo had argued the night before she disappeared, as well as the next afternoon? Did they have an altercation, whereby he physically assaulted her and then strangled her? Had Rick Pulley really been at the Dan River High School play the entire time? Or, at some time during or after the play, had he driven the short distance to the Hyco Creek Bridge and tossed her dead body?

On December 18, 2002, Isom e-mailed Connie at work to report that female remains had been found under the Hyco Bridge in Caswell County, North Carolina, eleven miles from where Patty Jo's truck had been found. He said they were waiting on the results of the dental records for a positive identification. That wait seemed longer than the whole 3½ years put together.

Finally, in a few hours, the dental records confirmed the skeletal remain collected under the bridge was Patty Jo's. Isom called the Gates County Sheriff's Department (GCSD) and asked them to dispatch a deputy to the home of Albert and Elva Mae Riddick. "I want you to tell them that their daughter's body has been found and that she is coming home for Christmas."

Chapter 44

For three years, Pittsylvania County Officer Keith Isom had waited for this day, when Patty Jo Pulley's body would be found and her husband would be escorted back to North Carolina to face the murder charges. Although the police had a good case against Rick Pulley, Isom knew there was no such thing as a slam dunk.

Isom said that before Patty Jo's body had been found, District Attorney (DA) Joel Brewer had been a complete stranger to him. Now, all of a sudden, when Patty Jo's remains were found in Caswell County, he had to trust Brewer with his case. And that was hard for him to do, especially after all the rumors that had been flying around out there. Isom had heard so much about Patty Jo being alive that he imagined once the trial had started, she would burst through the doors and blow the case wide open.

"In a homicide investigation, it is relatively simple," Isom explained. "Who was the last person with the victim? What did we know about Patty Jo Pulley? There was the possibility that she had run off with another man. And then there was talk about Patty Jo having a spinal leak that was supposedly diagnosed by a physician, and that possibly she could have collapsed somewhere and died. Besides this, there was not much at all. But what did we have on Rick Pulley? Phone records, misuse of church funds, past-due bills, an adulterous relationship, Internet pornography?

"Now, granted, it took a while to find these things out about Rick Pulley, but like any good divorce attorney worth their weight in salt, we had to ask ourselves a few questions: Did they have a good marriage? Did they have any credit cards? Were they financially strapped? Was there any undue stress? Did they own a computer? Were there extramarital affairs? It was Rick, more so than Patty Jo, that was under stress. But could he have snapped? Was he seeking adulterous relationships? His home life might have been duller than ditch water—we didn't know—and maybe that was why he snapped."

So what did Keith Isom *really* think of Rick Pulley? Isom would shake his head, then smile and say, "People like Rick Pulley are two of a kind. He was a little arrogant bully who grew up into a big arrogant bully."

During most of the investigation, Rick Pulley had succeeded in avoiding Officer Isom, but now that they had located Patty Jo's body, Isom knew Rick could not escape his notice forever. Patty Jo Pulley's remains had been found in a creek bed between the intersection of US Highway 119 and 158 in the Leasburg area. In the weeks that followed the initial discovery, Isom and other law enforcement officials were meeting with the Caswell County prosecution team and getting their ducks in a row.

On December 18, 2002—the same day Isom e-mailed Patty Jo's family that her remains had been found—Rick Pulley was shopping with a friend in an Abington, Virginia, Christian bookstore when he heard the news about Patty Jo. When he arrived home, he checked his phone messages and he had received a call from someone in the media. A news reporter wanted to know if Rick had heard about his wife's remains being found, and if he had any comments, to call the television station back.

Rick said he was devastated after he heard that message. "I was pretty much in shock as a result of that message." Rick later talked about it like it had happened yesterday. "I drove my friend home and then I went back to the house and listened to the message again. It brought everything back to the forefront again. I let Grace outside for a while and I just sat there and thought about what had happened in May 1999."

Rick had his back to the wall again. He was in another quagmire. What was he going to tell Donna Dotson? He had known Donna since the end of August, and during those months, he saw something in her that he valued. He saw something that he felt was very precious and special.

"Donna demonstrated a life and care for me that was wonderful, and I believed at that point that I never met anybody in her family, and she hadn't met anybody in my family. But I had already invited her to visit my mother at Christmastime on her way down to see her son in Fayetteville."

Now, how would he break the news to her about Patty Jo? What would he say to her? It was the same old dark cloud again—only, this time, Rick wondered, after it rained, would he see another rainbow?

The same day that Rick got the message from the television station on the telephone, he saw two detectives, Isom and Adkins, pull up in his driveway. They were there with the Lebanon chief of police to inform Rick that his wife's remains had been found.

"At that point, I didn't have much of a reaction at all," Rick said. "They asked if they could talk to me in my office and we went into my office. I sat down at my desk and they sat across from me. Sergeant Adkins started interviewing me again. While they were there, they said they wanted me to come down to the Caswell County sheriff's department and meet an SBI agent, and that was the result of the meeting."

The group of police officers met with Rick for an

hour. They then asked him to drive down to Caswell County so he could identify Patty Jo's clothing and jewelry. Rick would remark later that he never saw any of Patty Jo's clothing. All he was shown were a couple of rings and an earring.

"I was able to identify pretty certainly that one of the rings was Patty Jo's by looking at it. It was a ring that I had given her for some occasion—either Christmas, anniversary, or Valentine's Day. It was a gold ring with a ruby stone. The other ring I wasn't certain, nor was I certain about the earring."

Rick had agreed to release Patty Jo's remains to her family, even though by law a wife's body went to her husband. The family was grateful because they knew he didn't have any money and wouldn't have given her a proper burial. It seemed the only people he had to rely on these days were his church family, and he had long ago stopped asking them for money. The Riddicks sent word to Rick that he was welcome to attend the funeral, even though they knew some of their family suspected Rick had killed her and didn't want him there.

One of the Riddicks' relatives, Dr. Wayne Proctor, was a minister and he had agreed to perform Patty Jo's memorial and last rites. Out of concern for both Rick and for those who didn't want him to be at the funeral, the pastor advised Rick to pay his respects at a time when the family was absent.

Albert and Elva Mae had planed an ordinary funeral for their daughter. They ordered a beautiful white casket trimmed in brass and decorated it with daisies, her favorite flowers. At the head of the casket, they put her grandmother's Bible, Patty Jo's baby blanket, and a single red rose. At the foot of the casket, Patty Jo's remains rested in a small box. So everyone could remember what the *real* Patty Jo looked like, inside the casket, they put a framed picture of her.

For the first time since Patty Jo had been missing in

1999, the Riddicks sat down at the dining-room table and celebrated Christmas. She was finally at rest—finally at peace. It was a bittersweet moment for everyone involved.

On Christmas Eve, 2002, Patty Jo Pulley took her last ride through Gates County. After about 3½ years, she was finally coming home again. The Riddicks had been robbed of so much. Patty Jo would not even have a normal funeral, like she deserved. There would be no wake; no body to mourn; no hands to rub or face to kiss; not even the words heard so often at funerals, "Oh, she looked so peaceful, didn't she?"

Five days later, Patty Jo's casket was rolled down the aisles and past the pews at Sandy Creek Baptist Church, where she had sat as a little girl; her casket had been turned and opened at the front of the church, in almost the same identical spot where she had sung and played hundreds of times before. As the choir sang, the same spirit rose up as a mighty wind and filled the sanctuary as it had the day she had given her heart and dedicated her life to God.

The words to the song "Remind Me, Dear Lord" were printed on the inside of the funeral programs. No doubt, Patty Jo had sung this song at the church many times during her short lifetime: *Remind me, dear Lord, of the things that I love and hold dear to my heart are just borrowed, they're not mine at all. Jesus only let me use them to brighten my life.*

Over the holidays, Patty Jo's family drove to Caswell County and visited the area where her body was found. They prayed over the spot, took pictures, and placed a yellow-bowed wreath at the bridge.

Chapter 45

Rick Pulley did not attend his wife's funeral services. He had talked with Albert and Elva Mae on the phone and asked them, "Am I welcome at the funeral?" At that time, Rick said, he was told he was welcome, that the Riddicks had said that he could come.

"That it was the first time we had any contact for some time," Rick recalled, "it was all positive at that point and there was no animosity. I had received some messages from people in Patty Jo's family on my answering machine that wasn't positive. I wanted to make sure that I would be welcome and her parents said I could come at the time.

"In the end, the Riddicks never said I couldn't come. But I had a discussion with Patty Jo's cousin, who is a pastor—we had done some things with his church before—and I knew through the family that he was also going to be officiating at the funeral, and I discussed this with him about coming. I asked him how he felt about me being there, and if he felt like it would be more difficult upon the Riddicks if I showed up. I knew some of the family members were against it and had copped an attitude about it.

"So I had two of my friends from Lebanon and their

young sons drive me to Gates County. When we got to Sandy Creek Baptist Church, we circled around to make sure that nothing was going on at the church. I didn't know where the grave site was gonna be. I didn't know it was going to be at the family plot, I thought it would have been at the church. I hadn't really thought that through.

"But we were in cell phone contact with some friends of ours that we knew were going to be there. They were waiting for us at the grave site. When we found out that none of the family would be there, and we didn't think there would be a scene or any problems, we went to the grave site and sort of just had a time with my friends there. We prayed. We comforted one another. I believe one of the young guys had a guitar and we sang a couple of worship songs. We sang a song that was particularly one that we all knew was Patty Jo's favorite. It was an emotional time. Very emotional."

After their impromptu service, Rick and his friends drove back to Lebanon. He didn't ask to stop at the Hyco Creek Bridge and look at the site where Patty Jo's body had been found. He did, however, think about the last ring he had purchased and given to Patty Jo.

"I don't remember the exact occasion." Rick thought he had given it to her after Valentine's Day. "It was after she had lost her grandmother's ring. I think it's called an anniversary ring. It has a few little small diamonds— they're really small diamonds, four or five tiny diamonds that run across the top. She wore it most of the time, but she lost her original ring, the one her grandmother had given her. She lost that along with her original wedding band when we were doing a concert someplace. I think it was at Elon College. We were moving stuff and all of a sudden she noticed that her wedding band and her grandmother's ring weren't on her finger. She never found either of those. Right after that, we were on our way home from the concert and we stopped somewhere and I bought a wedding band for her."

While Rick was busy finding himself, the Riddicks were struggling to find closure. Nearly 3½ years had passed and they still had no answers. They had nothing that belonged to Patty Jo, except for her pink Christmas sweater that Connie had found at a yard sale. In one of her lone investigative trips, she had stopped at a yard sale between her home and Danville. It was on a Saturday morning, and the sale was being held in front of a large farmhouse. Out front, in the lawn, a sign read: MULTI-FAMILY SALE. The families were selling anything and everything. After browsing through all the clothes and knickknacks, Connie spotted something out of the corner of her eye. It was soft, pale, and pink—the same sweater Patty Jo had been wearing the last time she visited Gates County in 1999.

"Where did you get this?" Connie yelled, pointing at the pink sweater on the rack. Before the organizer of the sale could respond, Connie broke down and started crying. She pulled the sweater to her body and knew it was the same one by the scent. It was the very same homemade lilac fragrance that Patty Jo had on that day.

Where is Patty Jo? And how did her sweater get into this yard sale? How many more of her things were missing and would turn up in bits and pieces all over the state?

Connie was not going to give up trying to find Patty Jo. She was relentless. Late one night, she was surfing the Internet and pulled up the Web site for the River of Life Church. On the Web site, there were photos of different trips the church had taken overseas. In one particular photo album, taken at a hospital, Connie recognized a lady in a pink robe. It looked exactly like Patty Jo.

Patty Jo had always worn her wedding band on her middle finger. This lady in the pink robe wore a gold band on her middle finger.

Connie was ecstatic. She phoned a friend who happened to be a former Federal Bureau of Investigation (FBI) agent, who then put her in touch with the FBI.

The FBI forwarded the picture from the Web site, along with a picture of Patty Jo, to the National Center for Missing and Exploited Children (NCMEC). Connie also sent a letter Rick had written to the Riddicks explaining what had happened the night Patty Jo disappeared. Both the pictures and the letter were analyzed by the FBI Academy in Quantico, Virginia. Of course, there was no way of determining exactly when that picture was taken, but the results were encouraging.

The FBI mailed a letter to Connie and stated that the results of their analysis indicated that the two women in the pictures were more than likely the same. And they would investigate the incident if she could get a name of the hospital where the picture was taken.

Connie scoured the Internet until she found the name, and she passed on the information. But when the FBI questioned the authorities at the Romanian hospital, they stated they had never seen the woman before and knew nothing of the picture.

"That can't be true," Connie protested. "Patty Jo was there with her husband and a group of people from the church in March of 1999. I know they have to know who she is." When she went to access the church's Web site for more information on the picture, the Web site had been removed.

"I'm sorry, Connie," the agent apologized. "After seeing that picture, I would have bet my whole paycheck that my agents would have come out of that hospital in Romania with your aunt."

So what had really happened to Patty Jo? Did she run away to Romania? Was Rick going to join her later? Did she come back to the United States and somebody killed her, then dumped her body at the Hyco Creek Bridge?

In times like these, people get desperate and the mind will start to believe anything it suspects. But these were the questions Connie and the Riddicks were asking themselves, the very same questions they wanted Rick to answer. They desperately wanted to know what had happened to Patty Jo, and they were still waiting for someone to be arrested.

On February 12, 2003, Detective Isom called Connie Winslow to break the news that Rick Pulley had been arrested and was being held in a Russell County, Virginia, jail. "As soon as the handcuffs were on him, he cried like a baby," Isom related. "He kept saying over and over that he had not killed Patty Jo."

Chapter 46

Rick Pulley waived extradition and was transferred to the Caswell County Jail. It was here that Officer Keith Isom would finally have his way with Rick. During an interview at the jail, Isom pulled his chair close to Rick and got in his face. "Tell me now, Rick, how did it feel to watch Patty Jo take her last breath?"

Rick stared at Isom silently.

Isom let the silence stretch. Though he felt himself reddening a little, he asked coldly, "How did it feel to choke the very life out of her with your own bare hands?"

Rick raised up in his chair, made a motion toward Isom, then caught himself and quickly backed off.

For the first time, Isom saw the evil side of Rick Pulley. He stared at Rick with an odd, twisted little smile from the corner of his lips, as if to say, "Be sure your sins will find you out."

Even though Rick maintained his innocence, he was not doing well at all. He was worried about Donna and how she was handling his arrest.

Things were a lot different now from what Rick had told her, but she was confused. They had tried to communicate by mail, but she was dealing with her own emotional issues at the time. He talked with his lawyer, Theresa

Pressley, and she arranged to have Donna admitted to the jail so she and Rick could work through these issues. Rick needed all the support he could get at this time.

A federal inmate named Scott Harold had been detained by the Caswell County police and placed in a jail cell next to Rick's. Harold said he and Rick had had a lot of shallow conversations, and that led them to deeper ones.

"Naturally, we asked one another why we were locked up," Harold stated. "I told him my story and he told me his. He said at first that he was innocent. He said he did not kill his wife. I said, 'Yeah, everyone here is innocent.'

"For two days, we didn't say much to each other. He mainly talked on the phone during this time. When a preacher came and saw us, Pulley started acting funny. This struck me as odd, since he said he was a missionary. The following day, he told me that his wife had seen him and another woman—I think her name was Donna—and had threatened him, et cetera. This led into a story about . . . a blue pickup truck, his choking his wife, driving around looking for a place to hide the body, a low bridge, et cetera.

"Maybe he was pulling my leg or just lying. Who knows? I don't want any deals or time off. I just don't want to see someone get away with cold-blooded murder—if, in fact, they did commit it."

Harold had opened a can of worms. He wrote DA Joel Brewer and gave him the details of Rick's supposed confession.

Rick denied telling Scott Harold that he had killed Patty Jo. Harold was in a jail cell next to Rick's, and he said Harold was skinny and always looked sick and unhealthy. Rick stated they never had long discussions, and he didn't remember attending any preaching services with Harold.

"My lawyer came to visit me on those evenings the preachers came to the jail," Rick recalled.

"Harold was confined in the single-cell isolation area and they brought him in my same area. I never told Scott anything, nor did I confess to murder. I never even confided any details of the case whatsoever, but he confided in me that he had killed a man.

"It was pretty shortly after Harold got there that he told me that he felt like it was strange, but he could tell me anything. That he felt like I was a close friend—that I was one of the best friends he ever had. I couldn't think of any reason why he was saying that.

"I did buy him several packs of cigarettes. At first, he didn't know people could smoke in the Caswell County Jail. When I told him that was okay, I didn't realize he didn't have any money at the time. There was an air-conditioning unit outside of the single-cell area, and behind the filter, there was all kinds of trash, and just all kinds of nasty stuff, and it was filled with cigarette butts. He was going through there, picking out the cigarette butts. Said he was gonna make what you call a roll-up of those butts. I didn't realize he didn't have money, so I bought him a pack of cigarettes that day and bought him cigarettes frequently after that. I never saw him taking medication."

Brewer sent Officer Adkins over to the jail and asked him to check it out. While Adkins was there, he took pictures of Rick's jail cell wall. He noted there were no photos of Patty Jo on his wall, but there were photos of another girl, Donna Dotson. Apparently, Donna Dotson had been visiting Rick in jail. She had been introduced to Adkins as a girlfriend, but when he talked with the jailers, they all said Rick's lawyer, Theresa Pressley, had introduced her as a "counselor."

Pressley got hold of it and called the DA's office and gave them a fit about it. After a couple of rounds of "he said/she said," she finally admitted that was stupid of Rick to have those pictures of his girlfriend on the wall while he was still married to Patty Jo.

Chapter 47

Rick Pulley had been sitting in custody since being arrested February 12, 2003. His secured bond of $400,000 had been set on April 29 by Judge Narley Cashwell. Cashwell also gave Rick a trial date for August 23, 2004.

On May 4, 2004, Rick's court-appointed attorney, Theresa Pressley, filed two additional motions. The first motion was for a ruling on a speedy trial.

"The defendant requests that his trial be set at the next available trial session of June twenty-eighth, and that his case be given priority due to the age of the case and the other circumstances surrounding the case."

The second motion was to allow the defense to examine a piece of evidence. Pressley had asked that she be allowed to see the rope that allegedly was around one of the wrists of Patty Jo when her remains were discovered.

"The medical examiner told me law enforcement officials originally said that the victim's hands were tied behind her back," she added in the motion, "but later they changed their report that the rope was tied around the waist."

The evidence at the crime scene documented a nylon cord had been found underneath Patty Jo's back, near her clavicle area. Her hands were found several feet away from her body in both directions. At no time did the forensic report state the rope was tied around her hands or around her waist. Pressley wrote in her motion that the prosecution mentioned during the April 29 hearing that the victim's hands were tied behind her back.

"The remarks of the district attorney were highly inflammatory and do not appear to be backed up by evidence," Pressley countered, "and the defendant now has added need of discovery to see, observe, and photograph this rope."

On May 12, 2004, Rick Pulley was escorted to superior court again. At 10:30 A.M., he and Pressley stood in front of a judge and waited for several motions they had put before the court to be decided. Of course, the greatest importance was the motion to set the trial date.

"This delay has prejudiced us," Pressley argued. "We have lost two of our witnesses while waiting for this trial. One of our witnesses has suffered from brain damage as a result of a car accident, and our second witness, Mr. Pulley's aunt, who was to testify on his behalf, has died of a heart attack."

Even though Pressley argued the delay of a trial had put them at a disadvantage, superior court judge W. Osmond Smith III set August 23 as the start date for Rick's trial.

Caswell County DA Joel Brewer said that date was still probably too soon for the prosecution. He told the judge that new evidence had emerged that week that required his investigators to travel out of state, and that some witness protection issues were involved.

Brewer declined to elaborate on the details of either.

In October 2003, Rick was formally arraigned in Caswell County Superior Court. He appeared relaxed as he smiled at a couple of his supporters in the courtroom. When it came time for him to plea, he answered "Not Guilty" to the charges.

Joel Brewer said after examining all the evidence and discussing the case with members of both families, he would not seek the death penalty. He would not comment on any plea bargaining that may have take place prior to Rick's arraignment.

Patty Jo Pulley would have turned forty-three in July.

At the hearing, a reporter asked Patty Jo's mother, Elva Mae Riddick, what she hoped would come out in the trial.

"I'm just like everyone else," Elva Mae said. "I just want to know what happened and why it happened. We're just looking forward to having it over with. It's been a long time. It's been the hardest five-and-a-half years of our lives."

In preparation for the Rick Pulley trial, DA Brewer requested special SBI agent J. R. Bowman locate and photograph a 1991 Ford F-150 four-wheel-drive truck with a manual transmission, so as to compare the vehicle to Rick Pulley's. On August 18, 2004, Special Agent (SA) G. R. Thomas was assigned the task of locating a person, preferably a female with the same five-four stature as that of Patty Jo Pulley, and placing her in the front seat of the vehicle. The purpose of the activity was to determine if a person the size of Patty Jo would likely be able to operate a manual transmission Ford F-150, with the vehicle seat pushed toward the back glass of the vehicle.

The next day, Thomas located such a vehicle in Lexington, North Carolina, and found a female deputy from the Lexington Police Department who was the exact size of Patty Jo. With another special agent witnessing the investigation, Thomas took photographs and measurements regarding the placement of the vehicle's seat and clutch pedal. Based on his investigation, Thomas concluded that the female officer was unable to operate the vehicle when the vehicle's seat was positioned all the way back, toward the rear of the vehicle cabin. Thus, it was not Patty Jo Pulley who was driving the red truck when the doors were locked on River Bend Road.

Chapter 48

Caswell County chief district attorney Joel Brewer was a native of Georgia. Brewer graduated from the University of Georgia in 1972 and the university's law school in 1974. Pointing out that his nickname "the Bulldog" had more to do with his finesse in the courtroom than his attachment to the university mascot, Brewer was a North Carolinian at heart. After he graduated from college, he lived in Raleigh with his brother, a minister in the World Christian Church at the time, and worked in the construction industry. Before the summer was over, he had met and fallen in love with Pam Brown, a young, dark-haired Meredith College graduate (Meredith was also Patty Jo's alma mater). It didn't take Brewer long to figure out what he wanted to do with the rest of his life, and by the time he had graduated from law school and passed the bar, he was married and ready for a family.

Brewer's maiden voyage into the legal word began in Raleigh in 1975, when he worked as an attorney in a general practice. The next year, he signed on as a trial lawyer, when he and his family moved to Roxboro. For five years, he honed his craft as a private trial lawyer, until he opted in 1981 to take a job as a trial prosecutor for the state of

North Carolina. In 1984, Brewer became the elected district attorney of Caswell and Person County.

Until two weeks after Patty Jo Pulley's skeletal remains were found under the Hyco Creek Bridge, Brewer had never heard anything about Patty Jo Pulley's disappearance. But in mid-January 2004, he met with representatives from the Caswell County Sheriff's Office and the Pittsylvania County Sheriff's Office and several SBI investigators to put together as many pieces of the puzzle, which they had, to determine what they were going to do with the case. Several white boards were used to plot the different pieces of evidence each person had, so the group, as a whole, could start looking at the strengths and the weaknesses of the case.

Brewer believed the case would fall under his jurisdiction, since the victim's body was recovered in Caswell County. He knew there was a possibility other developments in the investigation might prove different, but he still wanted to treat the case as if it was under his jurisdiction. Thinking of ways police investigators could help him get a handle on the case, he divvied up a list of questions.

When the investigative team met with Brewer the following week, a number of those questions were answered. He then queried each person in the room, and asked for their opinion on what they thought might have happened to Patty Jo Pulley.

"This is what I want to know." Brewer wrote on the erasable board: *Has a crime been committed?* "Then I want to know . . ." *If a crime has been committed, who committed this crime?*

After talking with the investigators and reviewing the investigative reports, Brewer was satisfied a crime had been committed, and fairly certain police investigators knew who had committed the crime. The only pieces of the puzzle they hadn't figured out was how and why it had occurred.

Since Caswell County had the body, Brewer made the decision to go forward with the case. "I'm satisfied that we are going to be able to show a jury the determination about how the crime occurred in the state of North Carolina."

Brewer met with his prosecutorial staff and discussed the case.

"The Rick Pulley case is not a death penalty case," Brewer explained to his staff. "First of all, it does not have all the death penalty statutory aggravating factors. Secondly, it doesn't have the burden of proof beyond a reasonable doubt. I think if we are going to ask a jury to take someone's life, then we better have proof beyond all doubt."

Brewer passed out folders with summations and copies of police reports.

"Doubt doesn't really need to be an issue on a death penalty case," he continued. "Any case that lacks that overwhelming, compelling type of proof should not be tried as a capital murder. It is simply a waste of the state's time and resources."

Brewer's first capital case was in the mid-1980s. Including that first case, he had never lost a murder case. He attributed his wife Pam's knowledge in education as a big factor in shaping his career.

"My wife was the assistant principal at Person High School for years. A former North Carolina State teacher of the year, she helped me understand the importance of courtroom presentation and communication with jurors.

"In the 1990s, the O. J. Simpson case had a huge impact upon prosecution in the state of North Carolina and across the nation. From an audiovisual standpoint, it really raised the bar on how prosecutors present information and try their cases in today's courtroom. Civil attorneys had been improving their methods for a while, discovering the values of simple teaching methods. Our schoolteachers had known and used these methods for years, but these skills had not gotten to courtrooms until the 1990s.

"Now, if teachers thought they had it bad in terms of modern equipment, the court system was even worse. Our first projection machine was when we ran out and got a scratch-and-dent model to be used. What we discovered we needed was someway we could lay a hard exhibit, such as a weapon, to something as simple as a chart. We needed a wide screen for the Pulley case so that we could display our evidence and exhibits in the courtroom, so we went out and bought one."

As Brewer and his staff began organizing the Pulley case, they realized it was an enormous amount of detailed information. There were so many different facets involved in the case, it quickly became as complex a circumstantial case of murder as Brewer had ever been involved in. It was a herculean task just to assemble the raw data, assimilate it, digest it, and then regurgitate it back into some type of assembled, organized presentation.

The Pulley case would take Brewer and his staff an enormous amount of time to put together. In the weeks leading up to the trial, they would be in the office until as late as 2:00 A.M.

"There was an enormous amount of discovery in this case," Brewer recalled. "At one point, the defense was ready for trial and they were yelling for a trial. So we called the Pittsylvania County Sheriff's Office and asked if they had delivered us everything. When they said we had everything, my assistant, Hugh Willaford, asked if they were sure, that there was something that the defense was referencing that we don't have.

"'I will go back and see,' the technical officer assured him, but the next day, Hugh called me and said, 'I was just brought fifty-five boxes of evidence and that was all in response to a request for something as simple as a pair of pants.' So when the defense still wanted to go forward with trial, I told the judge it would be ineffective assistance for defense counsel because they wouldn't have the time to go through it, no more than we did. So the court allowed a continuance on both sides to sort through that material. But, even then, there was still so much material there to absorb."

If Brewer had a talent, it was for pulling material together and organizing the theme of a case, he believed. The good thing about his job as a criminal prosecutor was that he had the opportunity beforehand to put everything together.

"You do it in relationship to what your elements of the crime are," Brewer explained. "Prosecutors are routinely taught to understand what they have to prove. Judicial instructions are set by the North Carolina Supreme Court, so if we know what issues are going to arise in a case, then we know what instructions the judge is going to bring. These are the written instructions set by the state supreme court and they are all ready for us to review.

"For example, forty years ago, judges wrote their own instructions. They would sit down the night before and write out their own individual instructions they were going to give the next day. But today, we have what is called 'the patterns' and the judges now read the patterns as jury instructions.

"Occasionally some judge will go off and leave the pattern, but the good thing about the patterns is that, if they use the patterns, it keeps them from being reversed by the appellate courts. If they use their own, then they risk being overturned by the appellate courts.

"As my staff and I prepared for the Pulley case, we studied the patterns. We asked ourselves what the issues were going to be at trial, and discussed such issues as the pattern instructions for flight of the accused, on witness identification, on substantive element of the crime. We knew what the elements were going to be for first-degree murder, how many elements there were, and what we would have to prove. There are even pattern instructions for elements on premeditation, deliberation, specific intent to kill, and malice. All of those terms are explained.

"So if a prosecutor knows what he is going to charge, what he is going to try, if he has an indictment for first-degree murder, then he pulls the instruction pattern for first-degree murder—he can plan out his case. And then he may look through the patterns to see if there are any patterns for circumstantial evidence, such as photographs and charts. So one can use these as a framework into organizing your evidence, into what is the evidence of malice, what are the elements of premeditation and deliberation.

"One of the biggest issues in the Pulley case was the identity of the accused and the evidence as it related to the identity of the accused. We knew that. And we also knew that motive was not required to be proven to the jury, even though we knew it was going to be a huge motivator in Pulley's case. Again, there was a pattern of instruction for motive. Before the trial, we asked ourselves, what is it that we have as motive? We knew that Pulley was having financial and sexual problems, and we planned to develop later on everything from the elders' testimony about the credit cards and the police testimony about the overdue bills and phone sex charges, to the women he had relations with at the church.

"In a circumstantial evidence trial, we pull all of this information into what we call our 404 B evidence file. These were the past incidents and previous behavior in Pulley's life that didn't necessarily relate to his case, but they were other bad acts or activity that shed light on his character. Again, like the credit card use and the sexual telephone calls, there was an enormous amount of material on that."

Brewer had taught criminal defense tactics in a seminar for the North Carolina Academy for Trial Lawyers, as well as providing instruction and giving trial tips to the prosecutors at the state level. He believed that cases should be tried at their highest level many times. Prior to the Pulley case, Brewer had taught a couple of weeks each year at the National Advocacy Center (NAC) in Columbia, South Carolina. The NAC is the national training center for new state and federal prosecutors from across the nation. Their building is one of the finest buildings on the University of South Carolina campus and paid for totally out of drug forfeiture money at the federal level. The building houses ten courtrooms, two hundred bedrooms, several auditoriums, a cafeteria, and state-of-the-art teaching facilities. Most of the teaching is by done by volunteer, seasoned prosecutors from across the nation.

In the summer of 2003, Brewer was teaching nine new prosecutors, all with less than six months' experience, but he had as coteachers, one with thirty and another with thirty-one years of experience, not including his twenty-five years. With a one-to-three ratio, he and his colleagues taught, using video and critiques and doing mock trials, and tried to cover everything from opening statements and trial theory to closing arguments.

As the Pulley case drew closer to trial, Brewer tried the case before other people at the NAC. In the summer of 2004, he had gotten to class early and asked one of the faculty coordinators if there were any visiting prosecutors that could sit in and listen to his case. Brewer was fortunate enough to get help from prosecutors as far away as Alaska, Texas, Chicago, and New England, who helped him lay out his case. Because of the issues of all the different locations of where Patty Jo lived, worked, where the truck was found, and where the body was recovered, Brewer struggled with how to present it to a jury. It was difficult for him to keep it all straight, must less a jury. His colleagues showed him how to lay the case out geographically. Brewer planned to use the same program, both in his opening statement and at the end of the trial.

What was even more valuable was that Brewer, after meeting with his colleagues in South Carolina, came away with twenty questions he had never considered at that time, but ones that he knew the investigators either had the answers for, or could get the answers for.

"I was able to bring all that back to North Carolina with me," Brewer said, "all that wealth of seasoned, prosecutorial experience and use that to help build the fabric of Rick Pulley's case. Even before we went to trial, I could already see there was overwhelming evidence against Rick Pulley that would lead a jury to see the moral certainty of a guilty verdict."

Chapter 49

Rick Pulley's court appointed lawyer, Theresa Pressley, had pushed for a speedy trial. There had been three prior trial dates set and, on each occasion, Brewer had asked for more time. When Pressley complained about not receiving discovery materials on time, the DA claimed his office had such a heavy workload that it was difficult for him to get to all the material.

"I've already been before the judge twice," Pressley protested. "The defense has had to pay a private detective to gather material we should have gotten free from the prosecution as part of the discovery. We could have used the money we spent on something other than discovery materials."

Supposedly, a month before the trial, Brewer had communicated to Pressley he would offer a plea bargain if Rick would confess to manslaughter. As part of the plea bargain, Rick would be sentenced three to six years in prison, but would receive credit for the time he had already served in jail.

Rick was encouraged and believed the DA would have never made such an offer unless he had a weak case. But he was not interested in an plea bargain, as he would never agree to confess to something he did not do. Rick believed the prosecution did not have any evidence to support a conviction, that he would be found innocent, and that his name would finally be cleared.

The trial had been a long time coming, but, finally, it was scheduled to begin on Monday, October 18. The murder trial of Eugene Rick Pulley was considered big news in the small county of Caswell, North Carolina. The majestic Caswell County Courthouse was already nearly filled to capacity. As soon as word made it outside that a jury had been selected and seated, a handful of spectators darted up the twelve wide concrete steps in the front of the courthouse and rushed to the courtroom. Only a few people were left scrambling for seats in the gallery as the judge waited for the prosecutors and defense teams in this high-profile case to take their places behind the rich mahogany tables.

Rick Pulley sat beside his attorney, Theresa Pressley. She had defended a number of clients in capital murder cases and had a strong reputation as a hard-nosed fighter who had a soft heart for her defendants.

Those who knew Rick, but hadn't seen him for a while, were shocked to see how much he had aged. Over the last four years, he had ballooned up to more than three hundred pounds. His blue shirt, red-and-blue tie, and white trousers clung to him as if they were last year's wardrobe. His once dark and curly hair had turned completely gray—gone were his flamboyant smile and his quick handshake.

At Pressley's request, Rick was not handcuffed when he was in the courtroom. There was a restrictive device that fit between Rick's legs, which required him to keep his legs directly in front of him. It was clear Rick Pulley was no longer the man in charge.

For the most part, it was inconceivable that this calm, soft-spoken man could have killed his wife, tossed her under the Hyco Creek Bridge, and left her there to rot. By now, the case was already 4½ years old. Talk was cheap in the courtroom, and everyone was quick to throw in their two cents' worth.

"The state's got nothing to tie Rick to the murder," a dark-haired female reporter argued at the back of the courtroom. "They've got no motive, no weapon, and no eyewitnesses to the murder. All they have is circumstantial evidence, and that makes a weak case."

"Don't be fooled by appearances," her colleague said assuredly. "From all I have read and heard, it is a slam dunk."

Lines already had been drawn in the courthouse. Once the jury of eight men and four women was settled, the lawyers knew it was time to ante up. It was time for battle.

"All right, we're back in session," the Honorable W. Osmond Smith III announced, signaling this long-awaited legal contest would begin. "The state may proceed with an opening statement."

"Thank you, Your Honor," Caswell County DA Joel Brewer began. Brewer was a short, gray-haired man who spoke very slowly and deliberately. Even though he was a little pudgy around the middle, he had boundless energy and passion for what he did best—prosecuting criminals.

Brewer had all his material in front of him—the material he would need to keep the case organized and together. His system was not an elaborate one. In fact, he used an accordion file to keep himself organized. When he was handed pieces of information and slipped pieces of paper—whether it was scientific evidence, a police statement, material about a lay witness, the defendant's criminal record, or background information on the defendant—he would insert it in a folder and file it away.

As he began unfolding his organized presentation to the jury, he realized there was an enormous amount of detail he would have to tie together for them. He and his staff had been at this arduous task since December 18, 2002, shortly after Patty Jo Pulley's skeletal remains were discovered. It had taken him quite a period of time to sort through it and understand it all. With the proliferation of pretrial publicity, Brewer knew he had his work cut out for him.

Brewer began his opening statement by summarizing the lives of Rick and Patty Jo Pulley. He wanted the jury to know that most of the events he referred to took place on the North Carolina and Virginia line—and below the Virginia line, of course, was Caswell County. He used a geographical map to help the jury follow along. He then related the events of May 14, 1999, the day Patty Jo Pulley disappeared, and how Rick Pulley became a suspect.

To help him track through the plethora of names and dates, Brewer had a timeline prepared and he would flash it up on the screen. As he spoke, the jurors could follow the deadly timeline themselves.

Brewer told the jurors about two men who had spotted Rick Pulley on the shoulder of the road near where Patty Jo's red truck had been parked. Then, after the truck had been found, a PCSO officer interviewed Pulley and noticed right away three scratch marks across Rick Pulley's face.

"You're going to learn the actions on the evening of May 14, 1999," Brewer assured the jurors. "And you're going to learn during the course of this week what was going on in the lives of Rick and Patty Pulley. And you're going to learn of the actions of the defendant before May 14, 1999, and you're going to learn significantly the actions and statements the defendant made after May 14, 1999."

Brewer revealed some of what happened after May 14, and after Patty Jo Pulley was reported missing by her husband. Then months and years passed, following the location of the red truck, he related, until December 18, 2002, when Dana Goodnight, a surveyor, found her remains in a creek bed below the old bridge on Highway 158.

After several objections from the defense, Brewer continued his blow-by-blow account of how and why Pulley became a suspect in his wife's death. He mentioned briefly Rick's financial difficulties and his illegal use of credit cards belonging to the church where he pastored. Then he glared at the jury and told them how Pulley had sold the red truck and then sold within weeks after her death the most priceless belonging that Patty Jo owned.

"Rick Pulley sold Patty Jo Pulley's piano weeks after she disappeared," Brewer said emphatically. "Broke her mother's heart. Rick knew that Patty Jo Pulley would never play the piano again."

After revealing several other atrocities—like phone sex and adultery—Rick had committed, Brewer brought his brief opening to a close. In the short time he spoke, he wanted to make certain the jury knew that a crime had been committed, that Patty Jo had been murdered. And he wanted the jury to know the law enforcement agencies and his office were satisfied Rick Pulley had murdered his wife. Since the body was found in North Carolina, the only thing left for the prosecution to do in this case was to demonstrate how Rick had murdered his wife.

"Now, ladies and gentlemen of the jury," Brewer said in a soft, confident voice, "that's some of what the state intends to present in this courtroom in the coming days. There's other evidence, but we'll leave that for you to hear on first impression. One thing is for sure, on May 14, 1999, the Riddicks lost their daughter, but the defendant didn't lose his pickup truck."

Defense attorney Theresa Pressley pushed her eyeglasses up on the bridge of her nose and walked toward the jurors. The fair-skinned, neatly dressed lady walked in high heels and they clicked across the floor. Several female spectators seated throughout the gallery were giving odds on whether or not Pressley would last a week in heels.

Rick sat stoically at the defense table. Throughout the trial, he served as Pressley's assistant, as he seemed to know her case strategy and often helped her with her papers. Together, they vowed to prove without a doubt that he could not have killed Patty Jo.

Pressley's voice was quick and assertive. In a matter of

minutes, she encapsulated the events of May 14, 1999, and stated the evidence would show that Rick loved his wife and had absolutely nothing to do with her disappearance and death.

"The evidence will show that he spent three or four days without sleep looking for his wife, going to various places," Pressley said in rapid fire. "The evidence will show that all sorts of reports came in of sightings of Patty Jo and he went looking. The evidence will show that he met with officers repeatedly. The evidence will show that he participated in six hours and two minutes of polygraph examination. The evidence will show that after his wife disappeared, his life went into turmoil.

"His finances were worse off than ever. His depression level was horrible. Things fell apart. The evidence will show he stayed at that church until October, and then he moved to Lebanon, Virginia, where he and Patty Jo had visited several times. This was the church they were planning on moving to, and he became a part of that church, and he still wondered about Patty Jo. The evidence will show he kept his health insurance on his wife up until December 18, 2002.

"The evidence will show that he loved his wife, and that his life has changed forever. We thank you for listening to all the evidence. We ask you to consider each witness in their entirety and apply the law that the judge gives you to the facts that you hear."

The judge gave the jury a level look, then excused them for the rest of the evening. They were informed to report back the next morning at nine-thirty.

After the jury exited the courtroom, Brewer rose to his feet. He looked almost comically shocked.

"On the record, Your Honor," he said in a flat and disgusted voice, "I would hope that's the last time we hear the word 'polygraph' in this courtroom."

"Yes, I would like to confer with counsel," Judge Smith said with less grace than usual. "That's what I would like to confer with you about. Unless you want to be heard on the record, I'll confer with you both in my chambers."

The next morning, a television camera, cocked and loaded, squatted on its tripod in one corner of the courtroom. A cameraman from WSET, television channel 13, from Lynchburg, Virginia, hunkered over the camera, adjusted its lens, and made certain everything was in working order.

Judge Smith explained how a representative from the television station had submitted a request to have a camera in the courtroom. He had approved the request, as long as the applicable rules regarding cameras in the courtroom were met.

Smith then moved on to the matter of defense's mention of defendant's polygraph examination.

"The court is of the opinion that this is an improper reference to a polygraph examination," the judge said as if no one had anything to apologize for. "It is not evidence that would be admissible as the court understands the law and the current facts and circumstances. . . . The court feels like such an opening statement made by defense counsel would reasonably permit the jury to draw an inference that the defendant submitted to a polygraph examination and that the results were favorable to the defendant, which would be an erroneous conclusion."

After Smith advised both attorneys to refrain from any mention of a polygraph examination and exclude any testimony or information that inadvertently or otherwise referred to it, he asked the bailiff to bring the jury in.

As the jurors filed in and took their respective seats in the jury box, spectators whispered about the rumors they had already heard this morning in the courthouse about who was going to testify. It seemed as if everyone had an opinion on what was going to happen in the preacher's murder trial.

Brewer and his senior assistant, Hugh Willaford, had agreed prior to this court date that they had no reason to overtry this case. The facts were already there and stood on their own merits. One by one, the witnesses would be called and they would corroborate the facts. They would introduce to the jury everyone who was involved with the case and then argue their case against Rick Pulley: a husband whose life had gone out of control, a wife who was killed and tossed under a bridge, a murderer who tried to commit the perfect crime.

Willaford was a younger, brown-haired version of Brewer. Rising to call the prosecution's first witness, Dana Goodnight, to the stand, Willaford set the tone in the courtroom. With a narrator's voice, he staged the scene for Goodnight, a contract geologist for the North Carolina DOT, who told the story of how he was working on a bridge replacement project at Hyco Creek on December 18, 2002. He said he stepped on something, heard a crack, then looked down and discovered it was the skeletal remains of a human being.

As Goodnight described what he found and how the horrible scene played out, Rick sat still and reacted without any emotion. He listened as Goodnight said, "The thing that struck me the most was I noticed what appeared to be a bra stretched across the bones."

The photographs Willaford showed on the screen depicted the bridge and the area where Patty Jo's decomposed body was found. When he pulled up actual photos of Patty Jo's skeletal remains, her family hung their heads and silently wept.

Goodnight testified after finding the remains, he went to the Roxboro, North Carolina, Police Department and reported his discovery.

There was so much emotion in the courtroom after Goodnight's testimony, that Pressley wisely chose to ask Goodnight only a dozen questions.

Willaford asked a few more questions on redirect, then called Dr. Ralph Howell to the witness stand. Howell was Patty Jo Pulley's dentist, who had treated her since she was about eight years old. He had kept all of her records and had been able to match those up with the skeletal remains.

"I know this because of the fact that two number nines were slightly rotated and that she had restorations in certain teeth." Howell pointed to an X-ray of Patty Jo's teeth projected on the screen. "That the restoration in number eighteen was probably badly worn because of the material, and she had at the time tetracycline stains."

"Could you explain what that is?" Willaford instructed Howell.

"Tetracycline stain is a thing that children get due to taking tetracycline when they're small. This is not unusual back when Patty Jo was small."

The prosecution continued to build their case that the body found at Hyco Creek Bridge was indeed Patty Jo Pulley's. Her family members hung on every word as Clayton Myers, an investigator with the Caswell County Sheriff's Office, recalled being summoned to the Hyco Creek Bridge site around 11:00 A.M. that day. He testified he took a statement from Goodnight, then secured the site using yellow crime-scene barrier tape and started a log of who went in and out of the area. In his testimony, he recalled what persons were called to the scene and described the procedures that were used to remove the body.

The prosecution's fourth witness of the day, Earnest Burkes, was an oral pathologist. Burkes did consultant work with the North Carolina Medical Examiner's (ME) Office and served as an expert witness, who had testified in a number of courts as a forensic dentist. As expected, he sided with Patty Jo's family dentist, Dr. Howell.

"And what was your opinion, Doctor?" Willaford asked.

"My opinion, after completing the records that we had faxed from Dr. Howell, there were consistent patterns," Burkes stated. "In my opinion, the mandible and the maxilla were compatible with the person represented in the chart of Patty Jo Pulley by Dr. R. O. Howell. There is enough evidence there to prove without a doubt that the remains were hers."

Now that the prosecution had clearly established for the jurors that the remains belonged to Patty Jo Pulley, they needed to put the body together with the evidence collected at Hyco Creek Bridge, and then prove what might have happened to her. Brewer wanted the jurors to ask for themselves why she had died. Was it naturally, accidentally, or intentionally?

Caswell County sheriff Mike Welch then described for jurors how he had contacted the North Carolina State Bureau of Investigation. He then designated Investigator Mike Adkins as the case agent.

"I photographed these pictures of the area at Hyco Creek immediately after Patty Jo's body was found," Welch continued, "and we secured the crime scene."

"You keep saying 'crime scene,'" Pressley asked him on cross-examination. "Can you define 'crime scene' for me?"

"When you're dealing with a suspicious death, a crime scene is that particular area that you're investigating as a death," Welch said. "It could be a residence. It could be an open area. It could be a vehicle, but when you use the term 'crime scene,' you're referring to whatever is involved in that investigation."

Pressley pushed her glasses up on her nose. She then looked at Welch as if to say that she didn't believe his answer.

"And when you referred to this area as a 'crime scene,'" she asked, "there is nothing to denote that Patty Jo died here. Is that correct?"

"Based on my experience in the field of investigations and actually making that determination as the sheriff, that particular area was declared the crime scene for investigative purposes," Welch countered.

"So, in answer to my question, there is no actual evidence that Patty Jo Pulley died at that actual location?"

Brewer didn't appreciate Pressley's implications and

jumped to his feet with an objection. When the judge sustained, Pressley stated she had no further questions for the sheriff.

Investigator Michael Adkins followed Welch to the stand, as a person who had also photographed the scene. Jurors listened as Brewer questioned Adkins on what police had found at the scene. Adkins said they found jewelry, which Rick later identified as his wife's, and a fingernail, clothing, and a nylon rope.

"The rope was tied around Patty Jo's hands," Adkins testified, apparently confused.

Adkins said the SBI released the skeletal remains and other items to him late that evening. He testified that he transported the remains to the North Carolina Medical Examiner's Office the next day.

When asked if the remains had been altered in any way before they were transported, Adkins responded, "They were not changed. They were not altered. They were not tampered with."

In her cross-examination, Pressley bore down on Adkins, asking him if the rope found at the scene was entwined in the rib cage when it was discovered, or was it looped around the victim's hands? His answer was critical to her client's defense.

"At that time, did you tell the medical examiner that that rope was looped around the victim's hand?"

"Yes, ma'am. That's correct."

"But if the SBI reports and the pictures show that the rope was not around the hand," Pressley questioned, "then that information you gave Dr. Butts would have been incorrect."

"I'd have to see the pictures to know if that information was correct or not," he replied.

Pressley's implications were clear—the state had the burden of proving the defendant's guilt. Maybe the prosecution had been right about a lot of things, but they were wrong about this. She grilled Adkins further.

"So you've had the opportunity to look at them, isn't that correct?"

Adkins stood his ground. "Yes, ma'am. I've looked at them several times."

"And don't the pictures reflect that the rope was in a bind entwined to the wrist and not on the hand?"

Adkins stopped and thought about it. "I have not seen pictures that describe what you're saying."

"Have you seen all the pictures that the SBI took at the scene?"

"There's a lot of pictures, Miss Pressley."

"Was that a yes or a no, sir? Is it possible you haven't seen them?"

"It's possible that I have not seen them." Nothing could explain it more. Adkins was just stating his opinion.

"So, if the SBI records reflect otherwise, then you would assume the SBI records are accurate?"

"Yes, ma'am," Adkins said meekly. "The SBI records are accurate, and my records also."

Pressley saw then that she had Adkins right where she wanted him, and she wasn't going to let him off the hook.

"So, is it possible that quite by accident you gave the incorrect information to the medical examiner's office?"

"Objection," Brewer yelled out from his seat.

Before the judge could respond, Adkins admitted it was possible he could have given out the wrong information.

The prosecution watched as the defense tried to chip away at their solid case. In another tactical move by the state to convince the jury Patty Jo had been murdered in North Carolina, Brewer called out the name of Pat Daly, a crime scene specialist with the North Carolina SBI.

Daly described his investigation procedures after arriving at the Hyco Bridge scene that afternoon. Brewer then entered into evidence numerous photographs Daly had taken that day, displaying them for the jury on the projector screen. One of Daly's photos showed a brassiere lying on a rib cage. Another depicted a looped rope next to the brassiere. Several other photos showed all the skeletal bones of Patty Jo's body laid out in human formation. Another depicted a close-up view of the rope, which was tied in a loop with a circumference of 3½ to 4 inches.

"This is the rope that was found above the clavicle, or collarbone," Daly noted for the jurors.

Brewer then asked Daly if he had an opinion as to how the rope might have been used.

"My training and experience would indicate it was used for some type of restraint, hands or feet, or as a noose for purposes of strangulation," Daly responded.

Daly's testimony was particularly difficult for the Riddicks. As he described the process of separating and cleaning Patty Jo's bones and then demonstrated in the photos on the screen, it wasn't easy for them to absorb. They sat stone-faced throughout Daly's testimony; it was as if going numb was the only way they could survive the morbid slide show. They were not used to seeing pictures of Patty Jo in this fashion. They had only seen her when she was alive, clothed, vibrant, and happy.

While Elva Mae and Albert held hands and suffered through the endless parade of photographs, other family members cried or chose not to look. They never had imagined they could endure such a hardship, but they did it for Patty Jo's sake.

"Can you tell us how long Patty Jo's bones and her items had been there?"

Daly explained how the climate, the environment, and the water flow changes affected her body over the years, and how this had helped them to determine how long she had been there. It was a sobering thought that Patty Jo had lain there for almost 3½ years. The seasons, the winds, the waters, and many different kinds of animals had come and gone during that period. Her bones and her items moved and shifted with the changes.

Another important point Daly made was when Brewer asked how the body or the remains got there, and he answered, "Based on my training and experience, and based on the layout and on the terrain, I feel confident to say that the [victim's] remains were put there—they were not there of its own free will and natural state."

Pressley attempted to undermine Daly's testimony and asked him in cross-examination, "How did you even know those remains were even those of Patty Jo Pulley?" She also attempted to clarify the matter about Patty Jo's hands being tied behind her back, as had been testified earlier by Investigator Adkins. She asked Daly if the victim's hands had been found some distance from the rope.

Daly stated that some of Patty Jo's bones were missing, and, additionally, his observation had been that the rope had not been around the hands, which were at some distance from where the body was positioned, but instead it was above the rib cage, very close to the collarbone and one of the arm bones.

Brewer did not intend to let Pressley have the last word about the hands, so in redirect examination, he asked Daly if he had an opinion as to whether a cord, of the type found, could be used as a deadly weapon, used to kill, or used to restrain. In all three instances, Daly said, his opinion was that it could be used in such a manner.

"Do you have an opinion as to whether or not that rope has been used to restrain?" Brewer had asked.

"Through my training and my experience based on the condition the rope was in, the way it was knotted and looped, it would indicate that it was used for some type of restraint—either hands, feet, or possibly noose for the purpose of strangulation."

Pressley shot to her feet on cross-examination. "Could the rope be proven to have been there at the exact time as the skeletal remains?"

"I can say for a fact that based on its location," Daly said, "based on the position it was found within the remains, that they were there simultaneously."

Pressley shook her head. "So you don't know if they had been there for a long period of time, do you, Agent Daly?"

"No, ma'am. I cannot speculate as to how long the remains were there. No."

Pressley continued after him in her fast-paced, aggressive style. "Then you can't say that that rope was used as a deadly weapon."

"A deadly weapon, as in layman's term—" Daly tried to get in before he was interrupted.

"That's a yes or a no?" Pressley shot back at him.

Judge Smith intervened. "Well, actually, it wasn't a question," he stated, trying to keep both sides defused. "I'll let you rephrase it. It sounded like a statement. It was intended as a question, but if you read it in a transcript, it would not sound like a question."

Pressley took a deep breath, then started over again.

"Agent Daly, you could not say as an absolute fact, can you, that the rope was used as a deadly weapon?"

"No, ma'am."

Speaking slowly, as if she wanted everything on the record and out in the open, Pressley mused, "And, Agent Daly, you cannot say for an absolute fact, can you, that that rope was used for restraint?"

"No, ma'am."

Knowing that any good defense lawyer had the power to turn a good line of questioning into a three-ring circus, Brewer stepped back in on redirect. Sometimes, he found, he had to ask the same questions, but in a slightly different manner to drive home his point.

"Agent Daly, do you have an opinion as to whether or not that rope was used to restrain?"

"Yes, sir."

"What is your opinion?"

With information that was second nature to him, Daly tried to explain his answer again. "Through my training and experience based on the condition the rope was in, the way it was knotted and looped, it's my training and experience, it would indicate that it was used for some type of restraint—either hands, feet, or possibly a noose for the purpose of strangulation."

"And that's your opinion?" Brewer restated his position.

"Yes, sir."

Pressley wanted to make her viewpoint clear to the twelve jurors who, she believed, had come to this courtroom with an open mind. On recross, she again asked Daly, "You cannot say as a fact that that rope was even there at the exact time that those skeletal remains came to be?"

The muscles in Daly's jaw tightened. "I can say for a fact that based on its location, based on the position it was found within the remains, that they were simultaneous."

"But there are other items that are within that grid that you cannot say are linked to those skeletal remains. Is that correct?"

Daly nodded. "That would be correct," he stated. "Yes."

"So, once again I ask you"—Pressley paused for the effect—"can you say as absolute fact that that rope was there simultaneously?"

"No, ma'am," Daly admitted, "Not as an absolute fact."

The last testimony of the day belonged to NC chief medical examiner John Butts. Butts had performed over five thousand autopsies and been called upon over six hundred times to testify as an expert witness in the field of causes of human death. He told the jurors he had performed an autopsy on the remains found at the Hyco Creek Bridge and had concluded that they were those of Patty Jo Pulley.

"Her remains appeared to be most consistent with the kinds of injuries that might have occurred as someone had stepped on the bones," Butts said. "However, I did not see any evidence of a gunshot wound, any evidence of a stabbing, or other fracture that I would have associated with a blow or a blunt-force injury of that nature. Nor did I see any evidence on the remains of any old healed fractures or of other underlying conditions that she might have had prior to death."

Butts blinked slightly and continued his testimony before finally concluding that Patty Jo died as a result of violent injury or trauma of a homicidal nature—most likely, asphyxia, when oxygen fails to reach the brain.

Patty Jo's family believed they knew what had happened to her, but hearing the ME confirm it was agonizing for them. Their faces mirrored the pain they were experiencing.

Butts then told the jury how squeezing the neck can cause a person to become unconscious within six or so seconds, and how a continued shutoff of the blood supply to the brain brings death within a few minutes.

"Closing off the nose or mouth by smothering allows the person to be conscious for a longer time," he explained subsequently, "but continued suffocation causes irreversible injury to the brain and then death."

Brewer asked the doctor if the rope or cord found in evidence could be used as a deadly weapon or a restraint device.

Butts answered that it could be a deadly weapon, as a ligature to strangle someone, or it could be tied around a limb as a restraint. He also agreed with Brewer in that a fall from a twenty-seven-foot bridge could be fatal, regardless of whether a cord had been tied around the bones of the left hand or entwined with the rib cage near an arm bone.

In cross-examination, Pressley tried to establish that because Patty Jo's hyoid bone was missing from her throat area, she could not have been strangled.

Butts said that wasn't true. He stated he found no other evidence of cause of death, and, by process of elimination, he believed it to be strangulation.

When Pressley asked whether Patty Jo could have died from a heart attack or a spinal leak injury, such as the one she had suffered from years earlier, Butts said it wasn't likely.

In the early 1990s, Patty Jo was so weak, she could hardly hold her head up. After visiting a physician, she was told she had a spinal leak. In her diary entry, Patty Jo had written: *I've been too weak to write for the past week. A spinal leak, the doctor says. So much pain and fatigue—lucky to be alive. Can't begin to tell how it happened. It's always something. What will it be next? May God be with me.*

Pressley wanted to be certain the doctor understood Patty Jo's history. "Had anyone told you that she suffered from spinal injuries in the past?"

"I guess if she died of a spinal leak injury and someone decided they would put the body over there," Butts supposed, "but again, deaths from spinal leak injuries generally occur at the time you actually do the tap, if that's what you're referring to. And they don't occur, you know, days or weeks later."

"Could a spinal leak injury occur?"

"Only if you tap the spine again," Butts said with a hint of sarcasm.

Finally the jurors had heard the last testimony of a mentally exhausting day. The questions still loomed in their minds: Was Patty Jo Pulley murdered? Had she been drugged and thrown off the bridge? Had she been strangled? And, if so, by whom? And when?

After court was adjourned, Patty Jo's family filed out of the courtroom and talked about all they had learned during their first day of court. What they couldn't seem to shake was that during all those years they were looking for Patty Jo, she was lying somewhere under a bridge in the rainstorms, the summer heat, and the cold. It wasn't just an image that was imprinted upon their minds that they couldn't forget, it was more than that.

How could Rick Pulley dump Patty Jo's body and leave her there all this time? That was what troubled them about this whole matter more than anything else.

Chapter 50

According to the courtroom junkies—the armchair quarterbacks—it was the prosecution that had scored decisively in Tuesday's gridiron match. Although Pressley was clearly the underdog, she still was fighting a tough battle. By no means a pushover, she had, just by her presence, intimidated Patty Jo's family.

"Why does she cut her eyes at us and talk harshly to others while looking right at us?" Connie Winslow questioned. "She needs to smile a little more and look at the jury, but she doesn't need to look at us like we're the ones who put Rick on trial."

"There is a big difference between being aggressive and assertive," Connie's brother, Alan, remarked.

Day three of Rick Pulley's murder trial began with aerial photos of the places where PJ lived, where she went to church, where she worked, where her car was located, and the bridge area where her remains were found. The prosecution then tendered two witnesses, who, they believed, could pin Rick to the area where the red truck had been found the night Patty Jo was reported missing.

"All I can remember is it was like three seconds going by him," Dale "Cherokee" Purvis said. He had been given a laser pointer to show the jury where he lived, on the map, at River Bend Road. He also pointed out the Dan River, along with the bridge and the boat ramp, the city of Milton, the Pittsylvania County Fairgrounds, and the Virginia Highway 62, up from the state line to US–58.

Purvis said he had spotted Rick somewhere between eight and nine o'clock the night his wife had been reported missing. He noted that it was daylight saving time, still between light and dark, so he could see him pretty well. As he answered Brewer's questions, he described what he had seen, someone who looked like Rick walking away from the red truck.

Brewer asked permission to approach the defendant. He stepped toward Rick Pulley, then turned on his heels and stated, "The state would ask the defendant to rise."

Pulley frowned, as if his nemesis were joking.

"Objection," Pressley adamantly opposed.

Pulley sat motionless until the judge overruled and nodded at him. Rick then stood up.

"Mr. Purvis, compare the defendant to the person that you saw on the evening of May 14, 1999."

Purvis understood what Brewer was trying to get him to say. But, at the same time, he knew no one would quite understand what had happened unless one had been there. "I really couldn't make no comparison," he responded. "I went, like I said, it was one, two, three seconds driving by. I really couldn't compare him. You could stand there and he could stand up, and I couldn't make no comparison to be honest with you."

Brewer continued his examination of the witness, then tendered him for cross-examination. He had a second witness, Robert Rowland, whose testimony would not only support that of Purvis's but would positively identify Rick Pulley as the man they had seen walking down the road that night.

However, at a certain point in Rowland's testimony, the judge asked members of the jury to recess and reassemble in the grand jury room. Pursuant to a request by the defendant, and in response to a motion filed by the defendant in pretrial, the court had agreed to suppress any in-court testimony by Rowland of the defendant. Outside the presence of the jury, the judge agreed to hear the lawyers' opening statements as to their contentions on this matter, before hearing the evidence on voir dire.

Pressley contended Rowland's testimony had been tainted by neighbor Steven Keel. She claimed Keel had been motivated by a very substantial reward offered for the whereabouts of Patty Jo Pulley when he conducted his own private investigation of the case.

"The power of that suggestion with the ability of the witness to see the person who he was describing for only a short time," she argued convincingly, "and he could describe the face and then was shown one photograph by a person who was acting as an agent of the state is so suggestive to make any identification unreliable, and should not be allowed for the jury to consider, as it is so prejudicial and unreliable."

When the judge asked the state what was their position on the matter, Brewer stated he would prefer just to go forward with the evidence and let the court hear what was presented and preserve Rowland's testimony.

"Your Honor, we contend that he can make a positive identification and it's admissible, and that there's been no suggestive police procedure. Of course, adequate indicia of the things that we would ask the court to keep in mind are the tests under the United States and North Carolina Supreme Court decisions that the court is well aware of, which includes the opportunity of the witness to observe the person he's making an identity of." Brewer then spelled out those conditions for the court.

The judge asked for a short break. After the break, he brought Rowland back to the courtroom and asked to hear his testimony.

"Can you identify the man you and your brother-in-law saw on May 14, 1999?" Brewer asked the witness.

"That fella sitting right there . . . the white shirt, Mr. Pulley." Rowland assured the court that he was positive of his identification. He added that in 1999 Rick's hair was wet, longer, flatter on top, and black.

Pressley tried to trip Rowland up, asking him, "So if [Steven Keel] says you said it, 'It could be him and I'm about eighty-five percent sure,' is he telling a lie?"

"I don't know what he's going to say, ma'am," Rowland responded. "All I can tell you is when he showed me the picture, I said that was him."

Pressley couldn't shake Rowland's testimony. He finally had his day in court and got the opportunity to point his finger at the man accused of killing his wife, saying, "Yes, that is the man I offered a ride to. I'm one hundred percent sure that's who I was talking to that night."

Even though the jury wasn't there to hear this information, Rowland's testimony was devastating to the defense's case. In the jury's mind, it could put Rick at the scene where Patty Jo's truck had been found, and not at the high-school play, as he had previously claimed. Pressley moved to suppress Rowland's identification because Steven Keel had shown him a photo of Pulley shortly after Patty Jo's disappearance, possibly influencing the testimony.

But Rowland said the photo had nothing to do with his identification of Rick, that it was based on his memory of the night. "I remember something wasn't quite right about him. He didn't seem to be right, because his shirt was down and it looked like it was torn."

The judge would allow the jury to hear Rowland's testimony, saying Keel showed him the photograph and did not violate Pulley's right to due process. The prosecution scored a major victory when Smith denied the defense's motion to suppress Robert Rowland's testimony.

For good reason, Pressley had wanted to keep that information away from the jury. She knew it would be only a matter of time before they would hear this. Her strategy was to do as much damage control with Rowland's testimony and then confuse the jury with the state's next witness. She hoped she could cast doubt in the mind of jurors that Robert Rowland could be wrong in what he saw.

Even before the state called Steven Keel to the stand, it seemed everyone wanted to know all about him and what his connection was to the case. What had prompted a man like Keel to conduct his own neighborhood investigation? Was he really trying to clear Rick as a suspect, or were there other motives for him stirring up a hornet's nest?

"It occurred to me that I could clear this up," Keel said, explaining how he got involved in the case. "I could get Rick out of the picture in a minute. All I had to do was take a picture of Rick over there and show it to Rowland."

Pressley asked Keel a series of questions, insisting that what Rowland testified was completely contradictory to what he said.

The judge stepped in and admonished Pressley for her assumptions, reminding her that was for him and the jury to consider whether he recalled the witness saying it.

On Brewer's cross-examination of Keel, he said to the witness, "You have the right to remain silent. You have the right to an attorney. If you can't afford one, the court will appoint one for you. Do you understand your rights?"

Keel nodded his head. He understood.

"Did you take any actions in the state of North Carolina in regard to his case?" Brewer asked forthrightly.

Keel paused for a few seconds before answering, "No, not that I recall."

"You're very lucky. . . ." Brewer's voice trailed off without finishing his sentence.

The state would call a series of other witnesses, including several police officers, then recall Robert Rowland to the stand for the purpose of telling the jury his story and identifying Rick Pulley. After milking Rowland's testimony for all it was worth, Brewer called Samuel Scott Harold to the stand.

Harold had shared a jail cell in Caswell County with Rick Pulley and would testify that their relationship was more than the casual meet-and-greet type. He claimed that Rick had confessed to killing his wife and dumping her body. He said the defendant had related the events after a minister had visited him in jail. At which point, Harold said, he believed the defendant was on the verge of an emotional breakdown.

"I told [Pulley] that everyone I'd known who had committed murder bore an emotional scar. And I said, 'Ricky, you've got that scar on you.'" Later, Harold wrote to the Caswell County DA's Office, saying, *I don't want someone to get away with cold-blooded murder.*

Pressley later cast doubt on the credibility of the thirty-five-year-old former federal inmate, who at the time of writing this letter had already served twelve years for possession of a firearm. During her cross-examination, Pressley got Harold to admit he took Depakote and Zyprexa for, among other things, auditory hallucinations. And when she asked him if he was taking his medications at the time he said Rick had confessed to him, Harold said he had not taken his medications for several days.

Pressley recounted a phone call she said Harold made to her recently, at which time he had offered to now help Pulley in some way.

"Did you say you would help my boy out?" Pressley asked in a sneer.

"Something to that effect," Harold responded.

Pressley let it be known that Harold had either imagined this scenario with her client or had simply made it all up.

The state then paraded a host of police officers through the courtroom to testify and reveal details of their investigation. Particularly damaging was the testimony of Jimmy Lipscomb, formerly of the Pittsylvania County Sheriff's Office. Lipscomb described for the jury his analysis of Pulley's recovered truck and read from documents found in trash bags that were in the back of his truck. The documents reflected numerous debts and unpaid bills owed by the Pulleys in 1999. Among those items found in the truck was a $900 phone bill. The allusion to Rick Pulley's appetite for phone sex hung in the courtroom like dirty laundry on a clothesline.

All of what the witnesses were painting in court had not been an easy picture for Rick Pulley to look at. The places that the people had reported him being at, and the things that they had reported him doing or saying, were so unlike him. Throughout the day, he shifted his feet a lot and changed the expression on his face more than a few times. His attorney had pulled a few rabbits out of the hat, but so far, she hadn't made any of them hop.

Forensic pathologist Dr. Patrick Lantz, of the Wake Forest University Baptist Medical Center, testified that three scratch marks seen in photographs taken of Rick Pulley's left cheek the day after his wife disappeared could have been made by someone's fingernails.

"Based on the configuration and location of the scratches on the face, they are consistent with fingernail marks," Dr. Lantz said as blowups of the photos depicting Rick Pulley's face were projected onto a screen.

Lantz went on to say the facial scratches did not appear to be briar marks and that he believed the marks were caused during a physical altercation, adding that bruises seen on Rick's arms were consistent with grab marks. With a laser pointer, he described how the scratch marks were slightly squared off at the top, which, he said, was an indication that they were made starting at the top of the scratch. He told the jury all three scratches appeared to be fairly even on both sides and were about the same width and length.

On a photograph of Rick's right arm, Lantz pointed to what he characterized as superficial scratch marks, which were consistent with briar marks. He described those marks as more diffuse, interrupted, and tending to trail off at the ends.

The defense contended Rick's face was scratched when he chased his dog into briars on the evening of May 14. As Pressley extended Lantz's already long and drawn-out technical testimony, he confirmed his opinion on the scratch marks had not changed since the first day he looked at them. He again explained why he believed the scratches were from an altercation and detailed the differences between a real scratch mark and a briar mark. Rick had three of them on his face to worry about, as well as a few scratches on his chest and arms, in addition to a grab mark on his right bicep.

The state had organized a very strong case, even though at this point the only evidence they still had was circumstantial. It was time for Brewer to pull from his 440 B file.

Chapter 51

It would be a grueling experience for Rick Pulley. During the trial, he had learned to expect anything, and that he had to be ready to handle everything the state threw up on the witness stand. It was an emotional ride that proved almost unbearable, especially when certain people from his past were called to testify against him.

The River of Life Church pastor Randy Sudduth and his wife, Judy Sudduth, were called to the witness stand and asked to describe the role the Pulleys had played as members of the church, as well as the events that had occurred around the time of Patty Jo Pulley's disappearance. Pulley felt like a wooden stake had been driven through his heart when Randy, his former colleague and friend in the ministry, testified that he had made frequent trips into the woods by the volleyball court, but swore he didn't remember any briars.

As the trial continued on Friday, the state had set up a timeline of Rick Pulley's actions on a poster board, detailing all his actions on the day his wife, Patty Jo, had disappeared. Brewer and Willaford took turns calling witnesses to the stand, trying to poke holes into Pulley's claims that he was at a high-school play the night his wife disappeared. Witnesses swore that Rick told them earlier in the day that he would not make it to the play because Patty Jo was not feeling okay.

Reverend Randy Sudduth also recalled for the jury how Rick Pulley was using the church's credit cards to pay personal bills, and told how the couple was having marital problems. The state continually drove home the point that financial and marital problems had been Rick's motive for murder. They effectively used their witnesses to demonstrate how he had tried to establish alibis for his whereabouts on the day his wife disappeared.

Jamie Shackleford testified Friday that she saw Rick Pulley outside the Dan River High School auditorium the evening his wife disappeared. She and her daughter had participated in the school play *South Pacific,* on May 14, 1999, when she left shortly before the show ended to set up for a cast party she was hosting.

"As I was crossing the road, I believe, he rolled his window down and spoke to me," Shackleford said. "He said that it was a wonderful play and Jordan did a super job."

The prosecution contended that was unusual behavior for Rick to initiate a conversation with the Shacklefords, as they had had a falling-out at the church and Rick hadn't made a habit of being friendly with them.

Nor had Rick Pulley made a habit of calling Bethany Sudduth a liar. She testified that when Pulley found out what his then-sixteen-year-old neighbor had told police investigators when she called him earlier in the day to ask for a ride to the play, he was livid.

Bethany was asked in court, "And what did the defendant say to you on Saturday about that?"

"Uh, he called me a liar."

"And where did that occur?"

"Behind my house."

"And who was present?"

"I don't remember if anybody was present beside me and Rick and Mr. Isom."

Private investigator David Peters testified he had been employed by Patty Jo Pulley's family and described several visits to Rick Pulley after he had moved to Lebanon, Virginia, during the summer of 2000. After family representative Nathan Zachery informed Peters that a woman's body had been found, Peters says he relayed the information to Pulley, who asked where the body had been found. When Peters responded that he did not know, he said Rick pretty much shrugged his shoulders and said he would wait and see.

Peters testified further than when he returned two days later and told Rick the body's location, he said Rick responded casually, "That can't be Patty Jo. That's not the right area."

Under cross-examination by Pressley, Peters was asked about his investigative notes. Peters said he had met with Pittsylvania County Sheriff's officer Keith Isom in April 2001. At that time, he told Isom he couldn't find his notes on the case. He said he had completed his work for the Riddicks and had sent the originals of all his material to Zachery.

"Did Zachery ask you to beat up Rick Pulley?" Pressley asked, validating that the Riddicks had turned against Rick after Patty Jo had disappeared.

"Yes," Peters said as a matter of fact. "I just told him I didn't do that. That it was not part of my work."

Looking bright and efficient, and way more alert than Brewer imagined he probably felt, Keith Isom took the stand again and described a massive search for Patty Jo Pulley that took place one to two weeks after her disappearance. The delay, he said, was due to the unfavorable weather conditions in the Dan River. Isom admitted Rick Pulley took part in that search.

Isom also described searches of the Pulley home in Ringgold. He pointed out two sets of keys in a photo taken of the couple's dining room the day after Patty Jo disappeared, as well as a paycheck and pocketbook found on Patty Jo's dressing table.

Brewer wanted the jury to make the connection of why would a woman who had been denied the opportunity to use a check at the Winn-Dixie store the night before *not* cash her paycheck the next day, after she knew she was going shopping the next day?

There was a lot about Rick Pulley's behavior that wasn't kosher, and Brewer hoped the jury would see it the same way.

Isom displayed two sets of clothing worn by Rick the night of his wife's disappearance. He then showed the jury a search consent form for a subsequent search that Rick Pulley had signed, May 18, 1999, with the note—*20 minutes*—that Rick had written.

"That is all the time that Rick would allow us to search the home," Isom concluded.

Isom told the jury he did not get another chance to search the Pulleys' Ringgold home again until early fall, and only after Rick had left the house to move to Lebanon, Virginia. At that time, Isom said, he seized a hairbrush of Patty Jo's, hoping to get a DNA sample.

"Between these two searches of the Sonshine Drive home," Isom testified, "I spoke with Rick only a few times, and only once in person, and that was in the parking lot of River of Life Church."

During the same period of time, Isom said, he was in constant communication with Patty Jo's mother, Elva Mae Riddick, and with Connie Winslow, Patty Jo's niece. "Every other day, if not every day, I would hear from the family," he said.

Brewer's theory was that Rick Pulley should have been calling the police every day, or at least every other day, asking about the investigation, like the other people who loved her and were concerned about her whereabouts were doing.

Isom also described unsuccessful attempts to arrange

a meeting with Pulley after Pulley called Isom to tell him his new telephone number in Lebanon, Virginia.

As with any trial, there is often more going on in the halls and the lobby outside the courtroom than inside the courtroom. During a break in Randy Sudduth's testimony against his former youth and associate pastor, he sought refuge in a secluded area and cried profusely. Sudduth was concerned that his testimony about Rick's erectile dysfunction was a violation of the clergyman communication confidentiality.

Sudduth had testified that Rick was summoned to a meeting with Randy Sudduth, three other pastors, and an ordained elder to address concerns on Pulley's personal life, as well as some misuse of church credit cards during a Texas trip. During that meeting, the group asked Rick if he needed to discuss anything else, and he raised the issue of erectile dysfunction—as if the two incidents were somehow related.

But the day after that meeting, Sudduth testified, Rick again used the credit card at the Department of Motor Vehicles after he discovered the insurance had lapsed on his vehicle. Despite the misuses, Sudduth testified, to the best of his memory, Rick repaid every dime he took.

Prior to his testimony in court, Sudduth had attempted to invoke his clergyman's confidentiality privilege, saying that forcing him to testify would compromise the confidence his parishioners had in confessing to him, but Judge Smith overruled his objection.

"I am an ordained elder in my church, and I don't think of myself as a clergyman," Smith said. "Statements made in such a setting would not come within the clergy privilege, even though the community thought and believed that such communication would be confidential. Besides, the presence of an elder, who was not an ordained minister, compromised Sudduth's opinion that he could not be compelled to testify."

During a courtroom break, Patty Jo's family talked

about how much Rick Pulley changed in the mid-1990s. Prior to that time, nothing ever seemed to bother Rick, and all he did seemed to be about Patty Jo. But after their music ministry broke up and Rick was hired full-time at the church, the changes in both of them were painfully noticeable. Patty Jo rarely answered phone calls and e-mails unless Rick wasn't home. When they did come home to visit, which was on rare occasions, they were not as affectionate and lovey-dovey as they used to be.

As the Riddicks thought about Rick and how he had changed over the years, they remembered how preoccupied his mind seemed to be and how bitter he had gotten. One particular female relative sough help from Rick with a rather distressing situation. Instead of the usually calm, soft-spoken Rick that offered support and pointed out scriptural references, he became angry and judgmental. "You got yourself into this mess, now you can get yourself out of it."

In their last picture together, Rick and Patty Jo looked sad and distant. They had gone from laughing and joking to melancholy and detached. Patty Jo's weight loss made her sad disposition even more pronounced.

In her diary, Patty Jo had written about some of those changes: *Rick continues with his same duties, but spends much more time in the office, handling a lot of e-mails and phone calls. His work often has turned into a 2–3:00 A.M. situation. I wish he could spend more quality time with me. What has happened to us. And another $200 phone bill. I told Rick, again, this has to stop.*

The Riddicks considered why had Rick and Patty Jo had so much trouble paying their bills. Even though Rick's salary was low, the church was paying for most of their basic expenses. In addition to being a very frugal person, Patty Jo was working three part-time jobs. The question asked was "Could it be that Rick's expensive habits of phone sex were part of the problem?'

Chapter 52

The biggest slap in the face, as far as Elva Mae Riddick was concerned, was that Rick had sold Patty Jo's prized piano. Elva Mae knew nothing could bring her daughter back, but she had helped Patty Jo buy that piano. Rick had promised her that she could have it if they no longer wanted it or decided to trade it in on a baby grand. She would never forgive him for that.

The prosecution was not relying on Elva Mae Riddick's hurt feelings to win sympathy from the jurors; however, they wanted them to know that was of great importance to Patty Jo's mother.

On the sixth day of trial, Monday, October 25, 2004, Elva Mae Riddick testified tearfully about the last time she saw her daughter and the days that followed her disappearance. She said Patty Jo and Rick Pulley had visited her and her husband, Albert, for several days, the week preceding Patty Jo's disappearance. She said the couple came to her home to celebrate Mother's Day on May 9, 1999.

Riddick said she first learned about Patty Jo's disappearance when River of Life Church pastor Randy Sudduth called her around 7:00 or 8:00 A.M. on May 15, 1999. She said Sudduth instructed her to put her husband on the phone as well and then put Rick Pulley on the line from his end.

"At the end of the phone conversation," Elva Mae told the jury, "Rick told us, 'I love you.' We said we loved him. He said it was all right, that we didn't need to come there, and then he hung up. You can imagine what I did," she said when asked about her response to the call. "We went all to pieces."

Elva Mae paused, then dabbed a tissue at her eyes.

"I was surprised at how calm Rick sounded on the phone," she said, her voice shaky and trembling. "I thought he, of all people, would be devastated. I cried. I didn't know who had her. I didn't know what they were doing to her."

Elva Mae said when she told Rick later in the summer that she would like to have Patty Jo's piano—thinking she might still be alive—Rick informed her he had sold the piano because he needed the money.

"I felt like she might be alive," Elva Mae said. "I thought if I had the piano, I could save it for her. If not, I could keep it. I was crushed when Rick told me he had gotten rid of it."

Elva Mae said she had been able to retrieve some of Patty Jo Pulley's possessions from the Pulleys' home in the fall of 1999, such as dolls and a quilt Patty Jo had made with her family. But, she said, she had yet to receive photo albums she had requested from Rick.

Patty Jo's boss, Glenda Honea, of Danville, testified that Patty Jo had helped her clean her house that Friday she disappeared. Honea said when she left her home at 4:20 P.M. that day, Patty Jo was still there, but she said Patty Jo was not there when she returned home an hour later.

Honea said she had left a paycheck in her kitchen for Patty Jo to pick up and said the check was later deposited into a bank account. She testified she did not recall Patty Jo saying she was sick or calling her husband to ask him to pick her up.

Patty Jo's sister, Rita Corprew, said she had not seen Rick Pulley at Patty Jo's funeral. She also testified that she noticed Rick Pulley wasn't wearing his wedding band when she and her family went to retrieve Patty Jo's possessions in September 1999.

After entering its last exhibit into evidence, a North Carolina transportation map, the state rested its case.

The defense immediately asked that the court dismiss all charges against Rick Pulley.

"Respectfully, Your Honor, pursuant to General Statutes North Carolina 15-A1227A, the defendant moves for a dismissal at the close of the state's evidence and cites that there has been a lack of sufficiency of evidence to proceed on. The state has to prove not only substantial evidence on each element of the crime, but that the defendant was the perpetrator. Also, jurisdiction is not an affirmative defense. The evidence taken most favorable to the state, the only evidence that they presented that linked in any way the defendant to the death of Patty Jo Pulley, was Scott Harold. What Scott Harold testified was that allegedly the defendant's confession occurred in Virginia. There has been no other evidence tied directly to the defendant that the deceased, Patty Jo Pulley, died at his hands. While the state and defense counsel stipulate that the remains found were Patty Jo Pulley's, the cause of death was not conclusive. The time of death was not conclusive, and place or date is questionable under Scott Harold's testimony. We ask you to consider all these things and dismiss the charges. If Your Honor is not favorable to dismissing all charges, we'd certainly ask that the state not be allowed to go forward on first-degree murder."

After entertaining statements from both attorneys, Judge Smith denied defense's motion to dismiss at the close of the state's evidence.

"It's a matter for the jury now," Smith stated, knowing that one part of the long journey in the trial was over. The defense witnesses and evidence came next. He looked directly at Pressley and asked, "Will there be evidence for the defendant?"

"There will," Pressley answered, understanding she would now have to produce even more compelling witnesses to combat the physical and circumstantial evidence the prosecution had used to validate their rhetoric.

"Are you ready to proceed?" Smith asked further.

"I am," Pressley responded, indicating she was ready to present her case to the jurors.

Chapter 53

In the defense's eagerness to present their case and begin with the direct examination of their witnesses, Pressley called Richard Gardner, administrator at the River of Life Church, as her first witness. Gardner said he had been "rather close" to both Rick and Patty Jo in 1999. He said he and Rick Pulley had spent most of May 14, 1999, at the church, setting up sleeping arrangements for an upcoming conference. He remembered the 3:15 P.M. phone call that afternoon from Patty Jo.

Throughout the trial, each lawyer had proved they both had a mind geared for details. While one presented his or her case to the jurors, the other would hone in on the testimony and watch for any weak spots. Later, it would give him/her the opportunity to jump in with both feet on cross-examination and lessen the impact of a particular witness's testimony.

In the opening testimony of the defense's case, there was the simple discussion of the problem related to the prosecution's timeline and of Patty Jo's demeanor on the day she disappeared.

"She said, 'Hi, it's me. Is Rick there?'" Gardner answered the defense's questions carefully and without emotion. He recalled Rick then told him he was going to get Patty Jo and asked Gardner if he could cover for a 5:00 P.M. appointment Patty Jo had made. Gardner said that was when he returned to the appointment to his church office across from the Pulleys' home at 5:45 P.M., and saw both their vehicles parked in the church parking lot. He testified he received a phone call from Rick Pulley at 6:10 P.M., asking how the appointment had gone.

"While I was talking with Rick," Gardner continued. "I heard a voice in the background. I assumed it was Patty Jo."

Gardner said Rick told him that Patty Jo wanted his opinion as to whether she could drive the Pulleys' red truck. After joking for a moment, Gardner said he heard in the background what sounded like someone leaving the Pulleys' house. When he went to check his mail shortly thereafter, he said, he noticed both the Pulleys' vehicles were gone.

The following Saturday morning, Gardner testified, he visited briefly with Rick Pulley, saying Pulley looked distraught. Gardner said he had already driven several routes looking for Patty Jo when he heard someone say the Dan River had been broadening due to rain and decided to drive down River Bend Road, where he spotted the Pulleys' red truck and called 911.

Pressley's questioning of Gardner took a strange turn when she asked him to describe an incident that had happened two weeks before Patty Jo disappeared. Gardner said he and Rick were working on the east end of the large parsonage when a gentleman, approximately five-ten in height and two hundred pounds, fifty years in age, and of American Indian heritage, introduced himself to them.

Brewer objected several times to the defense's insinuation of third-party guilt. He clearly didn't want to give the jury the opportunity to consider a man who resembled Rick had anything to do with Patty Jo's disappearance.

Pressley was adamant this evidence should be admissible because Gardner had provided this information to Officer Keith Isom. The man was observed at the River of Life Church, was camping at the Hyco Lake Campgrounds, and when he said he was looking for a church to visit, Rick invited him to his home for dinner. Gardner said he saw the man a few more times, but did not see him again after Patty Jo disappeared.

After a lengthy discussion of the man's behavior and whereabouts, the judge asked if this man had ever demonstrated any violent behavior, to which Pressley answered no.

"And you contend that comes under this term, 'somebody else did it' theory?"

"Yes, sir," Pressley answered.

"All this suspicion about this man and his behavior is all hearsay, Your Honor," Brewer interjected. "There's nothing here that seems relevant to this proceeding in regard to this individual at the time on this showing."

When both the state and the judge did not warm up to her theories, Pressley presented what she thought were even more valid points to the court. When the judge overruled all her motions, she expressed her frustrations to him, walked back to the defense table, and then started snatching her papers from Pulley.

While Pressley steamed at her table, Brewer continued his attempt to disparage Rick. Under cross-examination, he questioned Gardner about the meeting they had with Rick Pulley in August 1999. Gardner said he and other church members had met with Pulley after he noticed he had not received several church credit card bills. He said he had requested copies from the credit card company and had discovered what he called "questionable transactions."

Gardner said he told Pulley explicitly that he was not to use the church credit card for personal purchases, and that Rick pointed out several instances where he had already used the card as such. Gardner said he then requested that Rick give him the card and he then closed the account.

"We made it clear to Rick that all those expenses would have to be reimbursed," Gardner said, adding that Pulley had repaid his debts to the church. But later, he said, he found six credit card bills in Rick Pulley's desk and trash.

The scratch marks were an important issue to the prosecution. When Brewer asked Gardner about those, he said when he first noticed the scratch marks on Rick's face, on May 15, 1999, he thought they looked like marks that might have been made by a dog's claws during play.

As if one "somebody else did it" theory was not sufficient to cast doubt on Rick's guilt, Pressley called Randy Glascot to the witness stand. Glascot was a neighbor of Rick's, who said he was probably at home four doors down from the Pulleys' the night Patty Jo disappeared.

Glascot stated he and Rick had never had any problems, but, the only thing the two men had in common was their physical size. In 1999, his height was about six-one and he weighed about 240 pounds. On cross-examination, he told Brewer he had not walked on Route 62 the evening of May 14, 1999, and he had neither kidnapped nor killed Patty Jo Pulley.

Still grabbing for straws, Pressley called Steven Keel to the stand. He acknowledged at one time he and Glascot had been friends. He also admitted during the course of his private investigation, he had talked with and written the police letters about Randy Glascot and how he, too, matched the description of the man Robert Rowland and Dale Purvis saw on River Bend Road.

When Pressley asked Keel if he felt at the time of Patty Jo's disappearance, there was more than one person he thought fit the description of the man Rowland observed, Brewer objected to the question. Before the judge could sustain Brewer's objection, Keel had already answered, "Yes."

Keel said that in one letter he wrote to the Pittsylvania County Sheriff's Office concerning his investigation, he mentioned Glascot as a possible suspect.

Working along those same lines, Pressley called her own private investigator, Tony Ropp, to the stand and asked him about his efforts to locate Randy Glascot before the trial. Ropp said he had some difficulty getting together with Glascot to interview him. And when the two men did meet, he said, he observed that Glascot's physical features were somewhat similar to Rick's.

Even though Ropp was not tendered as an expert witness in fingernail scratches, he was asked to look at the pictures of the scratches on Rick's face and give his opinion based on his experience.

After some confusion as to what an opinion constituted, Ropp testified he had seen fingernail scratches in previous cases he had handled and the scratches shown in the pictures of Rick's face appeared different from those he had seen in previous cases.

"The marks I have seen were elongated and closer together," Ropp clarified.

Willaford asked Ropp a few questions and then let him pass. His opinion on the fingernail scratches didn't carry any weight. There was just no way he could stack up to the state's professional forensic experts.

And as if to add further amusement for the prosecution, the defense called Charles Clayton, a Durham police officer, who could only testify that the only experience he had with fingernail scratches was when he and his wife got into an argument and she reached up and scratched him on the jaw.

Brewer didn't waste his time in cross-examination and quickly excused the witness. It appeared to him now that this was the way this long-awaited legal contest was going to continue. All of the complicated testimony on police procedure and forensic evidence was over. Despite all the pretrial media coverage, there were no startling revelations. No surprises. No bolts from the blue. And no voices from Heaven.

Remembering all the hard work he and his staff had

put into this case months earlier, Brewer relaxed. His eyes sliding away toward the defense table, he found a comfortable place for his mind to relax and waited for the tearful memories to begin.

Allowed now to speak for Rick Pulley, his friends and family would follow one another to the witness stand and speak about how loving a couple Rick and Patty Jo were. They recalled how Rick had reacted to the news of Patty Jo's death and how remorseful he truly had been. As Pressley moved through her witnesses, some more talkative than others, and some speaking haltingly because of their emotion, the presentation flowed awkwardly, as if all of the components of the case didn't fit. No one listening would have ever known how hard the defense team had worked to put all this together.

Pressley stood between the jury box and the defense table, and called for David Wilson, a longtime member of River of Life Church and a resident of the Sonshine South community in Milton, North Carolina, to take the stand. Wilson said Rick and Patty Jo Pulley had been like a brother and sister to him, that he and his wife and children were very close to them. Their families had spent vacations and holidays together, where they enjoyed long nights of conversations.

David Wilson described for the jury the day he had tried to console Rick as he ran toward the Pulleys' red truck the day it was discovered on River Bend Road. "Patty Jo! Patty Jo!" Rick was tearfully shouting, according to Wilson. In the days after her disappearance, Wilson said, Rick just went totally to pieces.

"He was distraught and emotional," Wilson noted.

When Pressley asked David Wilson how long he had observed Rick in this way, Wilson responded, "I've noticed that he's been in that state even today." He told the jury he might have received more than one thousand phone calls from Rick over the past eight months.

Pressley questioned David Wilson about several issues

the prosecution had related about Rick and Patty Jo's behavior. Wilson answered all her questions, stating that Patty Jo had driven the Pulleys' red truck to haul trash on occasions. He also said he had known the Pulleys' dog to run off and not respond to being called. In addition, he recalled seeing Rick wearing his wedding band after Patty Jo disappeared.

David Wilson further told the jurors that he also recalled seeing photo albums boxed for transport when he helped Rick Pulley move from his Ringgold home, and that Rick had sold his guitar and some furniture to him to alleviate some "financial distress," following his wife's disappearance. He also said there were thorns and briars in the wooded area next to the River of Life property's volleyball court.

Pressley asked David Wilson to identify some photos he had taken, which he said showed Rick and Patty Jo on trips abroad, at the beach, at home on Christmas. Wilson appeared to become overwhelmed as he described a photo of Rick and his dog wrestling on the floor. As the jury passed around the photographs, he removed his glasses and wiped away the tears from the corners of his eyes.

The defense then played parts of two videotapes that captured Rick and Patty Jo conducting missionary work abroad. In one, Wilson pointed to Patty Jo kneeling with some children at a hospital and to Rick playing his guitar while a group of children sang.

Patty Jo's family sat stoically throughout the presentation, but when the court broke for lunch, her mother and sister embraced and sobbed quietly along the wall of the courthouse lobby.

During cross-examination, Brewer held up documents and asked David Wilson if he had received 1,114 phone calls from Rick Pulley since February 2004. Wilson responded that he might have. When asked if Rick Pulley had called an average of four times a day over the past eight months, Wilson responded that Pulley had placed calls as often as he was allowed.

Pressley then asked Pastor Jeff Williams, of Lebanon Community Fellowship Church in Lebanon, Virginia, to speak on Rick's behalf. Williams said he had acted as counselor, friend, and theological buddy to Rick after Patty Jo disappeared.

Williams said, "He seemed to be a man in recovery. He was obviously emotionally attached by the chain of events." He recalled Pulley weeping when Patty Jo's remains were found.

Another friend of Rick's, Dwight Bailey, a Lebanon doctor, would concur with Williams's testimony. "Rick does have a passionate heart for the Lord, he's the most gentle man I've ever met." Bailey concurred, saying he and Pulley played golf and talked about the church's ministry. He had also witnessed Rick grieving when Patty Jo's remains were found.

"He was hysterical," he said. "He was tearful and crying uncontrollably."

Phillip Reams, a Roxboro, North Carolina, forest technician, testified that the marks seen on Rick's face looked like briar scratches to him. He identified locust brushes and floral roses in a photograph of the area near the church volleyball court.

"You can see some briars there," he said.

David Wilson's wife, Jo, testified that the purse identified in a photo by Investigator Keith Isom of Patty Jo's makeup table was actually a cosmetic bag, which, she said, she had emptied while helping Rick clean his house to move. Jo said she never saw disagreements or evidence of violence between the Pulleys.

During her five-minute interview, Rick's mother, Shirley Holiday, said that her son was "very upset" at the time of Patty Jo's disappearance.

The gallery and the media were growing bored with the defense's soft testimony. Everyone wondered if Rick

Pulley would actually take the stand. They eagerly awaited for him to take the stand and for Brewer to look him in the eyes and say the words that might bring him to his knees: "Did you kill your wife, Patty Jo Pulley?" For most people attending the trial, that was the real crux of the matter.

Earlier in the day, DA Brewer agreed not to offer evidence about a girlfriend Rick Pulley met in late 2002 in exchange for a stipulation from Pulley that the human remains found under Hyco Creek Bridge in December 2002 were those of his wife.

Brewer had begun questioning Caswell County Sheriff's sergeant Mike Adkins about pictures he took of Rick Pulley's jail cell. Brewer said Adkins's pictures showed photos of Pulley's girlfriend displayed on his jail cell wall, which, Brewer said, tended to contradict the defense's contention that Patty Jo Pulley was not dead.

Chapter 54

Things were not looking good in the defense camp. By Wednesday, October 27, 2004, it was obvious the hybrid defense that Pressley had constructed was not strong enough to match the attack the state had wielded. The defense witnesses had been weak—character witnesses, most of whom affirmed they were friends with the Pulleys. In a case that seemed to have become more and more convoluted as it progressed, the defense called several more witnesses to the stand, but none of them had made much of a compelling argument. Pressley was counting on Rick Pulley's testimony and hoped it would turn out to be the strong spot in the defense's weak front.

Several witnesses would testify Wednesday prior to Pulley taking the stand. Walter and Nancy Jackson spoke of Patty Jo's reaction to being asked to move to the smaller of two River of Life Church parsonages and about a trip she took with the Jacksons to a vacation home in Maggie Valley, North Carolina.

Nancy Jackson recalled a phone conversation she had with Patty Jo about a response to prayer she said Rick had had shortly before Patty Jo's disappearance. She recalled Patty Jo saying Rick had felt it had been conveyed to him that Patty Jo was going to be attacked or that he was going to be attacked through his wife. God had revealed this to him at the Hyco Lake Campground shortly before her death.

Brewer smiled, as if he had been handed another gift. Until this moment, he was not aware of Rick's revelation and how he thought Patty Jo would be harmed. He was looking forward to cross-examining Rick and would make a note to ask him about that.

Defense expert witness James Merritt was allowed to offer limited testimony about scratches that appeared in photographs taken of Rick, saying he did not believe the marks to be fingernail scratches.

Finally it was Eugene Rick Pulley's turn to take the stand.

Normally, in murder trials, the defense fights to keep their clients off the witness stand. They know when his own attorney is finished with the friendly questions, he will be slaughtered with questions on cross-examination. Any legal expert would have warned Rick Pulley not to testify, but he was frustrated. He had always been a likeable person, capable and able to talk himself out of a jam. He had done it so many times before. Apparently, he felt as if he was the most compelling evidence in the trial and that he needed to explain to jurors the reality of what happened on the night of his wife's disappearance.

The time had come for Rick Pulley to step up to the plate and take his swings. The time had come for him to testify. As he took the stand, though, he looked as if he were only a shade of what he had been in his earlier years in the music ministry, when just his pure presence stirred emotions in people and brought them to the saving grace of God. His hair was short and completely gray, and he had a round, jowled face and a barrel-shaped body. He did not wear an expensive suit. It was just the outfit he had worn in court before, purchased probably from Wal-Mart, at a cost of no more than $100.

As he stood at the witness stand and swore on the Bible—to tell the truth, the whole truth, and nothing but the truth—he could look directly at the prosecutors, and beyond them were his family and supporters. Adjacent to them were the faces of Patty Jo's family, who filled the benches on the left side of the courtroom.

When Pulley took the stand shortly after 3:00 P.M., he was clearly nervous. His eyes already glistening, he waited nervously for his attorney's first question.

The court transcripts of Rick Pulley's testimony would add up to a little more than 150 pages. That wasn't a lot of information for someone like Rick, who always had a lot on his mind. He still had a nice, soft, soothing baritone voice, reminiscent of his music and preaching days. He spoke directly to the jurors, but gave more of his attention to his lawyer.

Pulley verified the information everyone before him had been saying about his and Patty Jo's lives, then answered all the rebuttal questions Pressley had for him. Pressley relied on all the earlier testimony to jog Rick's memory and had him explain all the issues that had been discussed in the courtroom. Rick's memory was not all that it used to be and he fumbled through a lot of the answers. He could not remember all the answers to the questions and relied upon "I think, we might have, I believe" a little more often than he had probably been instructed.

When Pressley asked him about his financial and sexual problems, he started crying. He admitted his affairs and how money problems had strained their marriage. Pulley said that Patty Jo was disappointed in him and frustrated with him, but she forgave him. She had loved him and they had moved on.

"Our dream was to own a music ministry together," Pulley said, choking as he tried to utter the sentence.

Rick Pulley was clearly in a different world, a world to

which he never imagined he would belong. As pitiful as it was, it was only right to remember the opportunities he had been given to do something good, and what his life could have been. When Pulley admitted to doing something wrong, he looked up from the witness stand like a schoolboy confessing to his teacher and ashamed for doing something naughty.

Pulley had been unable to keep his secrets to himself, and his attorney made no attempt to downplay that. The question was whether Pressley had convinced the jury that Rick told the truth. He looked like such a broken man on the witness stand, but he was still Rick Pulley, the murder suspect, when he finished answering all Pressley's questions.

It had been an emotional two days in court for Pulley, as he had taken the stand on both days. He teared up again as he looked at pictures of him and Patty Jo. He testified they had a loving relationship overall. He also talked about the letters he had received after her disappearance with messages like, "I will always love you." It made him wonder if Patty Jo was still alive.

"It created more questions and I didn't know what to think," Pulley said, holding his hands out in front of him. "I was already at a difficult state of mind. And it just made things harder."

Brewer's cross-examination of Rick Pulley began with a patronizing approach. His intention had always been to discredit Rick. Of course, he wanted the jury to believe Pulley was a liar and a murderer. Pulley had done nothing heroic by testifying in his own behalf and admitting to his sins of the past. He had simply done what his attorney had asked him to do, so he could save his own skin.

Brewer elicited the information he needed from Rick Pulley to convince the jury he had murdered his wife. He played the tape that Keith Isom had recorded during his interview when he asked Rick to tell him about the last act in *South Pacific*.

"You got it wrong, didn't you?"

"A good bit of it," Pulley acknowledged. "Yes, sir."

"Mary Ann's boyfriend in the musical *South Pacific* was killed—reported dead at the end. Is that not correct?"

Brewer's examination got an objection out of Pressley, but it was overruled.

"That's right," Pulley answered softly.

"You've learned that since, haven't you?"

"No," Pulley said defiantly. "I knew that before."

Brewer was relentless. Now that he had Rick Pulley in the hot seat, he was going to make him burn.

"And you had an affair?"

"I did."

"And that affair lasted over a period of several months, ending sometime in the fall of 1994, is that correct?"

"Sometime in September or October. Yes."

"And that affair included at least two trips, one to a motel beside the Green Tree Inn. Is that not correct?"

"That's right."

"And one to the Swan Lake Campground?"

Pulley turned pale. His jaw tightened.

"There was more than one to the Swan Lake Campground. There were, um, maybe three or four trips to the campground." Brewer was smiling like a hero who had just received his medals.

"And during the most intimate of those occasions, you and this woman would disrobe and lay beside each other and rub each other. Is that not correct?"

"That's correct."

Brewer had one more important question for Rick Pulley.

"Now, you told investigators in one of your interviews when you discussed that marriage was for life, something to that effect. Is that not correct?"

"That's correct."

"No matter how miserable things got, you said, 'Till death do us part'?"

Pulley swallowed hard. "That's correct," he said, dropping his head and staring at the floor.

Brewer believed if he rattled Pulley enough on the stand, then he would fight. But Pulley never fought back, nor did he lose his temper once. He came off on the stand like a whipped puppy.

Most of the people in the gallery and the jury had no warning that the defense was ready to fold its tent, but after Rick Pulley's testimony, Pressley called only two more witnesses to testify. In a matter of minutes, she said to the judge, "Nothing further, your Honor. The defendant rests."

Chapter 55

Some of those in the gallery who knew little or nothing about trials learned on the day after the defense rests, the state, which has the final proof of burden, can call rebuttal witnesses. After seven long days in the courtroom, there was speculation as to how long it would take Brewer to finish his examinations. However, this would be his last day to build another mountain of inflammatory testimony, and he plodded gamely ahead.

Brewer had handpicked five of what he thought would be his best witnesses. He had seen the effect that Rick's matter-of-fact explanations were having on the jurors as he had tried to soften his image. Once more, as the testimony continued, the jury could not ignore the evidence of Rick Pulley's tangled web.

Eddie Garrett, one of Rick's church friends from Lebanon, was the state's first rebuttal witness. When Garrett had asked Pulley how he had gotten the scratches on his face, Rick told him he had gotten them from playing with his dog.

The state's second rebuttal witness was Mary Sue Fields. By now, she was married and had a baby, and was employed by the U.S. Department of State as a foreign service officer. Her testimony about Pulley's physical attraction and his attempt to control her was spellbinding.

The state's third and fourth witnesses were called to clarify earlier testimony. Judy Sudduth testified her daughter Megan had not been outside with her when Rick said he was trying to catch his dog. And Keith Isom confirmed a statement that Pulley had given him about an argument he and Patty Jo had on the day she disappeared.

It was the state's fifth and final witness that knocked the defense off its feet. Rita Corprew, Patty Jo's sister, was recalled to the stand and was asked about Defendant's Exhibit 61, which contained numerous letters addressed to Rick Pulley.

"All right, Mrs. Corprew," Brewer began, coaxing his witness. "Have you ever seen these exhibits before?"

"Yes, sir."

"When did you see them before?"

Corprew turned and stared at Pulley. "I saw them when I mailed them to Rick Pulley." A collective gasp came from the gallery. Before Brewer could respond, she asked, "May I say why I did it?"

Trying to protect his witness, Brewer ignored the question. He was more interested in the writing on the envelopes than her motive for writing them. "Whose writing is that?"

"That's mine," Corprew answered. She felt no compunction, and never had, apparently, about writing the letters.

Brewer asked Corprew to identify each card and letter inside the envelope, dating as far back as July 1999. "Do you recognize these exhibits?"

"Yes, I do."

Continuing her testimony, Corprew explained to the jury that she had typed some of the letters and mailed the envelopes from Milton and Danville. She said she had mailed a letter to Pulley when he lived in both Ringgold and Lebanon.

"Did you ever tell Detective Keith Isom?" Brewer queried.

"Yes, I did."

Corprew explained that she had, after she had written a letter to Pulley back in 1999. Apparently, she, better than anyone, knew Rick Pulley's Achilles' heel and was prepared to strike at it time and time again, until it brought him down.

The defense was stunned. Pulley had no inkling that Corprew had authored those mysterious letters that came to him after Patty Jo's death. Both his and his attorney's demeanor were entirely different now. His stare at her was icy. And when the judge asked Pressley for redirect, her pinched expression showed her irritation at the witness. "No further questions," she said in a faint voice.

Finally, on Friday, October 29, 2004, after two long weeks, and nine days of the court trial, the attorneys were ready for closing arguments.

Defense attorney Theresa Pressley fired the first shot of the last round, beginning her closing arguments with the statement "This case screams out reasonable doubt." She then referenced testimonies of several expert witnesses who said the marks on Rick Pulley's face were not fingernail scratches.

Pressley directed most of her frustration toward Steven Keel for Rick Pulley having been arrested. She maintained Keel was able to show Robert Rowland a picture of Rick and influence his decision.

Pressley also attacked the credibility of convicted felon Scott Harold, who admitted on the stand he suffered from auditory hallucinations.

"It just isn't possible for Rick Pulley to have murdered his wife, dispose of her body, and abandon his truck on River Bend Road in between times when," she said, "Rick or Patty Jo's whereabouts were accounted for."

She was very critical of the North Carolina medical examiner who ruled Patty Jo's cause of death was "most likely asphyxia."

"How can the state say that? They cannot say when, where, how, or why? There are so many possibilities."

In his 2½-hour closing statement, Brewer cited as justification for having the case tried in North Carolina, a revelation Rick Pulley recounted having at Hyco Lake that something tragic was going to happen to Patty Jo. Brewer painted a portrait of a burned-out, overly defensive man whose wife had become increasingly frustrated with his sexually related conduct and mismanagement of household funds.

Brewer said Rick Pulley's case hinged on three main points: one, the deep fingernail scratches found on his face the night Patty Jo disappeared; two, the inconsistencies in his whereabouts the day Patty Jo went missing; and three, his jailhouse confession to cellmate Scott Harold. He said there were two possible scenarios of Patty Jo Pulley's death at the hands of her husband.

"In one, Rick Pulley might have picked up Patty Jo from work in Danville the afternoon of May 14, 1999, got into a violent argument with her while driving down Route 86 into Caswell County, rendered her unconscious, and tossed her body over the edge of the Hyco Creek Bridge. Pulley might have then been able to return home shortly before six P.M. to begin the creation of an alibi for the evening's events.

"In the other scenario, Rick Pulley might have brought his wife home and tied her up, later killing her and leaving her at the bridge site sometime between ten-thirty P.M. and one A.M., when he went to seek help from Sudduth, who was working late at Domino's Pizza restaurant."

Referring to the biblical story in Genesis 4:15–16, Brewer likened the scratches he believed Patty Jo left on Rick's face, the night she disappeared, to the "mark of God" pronounced upon the biblical character Cain after he killed his brother Abel. He referred to Lebanon, Virginia, where Pulley moved after Patty Jo's disappearance, as his land of Nod.

After the closing arguments, Judge Smith offered the jury a verdict of not guilty and three verdict choices: first-degree murder, second-degree murder, and voluntary manslaughter.

Twenty-two years ago, Rick and Patty Jo Pulley had stood together at the altar in the Methodist church in Raleigh, North Carolina, in a candlelit ceremony, pledging their love and taking their vows of "for better or for worse, for richer or for poorer . . . until death do us part." Now many of these same people gathered on wooden pews and waited for a jury to decide if Rick Pulley took his vows seriously.

The jury deliberated only 2½ hours before they came back with a "guilty" verdict. Despite Pressley's repeated attempts to plant "reasonable doubt" within the minds of the jury, they found Rick Pulley guilty of killing his wife and dumping her body under a Caswell County bridge, where it was not discovered until three years later. Rick was asked to stand as the judge pronounced his sentence.

"Mr. Pulley, the jury having returned a verdict that you're guilty of first-degree murder, the court, having accepted that verdict, adjudicates you guilty of a class-A felony of first-degree murder. It is the judgment of the court that you be imprisoned for the rest of the remainder of your natural life of a term of life imprisonment without parole. That's the judgment of the court. The defendant is remanded to the custody of the sheriff for transmittal to the Department of Correction."

After the sentence was pronounced by Judge Smith, Patty Jo's mother read from a statement she had prepared for such a verdict:

"'We are so disappointed in our son-in-law,'" Elva Mae said tearfully, looking straight at Rick Pulley. Her expression showed heartbreak. "'We didn't know much about him when they were married, but we trusted Patty Jo's judgment. As we were around him more, we learned to

love him. We treated him like a son. In fact, the last time
they were at our house, we had traded cars, and I said to
him, 'Ricky, go and tell your daddy to let you drive his
new car.' He went out and they went down the road, with
Ricky driving. We are not rich people, but we tried to
help them out as much as we could. Patty Jo said they
were doing all right financially and not to worry about
that. We had such good times together, especially
Thanksgiving and Christmas. Now, when these holidays
come, we are very sad. Right now, we can't forgive. You
told us you did not harm Patty Jo, and the whole time
you knew she was deteriorating for three-and-a-half
years, leaving us to get back only a few bones to bury.
Patty Jo wanted to be an organ donor, and you took that
away from her. These things are hard to forgive. There
will always be a blank space in our family. You have hurt
us deeply, and not only our family, but yours as well.
There's nothing left to say but good-bye, Ricky.'"

Elva Mae lowered her head and walked slowly to her
seat. The only dry eyes in the courtroom belong to the defendant. As the officers of the court fastened their prison
jewelry to his hands and ankles, he turned to his sobbing
mother and mouthed, "It's going to be okay."

Epilogue

Caswell County DA Joel Brewer was very confident the prosecution would win the case against Rick Pulley. He said if he felt any demands or stressors, then it would have been self-imposed.

"The only demands came from within," Brewer would say, "to the extent I demanded of myself. I demanded excellence in myself as the prosecutor. Excellence from others involved in the investigation. And excellence in the trial preparation. Patty Jo Pulley deserved no less than our best and I am confident that is what we gave her."

Brewer said the case against Rick Pulley got better as it went along.

"There were surprises that came our way. There were people that came forward and pieces of evidence that we were not aware of, and that is not unusual in a trial. We didn't know that incident Nancy Jackson testified to where Rick had pulled off at the Hyco Lake Campground and received a message that something was going to happen to Patty Jo. That was a gimme.

"The defense had just called a couple of witnesses about what a loving relationship existed between Rick and Patty Jo. Ms. Jackson said when they had gone to Maggie Valley, Patty spoke to Rick over the phone and said, 'I love you,

Rick.' Then comes this witness interview with this lady about Patty Jo being confronted by Rick and that he had heard this voice of God. I had never seen this before, but we have wide open cross in North Carolina, as long as it is relevant. And because this was so golden, I approached the bench and told the court what I was fixing to go into. Of course, the defense objected, but the court allowed it.

"This is the same evidence, and the defense had just missed it. They had failed to see it, then put a witness on the stand who testified to it, and now it was going to come back and bite them in the butt. So for any event, I was allowed to cross-examine the defense about it, and I think it made some difference with the jury.

"Then, of course, one of the most compelling parts of the entire case was the scratches and the different explanations about where they came from. Was it a dog that scratched Ricky on the face, thorns, or was it Patty Jo?"

Brewer had some interesting insights into Rick Pulley's character.

"When you teach jurors in a courtroom, if you can get them to do something, like touch or feel something, then they usually get it. People are visual or auditory learners, and some are kinesthetic learners. What I knew we had to do was to appeal to all those senses of the jury and get what it was we were trying to get across.

"You see, defense attorneys are notorious for creating smoke screens or for running some rabbit to take the jurors' focus off the truth of the case. It may surprise you, but they use falsehoods. They deliberately mislead. But the prosecution has to stay with the truth.

"When you tell a lie, it is very hard for you to keep the story straight. When you tell the truth, it works in a different part of your brain. And that is the part of the brain that relies on memory. But when you tell a lie, that is the part of the brain that relies on creativity. And the part of the creativity doesn't go into the brain's memory as an event that was actually being participated in.

"When you're a defendant telling a story, it is hard for the memory part to tell the creative side over and over again what it had learned. And that was Pulley's problem. This piece of evidence came out of the blue, my Cain and Abel story—that he had gone off to the land of Nod—but he had played golf with the son of the church's secretary. That fellow liked him and said, 'I have been on the Web site and read about your case. Why is it that her family doesn't believe you? What is their beef?' Rick told this guy it was because he had gotten scratches on his face. He told him he had gotten them from his dog.

"Well, this guy had been listening and following the trial, and the defense had put on an expert witness that said it was consistent with a briar patch. We then got a call from western Virginia—sheriff said that there was somebody I needed to talk with. And the guy laid out the whole story for us.

"Also, we had this evidence of the private investigator, who had gone to see Rick. He had followed him around and observed his behavior. And then he told him about how there was a woman who was found at the zoo, and Rick says, 'No, that can't be Patty Jo. No, that wouldn't be her, she wouldn't be found there.'

"Rick had a memory of convenience. Some difficult details he could remember, but others he had no clue.

"I thought that we were pretty much winning the case by then, well before we got the slam dunk, the Cain and Abel story. After that, I would have been shocked, had the jury come back with a not guilty verdict. I thought the evidence of the disposition of the piano shortly after she was gone, and the telephone records to sex numbers, would have been of particular interest to the jury, so as to see motive. Beforehand, Rick is giving us this story that the marriage is going south, and when he was offered this sabbatical, he turned it down. Patty Jo is out there scrubbing and waxing floors and doing all this work, and when she encourages him to take a break, he was no. What was the big deal about it? He was going to get paid, wasn't he? And if they were in such bad financial position, then why didn't he just take the sabbatical and get a second job at Wal-Mart? Instead, he was at home running up $1,200 phone bills. We don't know if he hadn't gotten into the Internet sex yet, but he was big in phone sex.

"But I think the disposition of the piano and the selling of her clothes also did it for the jury."

Brewer said what was still confusing to him was the time Rick killed her. What really happened between four and nine on the evening she went missing?

"What I told the jury was that you have to remember that Ricky Pulley was doing everything in his power at that time that was confusing. He was attempting to create an alibi for himself. And that became a double-edged sword for the defense. That he had gone to certain lengths to be seen by certain people. He speaks to people he had never spoken to before. We were trying to get into that kind of detail. But what we really had to do was say, okay, we have all this overwhelming evidence, with him lying about the scratches and this other [thing], but if we can't show the jury how he did it, and there was a window with a possibility of time, then they are going to come back and say reasonable doubt. We had to find those time periods when it occurred, and we found two—afternoon and one late in the evening. We actually gave them two different choices and we gave them two different scenarios with a block of time [when] the crime could have been committed.

"One, he picked her up from work immediately, he got into an argument with her, then he went down into Caswell County—takes a little more time for him to come back and she was jumping on him about his telephone sex, those phone bills were in the truck. He slapped her and tossed her out.

"You could also make an argument, he had the struggle in the house, he subdued her and tied her up, then took her out later that night. That argument may have led them to believe he killed her in Virginia. But all the evidence tends to lead you to believe that Ricky killed her. We were satisfied he killed her that afternoon. The point is late in the evening he is already doing some things to try and cover up what he had done, like location of truck, walking up the side road down NC-57 and onto 62.

"Also, one of the most fascinating statements that we didn't get a lot of play out of, but was powerful, was when the minister's daughter—sweet, attractive little girl—takes the stand and talks about Ricky confronting her on that Saturday, after the sheriff's deputies talked with her, and demanding of her to know why she was talking to the deputies about him and accusing her of lying. It's those types of things that get a jury stirred up. If you read her testimony, she was one of those witnesses that the jury was going to believe whatever she was going to say, regardless. And for him to confront her on that Saturday and argue with her?

"What I argued to the jury was, again, was that a guilty man trying to cover his tracks? My strongest witnesses were, of course, my investigators—top-notch people, both from Virginia and North Carolina. And the fact that Keith Isom recognized this as a potential domestic violence situation from the beginning is awesome. When he saw Rick Pulley for the first time and he had his eyes wide open, he took photographs and documented evidence, and he recorded his interview, that was great. Then he also took photographs of a check on her counter, when we found out later she is living hand to mouth.

"And if she is living from hand to mouth and not feeling well, then why is she going shopping? She had tried to get her check cashed the night before and couldn't, so where is the money she is going to use to go shopping—where is it coming from?

"The fact that Isom handled this as well as he did in relation to domestic violence is the very key to foul play and it helped everything else fall in place. Isom was convinced from the very beginning that there was foul play involved in this case, and he believed Rick Pulley was involved. He became very aware of that during the entire year after her disappearance, especially when Ricky did not once call and ask about the progress of the case against his wife. I don't even think he visited the site where her body was found. I guess he didn't want to go there.

"The pathologist, Dr. Lantz gave us a good opinion about the cause of scratches. The others helped out a lot. I guess I wouldn't do anything any different than I did. Now that I look back over it, I don't know how I did it as well as I did. Of course, we had the two girls waiting in the wings—Angel Cox, the girl he had an affair with, and Cassandra Martin, the girl who heard Rick threaten to kill Patty Jo. But I realized we didn't need their testimony on rebuttal. Besides, it wasn't worth the cost of embarrassment to put those girls on the stand, so we chose not to put them on. At the time, it was a difficult [decision] to make, but as my case was getting better and better, I felt less compelled and worried about doing that.

"Of course, what troubled me about the investigation was this Steven Keel. I threatened to have him arrested for obstructing justice. When people want to get involved, they can sometimes do things that can irrevocably damage a case. There was logic in admitting the identification of the defendant and letting the jury make the decision about that. I wanted to let them consider the fact that the neighbor did all this, and ask was that what earmarked Robert Rowland's identification, or was that his actual memory?

"Ricky Pulley probably deserved the death penalty, but the statutes didn't lead us there. He will continue to live, and hopefully, his sentence will not be commuted. His family will go on living, but Ricky Pulley is the kind of person who writes people and continues to stir things up. When Ricky is dead, the victim's family won't have to listen to him talking about their daughter's death—he is not reliving it, talking about it, imagining it, or giving press conferences about it. When he dies, that part of it will be over.

"Yes, justice was done. Caswell County [was] caught with a brand-new sheriff, but yet he grew during this investigation. He was the first to hug my neck when the verdict came in.

"We got out of the case everything that we could have gotten out of it, and are pleased that the appellate courts have agreed with us. It was ironic that my opinion was filed the same morning as my reelection, in November 7, 2006."

Prosecutors are never given enough credit for believing in what they say.

After the trial was over, the police returned Patty Jo's clothing to the Riddicks, along with her cosmetic bag and some family photos. As Patty Jo's family sought closure in their lives, they still hung on to her memory. For Christmastime 2004, family members tracked down the piano man who had bought the black piano from Rick, and they bought it from him. They arranged for Elva Mae to be out of the house one evening and then slipped it in while she was away. When Elva came home from shopping, she discovered the piano, wrapped with a big red bow around it, in her living room.

The old Hyco Creek Bridge, where Patty Jo's skeletal remains were found, was torn down and replaced with a newer bridge. The bright yellow-bowed wreath that the Riddick family placed near the old bridge still stands on that spot as a reminder of this tragedy.

Rick Pulley's appeal in the North Carolina Court of Appeals for a new trial was denied.